THE GUIDE
TO
FRANCHISING

Other Titles of Interest

HUSSEY, D.
The Truth about Corporate Planning
Corporate Planning: Theory and Practice, 2nd edition

MENDELSOHN, M. & DRYSDALE WILSON, A.
The Law and Practice of Franchising

SASAKI, N.
Management and Industrial Structure in Japan

SASAKI, N. & HUTCHINS, D.
The Japanese Approach to Product Quality

TAYLOR, B. & HUSSEY, D.
The Realities of Planning

Related Journal

OMEGA*

The International Journal of Mangement Science

Chief Editor: Samuel Eilon, Imperial College of Science and
Technology, London, UK

OMEGA provides all specialists in management science with
important new developments in operational research and
managerial economics. Published material ranges from original
contributions to review articles describing the state-of-the-art in
specific areas, together with shorter critical assessments of
particular management techniques.

* Free specimen copy available on request.

THE GUIDE
TO
FRANCHISING

by

MARTIN MENDELSOHN
Solicitor

FOURTH EDITION

PERGAMON PRESS

OXFORD · NEW YORK · TORONTO · SYDNEY · PARIS · FRANKFURT

U.K.	Pergamon Press Ltd., Headington Hill Hall, Oxford OX3 0BW, England
U.S.A.	Pergamon Press Inc., Maxwell House, Fairview Park, Elmsford, New York 10523, U.S.A.
CANADA	Pergamon Press Canada Ltd., Suite 104, 150 Consumers Rd., Willowdale, Ontario M2J 1P9, Canada
AUSTRALIA	Pergamon Press (Aust.) Pty. Ltd., P.O. Box 544, Potts Point, N.S.W. 2011, Australia
FRANCE	Pergamon Press SARL, 24 rue des Ecoles, 75240 Paris, Cedex 05, France
FEDERAL REPUBLIC OF GERMANY	Pergamon Press GmbH, Hammerweg 6, D-6242 Kronberg-Taunus, Federal Republic of Germany

First edition 1970

Second edition 1979

Third edition 1982

Fourth edition 1985

Library of Congress Cataloging in Publication Data

Mendelsohn, M. (Martin),
The guide to franchising.
Includes index.
1. Franchises (Retail trade) 2. Franchises (Retail trade) —
Great Britain. I. Title.
HF429.23.M46 1984 658.8'708 84-1084

British Library Cataloguing in Publication Data

Mendelsohn, M.
The guide to franchising. — 4th ed.
1. Franchises (Retail trade) — Great Britain
I. Title
658.8'708'0941 HF5429.235.G7

ISBN 0-08-031282-9

Printed in Great Britain by A. Wheaton & Co. Ltd., Exeter

To Phyllis, Paul and David

Contents

Foreword

I HAVE been involved in franchising for over twenty-one years: first as a franchisee, then as a franchisor, and now seeing a wider picture as Chairman of the British Franchise Association. The rapid growth and development of franchising should surprise no-one, because it truly is a system which offers something for all, including the end consumer. For the franchisee, the opportunity to start a business using a tried and tested formula, with a proven record of success; for the franchisor, the ability to quickly build a business network of reliable and motivated partners; and for the consumer, the assurance of quality in a product or service and the genuine interest of a local businessman.

The growth of interest in franchising in the U.K. can be recognised in the increasing demand for Martin Mendelsohn's excellent book. He identifies the benefits and the problems that franchising has faced since his third edition. He writes in an enjoyable style which makes for good and interesting reading, and once again I became thoroughly engrossed in the contents, particularly appreciating the additions on consultants and of course the British Franchise Association which now has a chapter to itself.

I wish this book, the fourth edition of *The Guide to Franchising*, the success it truly deserves.

BRIAN A. SMITH PhD, MSc
Chairman British Franchise Association

Introduction to the Fourth Edition

In the introduction to the third edition in 1982 I commented on the increasing pace at which franchising was growing in the United Kingdom. Little did I realise that the fourth edition would be published in 1984 or that I would find so much to add.

In making revisions, only Chapters 1, 2, 3, 4, 8, 9 and 12 escaped any radical changes. Each of them has been revised in some way, ranging from tidying up explanations to adding small items. Each of the other chapters has been revised to a much greater extent, with perhaps Chapters 6 and 10 receiving more attention than the others. I have decided that the list which was formerly featured in Chapter 5 (What Can Be Franchised?) is better dealt with in a separate appendix. I have retained the eight founder members of the British Franchise Association for the case study section; they still represent good examples of the application of franchising principles in practice, and we have the difficulties experienced by Ziebart to examine.

There are two new chapters. In Chapter 14 I have featured some of the current developments and issues which have arisen as franchising grows. It did not seem appropriate or effective "to lose" these critical factors elsewhere in the text. I have also devoted a chapter to the British Franchise Association to reflect its growing influence.

Although I devote a chapter of this book to franchise contracts and refer elsewhere to legal considerations, this book is not intended to be a legal treatment of the subject. I have deliberately not gone into many interesting legal facets of franchising, since the purpose of the book is to provide what its title says—a Guide to Franchising. It is primarily intended for the businessman who needs to know what issues arise and will also assist the lawyer or other professional advisors in an understanding of the basic considerations of which understanding is crucial in giving advice. The legal aspects of franchising belong to a separate book which I am now preparing for publication and which will deal with the legal implications in detail and provide an extensive collection of precedents of agreements and clauses.

I have many people to thank:

—the eight founder members of the British Franchise Association for updating their presentations. I do not normally like to single out one person, but on this occasion I must thank Jan Hartmann of Ziebart International Corporation who spent a great deal of time with me in reviewing the problems they had encountered in the U.K.

—Tony and Christine Jacobsen and Tony Dutfield of the B.F.A. for their assistance.

—the Franchise Managers of National Westminster Bank, Barclays Bank, Lloyds Bank and of First National Finance Ltd., for their willingness to co-operate and for providing me with relevant information.

—John Stanworth and Jensine Hough for their help and consent to my use of their statistical information.

—my wife, my son Paul, my Secretary and Wendy Reed, my firm's word processor operator, for their assistance.

—Ann Harris for yet another excellent index.

—to my partners for their help and encouragement.

Introduction to the Third Edition

THE first edition of this work was published in 1970, the second in 1979 and now the third in 1982. This of itself illustrates the ever-increasing pace at which franchising is growing in the United Kingdom.

I have revised every chapter in this edition; some more than others. I have decided to separate the advantages and disadvantages from the different perspective of franchisor and franchisee. The chapter entitled "Setting up a Franchise" is much expanded and owes a lot to the series of articles which David Acheson and I wrote for *Franchise World Magazine*. There is a new chapter entitled "Franchise Advisory Committees" in which I deal with a trend which I feel will become more important. The last chapter, which was formerly entitled "How to Enter the U.K. Market from Abroad", has been changed to "How to Internationalize your Franchise" and has been completely rewritten. Many U.K. franchisors are now looking overseas for expansion and I felt it timely and appropriate to give this chapter wider appeal.

I have also commented on the suitability of Arbitration to many of the disputes which can arise in franchising and, with thanks to the Chartered Institute of Arbitrators, have incorporated the rules of the London Court of Arbitration in Appendix C.

I am again grateful to the eight founder members of the British Franchise Association for updating their presentations.

I also extend my thanks to my wife, my secretary and my firm's word processing operators for their assistance, and to Ann Harris for preparing the revised index with her customary skill.

Introduction to the
Second Edition

Since the first edition of this book was published in 1970 there have been many developments in the field of franchising in the United Kingdom. Indeed, it has become much more prevalent with the major part of the increased growth occurring within the last three to four years. It seems poised at the present time to enter a period of widespread growth.

In the first edition I made a strong plea for the establishment in the U.K. of a trade organisation. This has now occurred and you will find in Appendix A of this edition an extensive explanation of the aims, objectives, and procedures of the British Franchise Association so that its role may be assessed by those who will have contact with it.

I have extensively revised the chapter on "The Meaning of Franchise—Franchising" and included the definition of franchising which has been adopted by the British Franchise Association. I have also enlarged the chapter on "Franchising in Action" so as to embrace a wider field, and each of the eight founder members of the British Franchise Association has been kind enough to participate in this aspect of the book.

I have decided to drop the chapter of the first edition dealing with "Franchising in the U.K.—What Next?" Various other sections of the book have been updated and, where necessary, rewritten and expanded.

I am grateful to Dr. John Stanworth of the Polytechnic of Central London who has recently carried out a field study on three of the companies whose franchises I feature in Chapter 11. Dr. Stanworth has prepared and contributed the Appendix, summarising the results of his interviews with the respective franchisees of these companies. The statistics set out in Appendix B are, as far as I am aware, the only reliable statistical figures available concerning franchising in the U.K. and, as will be seen on reading them and comments I make in Chapter 11, they provided a very interesting insight into attitudes. In the wider sphere, despite the relatively small sample, these figures provide confirmation of many of the theoretical justifications for franchising which have hitherto been expounded.

I should like to express my gratitude to the following individuals and their companies for granting me interviews, where necessary, and for the contributions they have made to this book: John Lawrence of Budget Rent a Car; David Taube and John Gooderham of Dyno-Rod; John R. Corson of Holiday Inn; David Acheson of Kentucky Fried Chicken; Edwin Thirlwell and John L. Scott of Prontaprint; Brian A. Smith of ServiceMaster; Hugh Arthur of Wimpy; Keith Tarry and Peter J. Dunscombe of Ziebart; The British Franchise Association; Tony Jacobsen; Christine Jacobsen (Secretary of the British Franchise Association).

I am again indebted to my secretary who has coped so well with my handwriting and with the typing of manuscripts. Ann Harris has prepared the revised index and I am grateful to her for her help.

Introduction to the
First Edition

FRANCHISING is an industry which has achieved phenomenal growth rate in the U.S.A. and is now beginning to gain ground in the U.K. I feel that it will in due course achieve a rapid growth in the U.K. despite the many misgivings that some people have.

These misgivings arise out of a misunderstanding of the basic philosophy underlying this particular method of doing business. Also an element of mystery that seems to be attached to the use of the word "franchise".

This book is an attempt to break down and analyse what franchising amounts to. Its aim is to provide a quick ready reference guide to the basic principles. It must be appreciated that the scope of this book does not permit a study in depth of the various aspects of a franchise transaction. Indeed, many chapters in this book could form the basis of a separate study.

There are many people to whom I am indebted for assistance with the preparation of this book. My Partners, Bruno Marmorstein, Geoffrey Jacobs, and Bob Patten, for their help and encouragement; and Bob Rosenberg of Dunkin' Donuts of America for reading my manuscript and for his helpful suggestions. I am very grateful to the following individuals and their companies for granting me interviews and for the contributions they have made to this book: Messrs. Acheson, Sharman & Brooks of Pleasure Foods Ltd.; Mr. David Taube of Dyno-Rod Ltd.; Mr. Noel Evison of Five Minute Car Wash Ltd.; and Mr. Leslie Spears of Budget Rent a Car.

I am also indebted to Rogers Sherwood of National Franchise Reports of Chicago, U.S.A., for his immediate agreement to my use of information published by him.

My thanks also to Mrs. Ann Harris for the excellent index which she has prepared.

Lastly, but not least, my thanks to my wife, my secretary and some of the staff at my office who has assisted with the typing of manuscripts at various stages.

CHAPTER 1

The Meaning of Franchise—Franchising

FRANCHISING as a legal or marketing concept is not new. Nevertheless, it is a topic which has in the past aroused suspicion and hostility which it did not deserve and it remains misunderstood by many. As in many instances where adverse judgements are made, lack of understanding is the cause. There is no reason why franchising should arouse any more antagonistic feelings than any other type of business method. Franchising has proved over the last fifteen or so years in the United Kingdom, even through a period of economic slump, that it is a viable method and can have a revitalising influence on the economy. The advances made by the membership of the British Franchise Association in the six years of its existence are quite impressive (see Chapter 2). There has been a surge of interest within the last three to four years which is gaining in momentum, resulting in a rapidly expanding use of this marketing method.

Franchising has evolved out of a number of business transactions, methods, and practices which have been common and popularly known for very many years.

Among the basic features of these business transactions, methods and practices are to be found the following:

1. The ownership by one person of a name, an idea, a secret process, or a specialised piece of equipment and the goodwill and know-how associated with it.
2. The grant of a licence by that person to another permitting the exploitation of such name, idea, process, or equipment and the goodwill and know-how associated with it.
3. The inclusion in the licence agreement of regulations and controls

1

relating to the operation of the business in the conduct of which the licensee exploits his rights.

4. The payment by the licensee of a royalty or some other consideration in the nature of a continuing fee for the rights which are obtained and for any services with which the licensor will provide the licensee.

These features, as will be seen, among others, are also found in every single franchise transaction.

How then did franchising develop into what it is now? To put franchising into its proper perspective it is helpful to consider the well-known business arrangements which have been with us for so many years and then to compare franchising with them. It is evident, with the benefit of the hindsight we now possess, that franchising has grown or, one may say, evolved, as a consequence of the natural development of those arrangements. If this basic point is mastered at this stage it will considerably assist in an understanding of the meaning of franchising.

One of the most common of these business arrangements arises out of the invention of some new machinery. The inventor will wish to ensure that he enjoys the fruits of his invention to the full and will, as a first step, secure his exclusive rights by obtaining a patent.

He may not have the financial resources or the knowledge to achieve the maximum nationwide or, indeed, worldwide exploitation which his invention merits. He may overcome this problem by entering into agreements with others who do have the financial resources and the business acumen to take the best possible advantage of the invention.

He will enter into an agreement granting a licence (or permission) to the other party permitting the manufacture, sale or perhaps merely the right to use the invention in return for a capital sum, a royalty or a capital sum in addition to royalty. This arrangement makes the maximum use of the inventor's skills and know-how, on the one hand, and the financial resources, marketing and other abilities of the licensee, on the other hand.

Another common business arrangement arises out of the coining of a trade mark in relation to certain goods. The owner of the trade mark, for reasons similar to those which motivate the inventor with his patent, will grant a right to others permitting them to manufacture the goods which are identified by the trade mark. The technical name of the agreement employed in such a case is a "registered user agreement", or, if the trade mark is not registered, a "licence". A trade mark user agreement contains provisions which regulate the standards to be observed in relation to manufacture, preparation, presentation, marketing, sale, and the quality of the goods. These provisions are necessary to preserve the standards of quality and the reputation associated with the trade mark. So many of the elements of a franchise transaction are found in such an agreement that, for example, the Wimpy franchise contract is in fact a registered user agreement. The name "Wimpy" is indeed a trade mark for the hamburger sold in Wimpy restaurants.

On a slightly different level are those now very common arrangements whereby the use of a famous name in entertainment, sports, or even a cartoon strip character is licensed. This type of arrangment is referred to as "Character Merchandising". In each of these cases, by entering into licence agreements, the owners of the names and their licensees are both obtaining benefits which would otherwise not be available to either.

There are other transactions designed to benefit licensor and licensee which are worthy of mention. The appointment of a dealer by a motor-car manufacturer (this frequently is a business format franchise which is explained below); the appointment of exclusive sales distributors; the licensing of the use of the name of a large oil company on a garage; as to the latter, everyone is familiar with the Shell, Esso, or Mobil station, but no one would think that all garages bearing an oil company's name are necessarily owned by that company. In many cases the rights granted are now commonly called franchises by those in commerce.

These examples demonstrate that franchising is not new and has been evolving over many years.

What, then, is new? First, there is the wide use of the name "franchising" to describe generically "licence-type" transactions. Secondly, there is the "total business" concept whereby a person develops, as will be seen, a complete system for the setting up and conduct of a business, and licenses (or franchises) others to trade utilising the particular system.

Clearly, there are many types of transactions entered into, all described as a "franchise", each having a different application. The differences will be apparent after the main type of franchise has been defined. To avoid confusion the main type of franchise (i.e. the total business concept) will be referred to as a "business format" franchise, which is the name by which it is commonly known. Some also call it a trade mark/trade name franchise. It is the business format franchise which has been responsible for the rapid escalation in the type of marketing method and for the wider public knowledge of its existence.

The business format franchise involves the exploitation, not merely of goods identified by a trade mark or an invention, but the preparation of the "blueprint" of a successful way of carrying on a business in all its aspects. The blueprint must have been so carefully prepared as to minimise the risks inherent in opening any new business. For example:

—criteria will have been established by which the suitability of sites available for the positioning of the business will be judged. In the case of a mobile franchise, e.g. ServiceMaster, Home Tune, the criteria will be established by reference to the availability of potential customers within a given marketing area;

—the person buying the business will be trained in the business methods which make that business different from other businesses of its type;

—he will be trained, as may be appropriate, in any special methods of manufacture, or processes to be applied to goods, or (as with fast food operations) methods of preparation, or the manner of providing services;

—he will also be trained in the methods of marketing and merchandising which exploit the merits of the business to the full and, one hopes, avoid its pitfalls;

—he will, after training, be assisted in getting his business ready to open for trading; and

—he will acquire the right to use the description by which the business is to be distinguished from other similar competing businesses (i.e. the brand image) while at the same time the business is recognised by the consumer as a part of the larger organisation which comprises him and his fellow franchisees.

All this will be spelled out in the blueprint.

The seller of the blueprint (the franchisor) will have prepared and smoothed the way for a person (the franchisee), who has probably never owned or operated a business before, to open up a business of his own, not only with a predetermined and established format, but with the backing of an organisation which would not otherwise be available to him, i.e. the backing of an organisation characteristic of the head office of a large corporation without many of the disadvantages. For the acquisition of the franchise and the continuing services which the franchisee will obtain (see below) there will, of course, be a fee payable.

What we have then are the four basic features mentioned on page 1, namely:

1. The ownership by one person (the franchisor) of a name, an idea, a secret process, or a piece of equipment and the goodwill and know-how associated with it.
2. The grant of a licence (franchise) by the franchisor to another (the franchisee) permitting the exploitation of such name, idea, process, or equipment and the goodwill and know-how associated with it.
3. The inclusion in the licence (franchise) agreement of regulations and controls relating to the operation of the business in the conduct of which the franchisee exploits his rights.
4. The payment by the franchisee of a fee or other consideration for the rights which are obtained and the services with which the franchisor will continue to provide the franchisee.

But, in addition and fundamentally, there will always be a continuing relationship which should provide the franchisee with full support of a comprehensive range of expert knowledge in the operation of his business in the form of the "head office organisation" of the franchisor.

There have been many attempts at a definition of a franchise in the U.S.A., the home of modern franchising. Most of them seek to provide a concise expression of the elements of the transaction which has the effect of omitting much which should be included. It is not the function of this book to seek to establish a concise definition, for with understanding of the subject such a definition becomes unnecessary. However, there is at the end of this chapter a summary of the features which are essential elements in every business format franchise.

In seeking to achieve understanding it is of considerable assistance to look at some of the definitions which have been formulated. A great number of laws have been passed in the U.S.A., which affect franchising and each provides a definition. The definition in such a case, of course, is not seeking to provide a commercial understanding of the nature of the transaction; rather it is seeking to define business practices which the legislature wishes by the particular statute to bring under some form of regulation. It is proposed to analyse two definitions used by commercial interests. This first definition appears in the by-laws of the International Franchise Association (the I.F.A.), which is the trade association of American franchisors:

A franchise operation is a contractual relationship between the franchisor and franchisee in which the franchisor offers or is obliged to maintain a continuing interest in the business of the franchisee in such areas as know-how and training; wherein the franchisee operates under a common trade name, format and/or procedure owned or controlled by the franchisor, and in which the franchisee has or will make a substantial capital investment in his business from his own resources.

This definition is concise and quite comprehensive, yet at the same time it leaves many questions unanswered and omits features which should be included. The real meaning is hidden in the concise phraseology. For example, it refers to the franchisee making an investment in his own business, yet nowhere does it say that the franchisee must own his business. This point, which is a fundamental feature of a franchise, is implied rather than asserted. As excellent as the definition is, it will be far better understood by those who already have a working knowledge of franchising and of the type of transaction; it is not for those who seek an underlying understanding.

There are a number of significant phrases in the I.F.A. definition and each will now be examined in turn.

1. *"A franchise operation is a contractual relationship."*

Let us clearly establish at once that a franchise is a contract—just like buying a bar of chocolate is a contract. It is no different from any other formal contract in that the terms upon which the contract is made are expressed in the contract. Perhaps it is just that bit more important that a franchise contract contains each and every term which has been agreed, for it is a contract with which the parties are going to have to live for a very long while. Moreover, in most cases it is going to be the sole provider of bread and butter, and hopefully a little jam, to the franchisee, so that any material omission may have an effect on the whole course of his life.

2. *"The franchisor offers or is obliged to maintain a continuing interest in the business of the franchisee in such areas as know-how and training."*

Of course the franchisor must maintain a continuing interest in the franchisee's business, but first, at least, get the business started. This is the first point which is omitted from the definition.

It is the franchisor's obligation to introduce the franchisee to and initiate him in the business which he will be acquiring.

It is the franchisor's obligation to decide responsibly whether the prospective franchisee is in fact the right sort of person for that particular type of franchise. Nothing could be more disastrous for both parties than to place a square peg in a round hole.

It is the franchisor's responsibility by pre-opening training to introduce the franchisee to all relevant areas of know-how which he requires for the satisfactory conduct and operation of the business.

Know-how is one of those meaningless all-embracing terms, until one defines what is intended to be included in the expression. It will, of course, differ from case to case. Know-how for one fast food operation will differ from another, e.g. Hamburgers and Pizza. Also the know-how, even in one Hamburger operation, can differ from that employed in another. Before the franchisee opens for business this vital part of the blueprint which he is being sold must be given to him. Know-how covers suitable business organisation, merchandising as applied to the particular operation, application of the principles of business management appropriate to the nature and type of business, operational methods, introduction to the franchisor's secret and confidential systems, methods, and in some cases formulae. The franchisee must be fully trained in all these aspects before he is let loose in his own business, and when he is let loose he should have any necessary on-the-spot opening help in getting off the ground.

Having reached this stage, the franchisee should have a full grasp of know-how applicable to that particular business; the franchisor should continue to maintain these services on a regular and updated basis coupled with the provision of a trouble shooter or field operations man to assist the franchisee through any difficulties which he encounters and promotional assistance to help maximise the beneficial exposure of the operation to the public to the mutual advantage of franchisor and franchisee.

3. *"Wherein the franchisee operates under a common trade name, format and/or procedure owned or controlled by the franchisor."*

This brings us to the crux of the matter. This relates to the central feature around which the blueprint is developed. To put this into more practical terms it is helpful to refer to the "Wimpy" franchise. In that case the common trade name is Wimpy (it is also a trade mark as mentioned above), the common format is the identical nature of the business carried on by all Wimpy franchisees wherever they are in each of the two categories under which they now operate. Included in this format are the similar shopfronts, the similar shopfittings and decor, even menus and menu cards. The procedure common to all Wimpys is the preparation of the food and the identical nature of the Wimpy one would buy in any Wimpy store in any part of the country, whatever the category of restaurant.

This part of the definition refers to those matters which constitute the basic operation, and by which the public clearly identifies the individual operation as being part of a larger group of similar operations while, of course, the operation and all its counterparts have the advantage of being run on a day-to-day basis by its owner and not by a manager.

The fact that the trade name, format, and the procedure are owned by the franchisor and used by all franchisees in common with each other is what makes an element of control over the franchisee's business essential. Whatever degree of control is exercised by the franchisor over any franchisee should not be looked at by that individual merely as a restriction of his scope to run his business as he thinks fit. He is too close to the problem. To put it into the correct perspective, the only way in which he can fairly consider the matter is to appreciate that the franchisor and all franchisees (including himself) are dependent upon each other for success. A customer lost at one outlet can be a customer lost to all the others also. In effect, the franchisor and all the franchisees are presenting a combined operation to the consumer. As a satisfied customer whose loyalty has been gained by good quality products and/or good service moves about the country he will patronise an operation apparently part of the group which has looked after him well before, rather than that of a competitor.

4. *"And in which the franchisee has or will have a
    substantial capital investment in his business from
    his own resources."*

As mentioned before, the franchisee must own his business. The franchisee has the right to own the business for which he is paying and he must have the right to sell the equity which he has developed in the business.

There may be certain limitations on the exercise of the right to sell; for example, the franchisor may require an option to purchase or he may require first to vet and train any prospective purchaser to satisfy himself that the purchaser satisfies the basic qualifying standards for a franchise and is not going to be a square peg in a round hole. It is also likely that the franchisor will have a waiting list of prospective franchisees to whom the business could be offered for sale.

The reference to the capital investment is not superfluous. It is important that a franchisee makes a substantial capital investment from his own resources. This goes a long way in providing him with the necessary motivation. A person who has his own money at stake, and who can see that he has the opportunity to control the destiny and growth of his asset by his diligent attention to the correct operation of the business, will put everything he can into the business and not the half-interest of a manager.

So far there has been no mention of payment. No franchisor is going to give anything away for nothing. If it appears that he is doing so, this is something which should be investigated. No one is in business to make gifts of his products or services. The franchisor is no exception to this general rule. Payment is made to the franchisor in any number of ways. He may ask for a franchise fee by name. He may sell a package which has the franchise fee included in the price. He may receive a fee calculated as a percentage of the franchisee's gross receipts. Whichever way the fees are to be taken by the franchisor he will be paid both for his initial services and for the continuing service which he provides. One other factor which must be touched upon at this stage is the problem of territorial rights, which is dealt with in more detail later in this work. This is a subject on which there can be no general rule, save that the franchisee must have some assurance that the area surrounding the site of operation will not be over-saturated to his detriment. This is a very difficult matter, for some franchised operations will thrive upon a massive saturation of an urban area while others will, by their nature, require a carefully defined and protected area of operation. A further difficulty can arise from the legal point of view in the light of the provisions of the Restrictive Practices legislation.

The second definition which is considered relevant is that which has been adopted by the British Franchise Association. The British Franchise Association defines a franchise as:

A contractual licence granted by one person (the franchisor) to another (franchisee) which:

  (a) permits or requires the franchisee to carry on during the period of the franchise a particular business under or using a specified name belonging to or associated with the franchisor; and

  (b) entitles the franchisor to exercise continuing control during the period of the franchise over the manner in which the franchisee carries on the business which is the subject of the franchise; and

   (c) obliges the franchisor to provide the franchisee with assistance in carrying on the business which is the subject of the franchise (in relation to the organisation of the franchisee's business, the training of staff, merchandising, management or otherwise); and

   (d) requires the franchisee periodically during the period of the franchise to pay to the franchisors sums of money in consideration for the franchise or for goods or services provided by the franchisor to the franchisee; and

   (e) which is not a transaction between a holding company and its subsidiary (as defined in Section 154 of the Companies Act 1948) or between subsidiaries of the same holding company or between an individual and a company controlled by him.

Apart from paragraph (e), which clearly has a technical basis, and is calculated to exclude "in house" arrangements, the definition embodies much of the I.F.A. definition which has been analysed above. The following points of comparison will be of interest:

   (i) the definition confirms the contractual nature of the relationship;

  (ii) it asserts the right or the licence granted to the franchisee to carry on the business, although it does not provide that the franchisee must own his own business, nor does it state that the franchisee must provide for his investment out of his own reserves, and it does not confirm that the franchisor will be obliged to provide initial training;

  (iii) it deals with the question of control by the franchisor over the manner in which the franchisee carries on the business;

  (iv) it confirms the obligation of the franchisor to provide the continuing assistance which is so essential; and

  (v) it deals with the question of the payment of franchise fees.

As with all definitions it is one which has been coined for a particular purpose, and no doubt it was the intention of the Association to frame its definition on such a basis that membership will be available to companies whose franchise, while not strictly a "business format" franchise, is still a franchise of a more limited nature (see Chapter 5 for a discussion on other types of franchise).

Membership of the Association carries with it responsibilities, and it is clearly in the interests of the Association and of the members of the public that, so long as the business to be conducted is what may be reasonably described as a franchise within the generic sense in which the term is understood in business circles, such a franchisor should have the ability to join the Association. The Association is dealt with in detail in Chapter 15. It is significant that the definition omits reference to the initial training in setting up the business, and it is also significant that the definition omits the requirement that the franchisee should have made a substantial capital investment out of his own resources in the business he would operate. The parallels between the two definitions are quite clear, and from these definitions and this discussion emerge the following basic features which must be present in every "business format" franchise:

1. There must be a contract containing all the terms agreed upon.
2. The franchisor must initiate and train the franchisee in all aspects of the business prior to the opening of the business and assist in the opening.
3. After the business is opened the franchisor must maintain a continuing interest in providing the franchisee with support in all aspects of the operation of the business.
4. The franchisee is permitted under the control of the franchisor to operate under a trade name, format and/or procedure, and with the benefit of goodwill owned by the franchisor.
5. The franchisee must make a substantial capital investment from his own resources.
6. The franchisee must own his business.
7. The franchisee will pay the franchisor in one way or other for the rights which he acquires and for the continuing services with which he will be provided.
8. The franchisee will be given some territory within which to operate.

Mention has already been made of the fact that there are different types of franchise. This aspect will more appropriately be dealt with in Chapter 5. What one must now consider is how and why franchising works in practice.

CHAPTER 2

How and Why Franchising
Works in Practice

ONE fact which is clearly demonstrated in Chapter 1 is that a franchisee opening for business is in a very different position from any other person who does so. The difference arises because of the pre-opening training guidance and preparation for the prospective business and the existence of an organisation to provide the necessary continuing training and guidance which the franchisee obtains while the business is running. This difference, and all it involves, is one of the two major features which lie behind the successful functioning of franchising in practice.

The other feature is the personal involvement of the franchisee as the owner of the business. From the franchisor's point of view it is the difference between dealing with a manager of a branch, with all the difficulties of motivation control and responsibility, and dealing with the owner of a business. The motivation and responsibility of the owner of a business should rarely be in issue, particularly if the franchisor's selection methods are good. The problem of control is not eliminated, but the nature of the problem and the relationship between the parties are different.

A person who opens a new business, particularly if he has no previous experience, runs considerable risks. The effect of these risks can best be demonstrated by statistics, and the figures which have hitherto been quoted as being applicable in the U.S.A. are not regarded by many as being completely reliable.

However, it certainly appears to be the case in the U.S.A. that the failure rates for franchised businesses are substantially less than the failure rates for non-franchised businesses. The most frequently stated figures in the U.S.A. suggest a 90% failure rate for non-franchised new businesses over a five-year period compared with a 10% failure rate in the case of franchised new businesses in the same period. As stated above, these figures are not regarded by many as being completely reliable, and the failure rate for non-franchised businesses was said, at a recent I.F.A. symposium to be 65% over a five year period. However, there certainly is a vast contrast between the failure rates of non franchised businesses compared with those which are franchised. This must, to some extent, account for the remarkable success of franchising in the U.S.A. The U.S. Department of Commerce statistics state that sales of goods and services through franchised outlets in the U.S.A. in 1981 amounted to a sum in excess of $376 billion and that the number of franchised establishments were in the region of 442,418, of which more than half were business format franchises. Indeed, over one-third of all U.S. retail sales are generated through businesses operating under the franchised system. In 1984 it is forecast that the sales total will reach $457 billion and that the number of establishments will rise to 462,000.

Even allowing for the differences which exist between the U.S.A. and U.K., these figures reveal that franchising has achieved great success in the U.S.A., and there is no reason to doubt that proportionately similar success cannot be achieved in the U.K.

In the U.K. there remain no statistics related solely to franchising beyond these which are published from time to time by the British Franchise Association. These are very limited in scope and only relate to the experiences of members of the British Franchise Association.

However, in relation to new business generally, there are the statistics available through the Department of Trade and Industry relating to the lifespan of businesses registered for V.A.T. since 1974. The fact that a business ceases to be registered for V.A.T. does not of itself mean that the business has failed. These statistics show that 40.2% of newly registered businesses ceased to be registered before the end of 1982. Of those, 64.5% ceased to be registered within thirty months of registration and after five years this increased to 91.3%. Of these businesses which are going to fail, the vast majority do so within two and a half years and almost all within five years. This degree of risk in the early years is what franchising seeks to minimise.

From enquiries made by the author, the overall failure rate experienced by franchisees of reputable U.K. franchise companies is negligible and supports the view that in the U.K., as in the U.S.A., franchising is a markedly safer way for a new business to be launched.

It is reasonable to conclude that reputable franchising does work in practice to a considerable extent in overcoming the risks inherent in any new business venture. There is no real reason to suppose that when wider statistics do become available in the U.K. they will reveal a substantially different picture from that revealed by the author's enquiries.

It is also the case that there exist in the U.K. far more franchise operations than most realise, and that franchising in the U.K. is already making a significant economic impact in both the retail and service sectors. The impact is also noticeable in the area of job creation.

Recent surveys of its members by the British Franchise Association (B.F.A.) have revealed some interesting facts. (The most recent survey was in October 1982 and covered forty members).

—the number of retail outlets operated by B.F.A. members doubled from 1,906 in 1978 to 3,969 in 1980 and rose to 4,300 during 1982;
—annual retail sales by B.F.A. members have grown from £154 million in 1978 to £285 million in 1980 and reached £400 million in 1982;
—the total number of staff currently and directly employed in franchising by B.F.A. members is more than 31,000: an increase of 50% since 1981;
—the average initial cost of a franchise is £16,000, excluding fast food, for which the average cost requirement is £55,250. Opportunities vary from an investment as low as £2,500 for a domestic cleaning business to as much as £250,000 for a major fast food operation;
—franchisees' initial cost requirements are obtained in the following way:

> (a) savings or redundancy $\qquad$ 31%
> (b) bank loans $\qquad$ 24%
> (c) finance company loan $\qquad$ 7%

—franchisees come mainly from:

> (a) the employed $\qquad$ 56%
> (b) the unemployed or redundant executives $\qquad$ 8%
> (c) previously self-employed $\qquad$ 36%

It is interesting to note that married couples account for 29% of franchisees and individuale female franchises for only 5% of the total. The intake from unemployed executives is on the increase.

The B.F.A. estimates that business format franchising by members could achieve annual sales of £1000 million by 1985.

Bearing in mind that the B.F.A. survey only covers its membership, which perhaps constitutes only 25–30% of all business format franchises, the potential economic effect which is growing is self-evident.

The European Franchising Federation estimates from its enquiries that the following table indicates the extent of franchising in Europe. It is emphasised that the figures which follow are estimates.

Country	Number of franchisors*	Number of franchised outlets	Sales by franchisees
Belgium	84	2,796	£772 m
France	450	22,000	£5.4 bn
Netherlands	178	4,308	£1.23 bn
German Federal Republic	240	33,400	£2.1875 bn
United Kingdom	250	16,300	£1.295 bn
Totals	1,202	78,804	£10.8845 bn
Denmark, Norway, Sweden, Italy, Greece and Spain			£3.6454 bn
Total sales			£14.5299 bn

* Automobiles and retail excluded.

When a new business fails or experiences difficulties it can be caused by any number of factors, e.g. lack of adequate working capital, a bad business concept, poor trading position for that type of business, lack of basic essential knowledge, poor controls, failure to recognise the danger signals, and so on. None of the factors within these categories should, of course, apply to a franchised operation. The franchisor's know-how should have ensured that the risks arising from these factors are anticipated and by the provision of his continuing services should enable the problems to be avoided or ensure that they were tackled at the appropriate time.

The other type of factor which involves the suitability or otherwise of an individual for a particular type of business, or indeed, owning any business at all, is one which often will only emerge after business has commenced and the die cast. No matter how careful the franchisor is in his selection of franchisee, in some cases he will not know until this point in time that an individual is inadequate in this respect. Some franchisees have a wrong attitude to self-employment. There have been a significant number in practice who have, despite training and warnings, assumed that self-employment does not involve hard work; a "boss" does not work! In this category also come those franchisees who expect the franchisor to do the work for them while they wait for their expected rewards.

There is a marked contrast between a franchisee and a non-franchisee when the business runs into difficulties.

The franchisee has the franchisor to fall back on: he should be guided by experts in his type of business and his losses minimized. He should be given the benefit of further training to see whether the problems can be overcome; he should also be given on-the-spot assistance. Lastly, if all else fails, the franchisor may buy the business back from him as a going concern or, alternatively, introduce a prospective franchisee from his waiting list who will buy the business at the current market price. There have been cases where a franchisor has assisted a franchisee who cannot cope with the responsibility, by providing a back-up team who have got the business back on its feet, to assist the franchisee in effecting the maximum recovery of his capital. There have also been instances where offers to franchisees of that sort of assistance have been rejected where the resulting losses have been so much greater. It is not suggested that the unsuccessful franchisee will not lose any of his investment at all, but at least steps can, and should, be taken to assist in mitigating his loss. The author is also aware of cases where franchisors have provided considerable operational support and thereby helped an initially unsuccessful franchisee to recover and become successful.

How does the non-franchisee stand when he meets his difficulties? Indeed, it is quite likely that without the supporting facilities which the franchisee has available to him he will not even realise for some time that he is trading at a loss. Alas! In many instances too late. Even so, to whom can he turn for advice? His bank manager, his accountant, his solicitor? None of these gentlemen, however skilled, will be able to provide the same guidance as someone who knows his type of business inside out and who, from wide personal experience in that type of business, can quickly analyse the problem and recommend the appropriate action.

It is suggested that there are three elements present in a franchise transaction which provide the key to the probable success of the franchisor/franchisee relationship.

1. The Preparation of the Franchisee

There are very many who embark upon a first business venture knowing what they hope to achieve, but

—without having had any formal introduction to the basic skills required;

—without any formal training in the management of a business;

—without any experience of the controls which it is essential to introduce to ensure that the business is running on a proper profitable basis, if at all;

—without knowing what are the minimum or even maximum margins which they should be achieving;

—without knowing their way around in their dealings with suppliers and what terms of business to expect;

—without having any standing or reputation with suppliers;

—without any real idea of what to expect their staff to be capable of achieving; and

—they may not even know what are the proper rates of pay.

There will always be many with whom they will deal who will be only too anxious to part them from their money.

As we have seen, some of these new businessmen will be successful, but very many of them will pay very dearly for the mistakes which they inevitably will make; their mistakes will be fatal and their business lost before they can apply what they have learned by their experience.

The franchisee, on the other hand, will open for business having been completely and thoroughly trained in all the relevant aspects. He will already, by his purchase of the blueprint, have paid for the knowledge and guidance to prepare him so that he will be able to cope with the problems which will arise. Hopefully, within the framework of his natural skills combined with those acquired in learning he will be able to provide the answers. If these fail him he has the relationship described in the next element to support him.

2. The Continuing Relationship Between the Franchisor and Franchisee

The franchisee, having received all his essential pre-opening training and having been assisted in opening, is not then left to himself.

He should have the assistance of a trouble shooter from the franchisor's head office behind him. If this head office is functioning correctly it should be giving the franchisee the benefit of the cumulative experience of the franchisor and of all the other franchisees in the network. This experience will invariably be presented to the franchisee in well-collated training, instruction, and operating manuals. The franchisee is thus learning by the practical experience and innovations of others and is also making his own positive contribution, both to his own and to his fellow franchisees' success.

There are six elements in this continuing relationship. The franchisor provides:

(a) an operational supervisor in the field (trouble shooter);
(b) the equivalent of a head office organisation which for an individual just would not otherwise exist;
(c) manuals containing the training guidance and advice he has given the franchisee. These will invariably contain a detailed description of the franchise system with full operational instructions;
(d) marketing and promotional advice;
(e) advertising on a corporate basis;
(f) continuing research and development.

The franchisor and franchisee have a mutual interest in the franchisee's success. The franchisee's interest is obvious—it is his own business. The franchisor wants the franchisee to succeed because it will help his own successful growth and benefit the development of the franchised chain. Franchisors and franchisees have a high level of interdependence.

The franchisor's trouble shooter should contact the franchisee even if not asked to call. He will be concerned not only with any problems which the franchisee has, but with ensuring that the franchisee maintains the necessary standards.

He should be competent to analyse its flow of financial information which is received from the franchisee. Very often the breakdown of financial information provides the early warning signs of difficulties for one thoroughly familiar with the business. Certainly it will be possible to check that the margins and expenses are being maintained at the proper proportionate levels. With this information and the keen eye of observation he may be able to spot a problem before it has developed to the point of causing serious trouble or even before the franchisee has realised it exists.

The trouble shooter should be backed by a head office type organisation with specialists in the various fields in which the operation is involved. Examples of the fields which the experts might cover are:

—promotion,
—advertising,
—merchandising,
—product innovation,
—quality control,
—business methods,
—accountancy,
—equipment.

These experts can be called in to assist, and it may be that in arriving at the solution of a problem met by one franchisee the same problem can be avoided or mitigated for all other franchisees.

It is said that necessity is the mother of invention; a franchisor under the pressure of having to help an ailing franchisee succeed may have to experiment and thus develop his blueprint still further and introduce improvements and refinements much more rapidly than would otherwise be the case. This sort of intervention is an example of the greater financial and management resources made available to a franchisee than would be available to a non-franchised individual.

The manuals with which the franchisee would be provided should contain a record of the initial training received. They will also contain advice on how to deal with situations which arise in practice, e.g. what to do if equipment breaks down and whom to contact. Supplements should be produced from time to time to keep all information up to date, as equipment and methods are changed or improved upon.

3. The Franchisee Owns the Business

This, together with the franchisee's financial investment, is what makes the franchisee work harder and better than a manager; he will receive the benefit of the increase in the value of the equity in the business. Indeed, there are many instances where franchisees have opened and developed a franchised business and sold it. The profits made in effecting such a sale have been quite remarkable and, in some cases, substantial. There will always be a ready market for the ethical and well-run franchised business, not only through its franchisor but also on the open market where the attractions of buying into a demonstrably successful business under a nationally known brand name are obvious. Indeed many franchisors have bought in franchised businesses from successful franchisees to operate in future as company-owned outlets.

Thus a considerable incentive exists for the franchisee, for he knows that the greater success of his business operation the more money he will eventually put into his own pocket. For the franchisor, although he will probably earn less from a franchised outlet than from a managed branch, he has far fewer problems. It is not his worry if staff fail to turn up; he does not need vast capital sums to finance the growth or development of his outlets, and he is not critically involved in the day-to-day management problems.

These factors combine to provide a support organisation for the franchisee to ease him through the problems of opening and running his business. If the incentive and application of the franchisee is added, it is seen that a very powerful partnership has been created to ensure, so far as is humanly possible, that the operation will work to the maximum advantage of both franchisor and franchisee.

The nature of the relationship which initially exists and then develops between the franchisor and franchisee is one which both parties must understand and appreciate. It is dealt with in more detail in Chapter 9.

However, franchising is not the answer for everyone; it has its advantages and disadvantages for both franchisor and franchisee. These are respectively considered in the next two chapters and will assist in the formation of a balanced view of the overall picture.

CHAPTER 3

The Advantages and Disadvantages of Franchising to a Franchisee

A PROSPECTIVE franchisee is going to become a businessman capable of making decisions, and before embarking upon his venture he has to make two vital decisions. The first of these decisions is whether or not to embark upon a franchised business. The second is what particular business to select.

In making a decision about the former, an assessment has to be made of the advantages and disadvantages of franchising from the franchisee's point of view compared with a non-franchised business.

Many of the advantages have been touched upon in the previous two chapters, but it will be useful to summarise and expand them again.

Advantages to the Franchisee

1. The franchisee's lack of basic or specialised knowledge and experience is overcome by the training programme of the franchisor.
2. The franchisee has the incentive of becoming the owner of a business supported by the background of assistance from the franchisor. He is an independent businessman within the framework of the franchise agreement and can, by his own hard work and effort, maximise the value of his investment.
3. The franchisee's business opens with the benefit of a name and reputation (a brand image) and goodwill which is already well established in the mind and eyes of the public.
4. The franchisee invariably requires to commit less of his own

capital than is required in setting up independently by reason of the assistance given by the franchisor in obtaining finance. Moreover, the capital required should be more effectively deployed with the franchisor's guidance than it would be by a trial and error first venture. However, many franchised businesses are organised in a highly sophisticated way, and a franchisee may well have a larger investment to make than he would if he were to open for business without the franchise umbrella. Then again, a more modest investment may be inadequate and jeopardise the success of the business.

5. The franchisee should (where appropriate) receive assistance in:

   (a) site selection;
   (b) preparation of plans for remodelling the premises, including the obtaining of any necessary town planning or by-law consents;
   (c) obtaining finance for the acquisition of the franchised business;
   (d) the training of his staff;
   (e) purchase of equipment;
   (f) selection and purchase of stock;
   (g) getting the business open and running smoothly.

6. The franchisee receives the benefit on a national scale (if appropriate) of the franchisor's advertising and promotional activities.
7. The franchisee receives the benefit of the bulk purchasing and negotiating capacity of the franchisor on behalf of all the franchisees.
8. The franchisee has at his fingertips the specialised and highly skilled knowledge and experience of the franchisor's head office organisation in all aspects of his business while continuing in a self-employed capacity.
9. The franchisee's business risk is reduced. However, no franchisee should consider that because he is coming under the umbrella of the franchisor that he is not going to be exposed to any risk at all. Any business undertaking involves risk, and a franchised business is no exception. To be successful, the franchisee will have to work hard, harder than ever before perhaps. The franchisor will never be able to promise great rewards for little effort. The blueprint of a way in which to carry on business successfully and profitably can rarely be the blueprint to a way of carrying on business successfully without working.

10. The franchisee has the services of trouble shooters or field operational staff provided by the franchisor to assist him with the many problems which may arise from time to time in the course of business.
11. The franchisee has the benefit of the use of the franchisor's patents, trade marks, trade names, trade secrets, knowledge and any secret process or formulae.
12. The franchisee has the benefit of the franchisor's continuous research and development programmes designed to improve the business and keep it up to date.
13. The franchisor obtains the maximum amount of market information and experience which circularised for the benefit of all of the franchisees. This should give him access to information which would not otherwise be available to him.
14. There are sometimes some territorial allocations in appropriate cases to permit the franchisee to operate within a defined area around the franchisee's business address. This is an area (see Chapter 10) which can give rise to legal difficulties which, unless handled with care, can bring the transaction within the scope of the Restrictive Trade Practices Act 1976.
15. With the entry of the Banks into franchisee financing (see Chapter 14) the franchisee will have access to lending sources and terms which otherwise would not be available.

Disadvantages to the Franchisee

1. Inevitably, the relationship between the franchisor and franchisee will involve the imposition of controls. These controls will regulate the quality of the service or goods to be provided or sold by the franchisee. It has been mentioned previously that the franchisee will own his business. He will, but the business is one which he is licensed to carry on in accordance with the terms of his contract. He must accept that for the advantages enjoyed by him, by virtue of his association with the franchisor and all the other franchisees, control of quality and standards is essential. Each bad franchisee has an adverse effect not only on his own business but indirectly on the whole franchised chain of businesses and all other franchisees. The franchisor will therefore demand that standards are maintained so that the maximum benefit is derived by the franchisee and indirectly by the whole franchised chain from the operation of the franchisee's

business. This is not to say that the franchisee will not be able to make any contribution or to stamp his own personality on his business. Most franchisors do encourage their franchisees to make their contribution to the development of the business of the franchised chain and hold seminars and national or regional franchisee meetings on a regular basis to assist in the process.

2. The franchisee will have to pay the franchisor for the services provided and for the use of the blueprint, i.e. franchise fees.

3. The difficulty of assessing the quality of the franchisor. This factor must be weighed very carefully by the franchisee, for it can affect the franchisee in two ways. Firstly, the franchisor's offer of a package may well not amount to what it appears to be on the surface. Secondly, the franchisor may be unable to maintain the continuing services which the franchisee may need in order to sustain his efforts.

4. The franchise contract will contain some restrictions against the sale or transfer of the franchised business. This is a clear inhibition on the franchisee's ability to deal with his own business, but, as with most of the restrictions, there is a reason for it. The reason is that the franchisor will have already been most meticulous in his choice of the franchisee as his original franchisee for the particular outlet. Why then should he be any less meticulous in his approval of a replacement? Naturally he will wish to be satisfied that any successor of the franchisee is equally suitable for that purpose. In practice there is normally very little difficulty in the achievement of successful sales or transfers of a franchised business.

5. The franchisee may find himself becoming too dependent upon the franchisor. This can affect him in a number of ways; for example, he may not achieve the motivation that is necessary for him to work and build his business to take full advantage of the foundations that the blueprint provides.

6. The franchisor's policies may affect the franchisee's profitability.

7. The franchisor may make mistakes of policy; he may make decisions relating to innovations in the business which are unsuccessful and operate to the detriment of the franchisee.

8. The good name of the franchised business or its brand image may become less reputable for reasons beyond the franchisee's control.

These, then, are the advantages and disadvantages which every franchisee must weigh up and consider before making the decision on whether or not he wishes to enter into a franchised business. In Chapter

11 there is contained detailed guidance on selection of a franchise. The advantages and disadvantages listed here must be taken into account when considering the factors mentioned in that chapter.

CHAPTER 4

The Advantages and Disadvantages of Franchising to a Franchisor

FROM WHAT point of view, then, should a prospective franchisor approach the position? What are the advantages to him of franchising as opposed to building, developing, and operating his own chain?

Advantages to the Franchisor

1. A small central organisation, which consists of a few highly skilled experts in the various aspects of the business with which the organisation is concerned, can earn a reasonable profit without becoming involved in high capital risk or in the day-to-day detail and problems which arise in the management of scattered small retail outlets.
2. There is not the need for injections of vast amounts of capital to achieve a rapid growth rate. Each outlet which is opened utilises the financial resources of the individual franchisee.
3. It follows quite logically, therefore, that such an organisation has an ability to expand more rapidly on a national or, indeed, international basis using a minimum of risk capital and management resources.
4. It will also be easier to exploit areas which are not already within the scope of the organisation, as franchisees with local interests and knowledge can be obtained.
5. A franchisor has less staff problems with which to cope, as he is not involved in the staff problems of each individual outlet.
6. The local management of each franchised outlet will be keen, well

motivated, and extremely alert to minimise costs and to maximise sales: much more so than would be the case with a manager.

7. A franchisor can achieve wider distribution and ensure that he has secured outlets for his services and products. This is particularly the case in a franchise organised in the manner, for example, in which the Wimpy franchise is. Each Wimpy franchisee has to buy his Wimpy hamburger and certain other items from his franchisor. No other product which he can obtain anywhere on the market can be described as a Wimpy. Any attempt to do so would be an infringement of the franchisor's trade mark and a breach of the franchise agreement.

8. Certain types of franchise schemes, such as the Dyno-Rod drain-cleaning franchise, are able more easily to handle accounts on a national basis. There are many organisations which require the services offered by Dyno-Rod who are able to negotiate with large industrial concerns having a number of factories and premises throughout the country arranging for each local franchisee to handle the work which arises on the premises of the branch of that company within his franchised area. None of the franchisees would have the ability or the capacity to negotiate or service arrangements of this nature on his own, yet the group as a whole has the capacity to do it, and each franchisee by the service which he provides to the franchisor's customer ensures that the group as a whole retains the business of the large national multiple branded company.

Disadvantages to the Franchisor

1. The franchisee very often and very quickly develops a feeling of independence; he is being successful; his business is running well and he is earning what he was told he could expect to earn or perhaps even more. He tends to wonder why he needs the franchisor at all. He becomes convinced that the reason for his success is that he is running his business well on his own initiative. This is a big problem for the franchisor. After all, he may be doing his job well and helping his franchisee achieve success only to find that the franchisee now thinks that he is the person who was responsible for his success and the franchisor is superfluous to his requirements. This is a matter which requires careful handling and skilled supervision.

2. A franchisor has to be on his toes to ensure that standards of quality, services, and goods are maintained throughout the

franchised chain. His trouble shooters will act as supervisors of these standards as well as doing their trouble shooting.

3. There is the franchisee who is not alive to the opportunities with which his business presents him. This again is a matter for careful handling by the franchisor, for the franchisor must never forget that the franchisee does own his business. The franchisee has to be educated and coaxed into accepting that the franchisor's suggestions on which action is needed do amount to sound advice. It is not the same thing as saying to the manager of a business "it is now company policy that so and so should be done and therefore you must do it". The franchisee can never be treated in this way. If the franchisor's reasoning and explanations are good, it should be possible for him to make the franchisee see how much more sensible he would be to do what he is advised by the franchisor to do.

4. There may arise a lack of trust between the franchisor and franchisee arising out of the incompatibility between the franchisee and the individual within the franchisor's organisations with whom the franchisee has to deal.

5. The franchisor may feel that by all the work and effort he is putting in to training the franchisee he is in fact preparing a possible future competitor.

6. The franchisor must be sure that the person selected for the franchise is suitable for the particular type of franchise or, indeed, has the capacity to accept the responsibility of owning his own business. The franchisor owes a great deal to prospective franchisees and to the growth of his own business to ensure that no one who is unsuitable is allowed to take a franchise.

7. There is often difficulty in obtaining the co-operation of the franchisee in decorating and renovating his premises or enforcing other operational standards so that the public is always given service in the manner stipulated in the franchise agreement and in a manner consistent with the brand image of the franchisor.

8. Problems can also arise where the franchised business forms part of a larger business which is carried on by the franchisee. The franchisee can find certain interaction and conflicts between the staff of the two types of business which may operate to the detriment of either or both. The franchisee can also be faced with split loyalties.

9. There is the problem of communication between the franchisor and franchisee. It is vital that each should appreciate the

importance of communication. The franchisee should appreciate that the franchisor cannot read his mind; he cannot know what is troubling the franchisee unless the franchisee tells him. Likewise, the franchisor should not assume that the franchisee has kept himself up to date. It is for the franchisor to ensure that he has communicated his information to the franchisee and that the franchisee has understood and acted upon it.

10. While the headaches and capital requirements are greater, a company-owned unit will be more profitable in cash terms than a franchised unit.
11. If the franchisee is paying his franchise fees calculated as percentage of gross income, he may not be fully disclosing his gross income.
12. There may be difficulties in the recruitment of persons who are suitable for the particular business.

In summing up the disadvantages with which a franchisor is faced, one might say that most of the franchisor's problems of a disadvantageous nature arise from his dealings with the franchisees as an individual and the personalities who are involved. This is a problem with which the franchisor would be faced in running his own business. However, there is a vital and subtle distinction for the franchisor between running his own business and running a franchised business, in that the franchisee is running his own business and he will resent the franchisor trying to run his business for him as if it were merely a branch of the franchisor's company. Each party must appreciate how essential are co-operation and mutual dependence and a tolerance and understanding of the way in which the other thinks.

CHAPTER 5

What Can Be Franchised?

As WILL be appreciated, this work is concerned to a large extent with the business format franchise which is described and analysed in Chapter 1. It has already been explained that there are other types of franchise. Franchise arrangements, in the widest commercial use of the word, are those transactions in which one person grants rights to another to exploit an intellectual property right involving, perhaps, trade names, patents, trade marks, equipment distribution, but not amounting to the entire package, or business blueprint, which is the essential feature of the business format franchise.

These transactions have involved all levels in the manufacture and distribution of goods or products. Thus we see involved in these wider franchises, manufacturers, wholesalers, and retailers, and a complete interchange between all three levels in the distribution and marketing chain.

There are thus franchises involving transactions between:

(a) manufacturers and wholesalers;
(b) manufacturers and retailers;
(c) wholesalers and retailers.

There is also a fourth category namely that between *retailer* and *retailer*; this category is the one which has possibly contributed more than any other to the explosive development of the business format franchise. This would be in the case where the retail business has been a marked success and proprietor makes the conscious decision to expand his chain by the franchise route.

In order to illustrate the three categories of transaction there follow examples of the types of arrangement involved in each case.

(a) *Manufacturers and Wholesalers*

The best-known franchises of this type are, perhaps, the soft drink bottling arrangements entered into by, for example, Coca-Cola and Pepsi-Cola.

(b) *Manufacturers and Retailers*

This category is involved with what are frequently described as "first generation franchises" and includes some of the oldest of this type of franchise arrangement and is effectively limited to the automotive industry. Thus we find the arrangements made by the motor vehicle manufacturers with their network of dealers. We also find the arrangements made between the petrol companies and their filling stations proprietors. So many of the elements of the business format franchise are present in these arrangements that they may appear to be quite close to achieving that status. Indeed, many motor manufacturers' "Main Dealer" arrangements are business format franchises. There are within the scope of the petrol companies' arrangements with filling station proprietors, different types of transaction ranging from a licensee or tenant of premises owned by the petrol company to a sales agreement with the owner of the filling station which may or may not be exclusive.

(c) *Wholesalers and Retailers*

This category is not so clearly capable of identification, at a glance, as being distinctly different from the manufacturers and retailers category. There can really be no commercial reason to differentiate between them except that the franchisor is a wholesaler rather than a manufacturer. These franchises are also not so easy to identify with any we have in the U.K., but they include hardware stores or chemist's shops or perhaps a supermarket. In the U.S.A. the motor vehicle accessory or spares store is clearly identified within this category.

So far as the fourth category is concerned, one need only look as far as the traditional well known business format franchises. Rather than look to the U.S.A. for examples, there are some well known U.K. franchises which illustrate this type of growth. The Protaprint franchise is a good example. This was started as a pilot operation which was expanded to three stores and then, as was the intention from the outset, the concept thus developed was franchised. Another U.K.

example, a mobile franchise, is the Home Tune franchise. This started off as an operation offering the service to the consumer and then expanded by the use of the franchise system. The vast majority of "High Street" franchises have developed in this way—franchising has been chosen as the marketing method most suited to the expansion of the concept.

It will be appreciated that the above categories do not amount to some of the traditional methods or practices described in Chapter 1 as being the business methods from which the business format franchise evolved, namely agencies, distributorships, licensing, and know-how agreements. We shall therefore briefly examine the nature of these arrangements and compare them with franchising.

In the first place there are agencies. What is an agent? An agent is a person with either expressly given authority to act on behalf of another person or one who, by the nature of his relationship with that other person, is impliedly authorised to act on his behalf. The authority given may be a special authority which is limited to doing one or two specific acts or it may be a general authority giving the agent unrestricted power to act. Fundamentally, an agent throughout does not act on his own behalf. He acts on behalf of and in the name of his principal. There is no separation of principal from agent in the eyes of third parties dealing with them. Whatever the agent says or does is completely and effectively binding upon his principal. As between the agent and the principal, of course, there are duties which each owes the other, but the third party is not usually concerned with whatever these private arrangements may be.

In all franchise arrangements the parties usually go to great lengths to ensure that no agency relationship arises. Indeed, invariably in franchise agreements there is specifically a provision that the franchisee is not the franchisor's agent or partner and has no power to represent himself as the franchisor's agent or as being empowered to bind the franchisor. Some agreements even require the franchisee to state prominently that he is a franchisee or licensee of the franchisor so that the consumer or others who deal with the franchisee are in no doubt as to the position.

The expression agency, like the expression franchise, is used quite often in the wrong context. It is, in fact, often used in the context of distribution arrangements. A distributor is, in essence, usually a wholly independently owned and financed wholesale operation which is granted certain distribution rights in relation to a product.

The real relationship between the parties is that of vendor and purchaser. The distributor is a completely independent businessman. Unlike the agent, in his dealings he does not bind the person by whom he has been granted the distribution rights. He may carry a range of products in respect of which he has a distribution agreement, and he may have competing or conflicting lines. The business he conducts is his own business, and he is no doubt motivated purely by commercial considerations deciding whether or not to accept any restrictions which may be imposed upon him in a distribution agreement. The vendor and purchaser relationship may also be present in a franchise agreement, but in most cases it should only be a feature and not the whole substance of the arrangement.

Licensing and know-how agreements are, invariably, the same thing. A licence is descriptive of the nature of a transaction by which one party authorises another to carry out or perform certain functions. A know-how agreement is a particular type of licence agreement and is most widely to be found in relation to technology transfer. These types of arrangement largely arise out of patent or trade mark exploitation and will usually authorise the manufacture of a product or a piece of equipment. It is not necessarily the only business carried on by the licensee. He may well be combining his activities under the licence or know-how agreement with many other activities. It may be that the product which is being manufactured under licence is complementary to, or an accessory of, something else that he does or makes. Alternatively, it may just make a useful addition to his existing range. Again, unlike the agent but like the distributor, he is an independent businessman. He runs his own business; he does not act by or on behalf of the person who granted him the rights. This type of transaction is the closest analogy there is to a business format type of franchise.

How does franchising differ?

Let us take as a simple example a company which manufactures meat products which introduces a hamburger as one of its new lines. Experience shows that the hamburgers sell well and are very popular. Some bright young man in the marketing division says "Why don't we open up our own restaurant to sell our hamburgers?"—so they do.

They could, at that point in time, have decided to get a wider distribution for their product by entering into a licensing agreement with other meat manufacturers for the same hamburger to be manufactured according to the same recipe in various parts of the country or territory with which we are concerned. They may do this in any event. They may have a distribution network of their own or they may distribute through meat wholesalers under distribution agreements.

In this case, however, they have decided, in addition to those traditional methods, to open up a retail outlet, and they develop a limited menu fast food operation built around their hamburger. They have provided an additional method of exploitation of their product and secured retail outlets for its sale. They have gone direct into the retail market, but they do not have sufficient, or do not wish to commit a large amount of, capital to open rapidly a chain of what could prove to be very successful hamburger bars.

So what do they do? They decide to exploit the distribution of the product at retail level by granting franchises or licences to others who will run identical hamburger bars modelled on exactly the same basis as the pilot operation which the manufacturer has set up. The franchisees would trade under the same name which has become established, the same format, the same procedures. They will sell the same product. A consumer should feel on entering each store that it is part of the same organisation and that the service and product is identical in each store. In other words, they establish a business format franchise.

The manufacturer has expanded its distribution network; it has secured additional selling points; at the same time it is utilising the staff and facilities of its head office by providing a back-up to the franchisees in various stores. It is therefore making a far more economic use of the amount of expertise available in its organisation. A very rapid growth of the retail outlets can be achieved without the franchisor having to make available a vast amount of capital resources or to stretch its manpower resources which it can ill afford or which it is reluctant to do.

So far as the franchisee is concerned, what is his position? He is certainly not an agent. He is not acting on behalf of the franchisor and he is not binding or committing the franchisor. He is his own man. He owns his business, he is an independent businessman, he puts the necessary capital into the business and he runs it and manages it. He is not a distributor in the ordinary sense, although he is part of the franchise distribution network. His position is not incompatible with a distributorship, for he is certainly buying a product and selling it, but he is applying a process to the product before resale. He performs his activities as a principal. He does not have other lines; he is not running any other business independent of this arrangement. What he has got is a complete business concept which is, in effect, being sold to him as a package. So there is a contrast with a distributorship, although there is clearly a common pedigree.

How does this franchise compare with licensing and know-how

agreements? In fact the same sort of contrast can be found as exists with the distributorship, although licensing and know-how agreements are even closer relations of franchise transactions than a distributorship. One is inclined to the view that the business format type franchise is directly analogous to the know-how and licensing arrangement. Let us therefore take another look at the franchise arrangement which has been described.

Certainly, there is a licence granted permitting the franchisee to trade under the trade name and in the particular format. There is certainly a know-how agreement. Know-how is imparted in all aspects of the franchised business. Before he is established in business the franchisee will require to be trained in the basic business skills relevant and limited to this particular type of business and in the operational requirements. He will also expect assistance in site selection, design and remodelling of the store, equipment, marketing, and promotion. The franchisee will also expect a continuing interest to be taken in him by the franchisor providing guidance when needed, promotional activities, innovation, and so on. These are the areas in which franchising is providing so much more than the traditional arrangements and which demonstrate the extent of the evolutionary process.

> *With traditional arrangements the agent, the distributor, or the licensee has his skills and experience which he is making available within the framework of the agency distributorship or know-how agreement. In the franchise arrangement the other party (i.e. the franchisee) does not have the skills, or experience, so he is to be given them and then sustained to the extent that he needs it.*

There is also the distribution element in that the franchised retail outlet is part of the franchisor's distribution network, but at a retail rather than a wholesale level, which is normally the case with a distributorship.

One element that is missing from the equation is the agency element, and agency is used in the strict sense. In the loose sense in which it is applied to distributorships it could be said that the franchisee has an agency as well. But certainly no franchisor would want to enter into a franchise arrangement in which the formal relationship between him and the franchisee was that of principal and agent. If that were the case, with all the inherent risks, he might just as well operate his own branch and employ a manager.

Franchising, therefore, is not merely an alternative, it is in reality another weapon in the armoury of the manufacturer, wholesaler, or retailer, which can be utilised to expand his business in addition to the other methods available to him.

It will therefore be appreciated that there is very little that cannot be franchised. Any business which is capable of being run under management is capable of being franchised. This does not mean that any such business will franchise successfully. The successful franchises are usually built round novel concepts, patented equipment, and trade mark associations. They are invariably novel approaches to an existing concept and, indeed, the food industry demonstrates this factor more readily than most.

A restaurant or a cafe is a class of business which has existed for many years, yet when Wimpy emerged on the market in the U.K. in the 1950s the new type of approach—the limited menu concentrating on doing a little but well—brought immediate success. A further illustration of this point is that in the U.S.A. there are at least nineteen different types of food operation under franchise.

The franchise scheme should aim to fill the gap in the market by providing a service or product which is not readily available or available at all. Its introduction should also be timed correctly, for there is no point in introducing a franchised scheme for a service or product which the public have outgrown and do not want or which is on the wane. Temporarily fashionable "FADS" should also be avoided; they will not have staying power.

The clearest idea that can be obtained of what can be franchised is to examine the experience in practice of others. There have over the years been published many lists and classifications of business under franchise in the U.S.A. The following list was published in the first edition of this work in 1970 and remains valid.

1. Accounting/Tax Services. This embraces tax preparation, computerised accounting systems for specialised professions, small business, and traders.
2. Agribusiness.
3. Art Galleries.
4. Auto Diagnostic Centres.
5. Auto Rentals/Leasing.
6. Auto Supply Stores.
7. Auto Transmission Repair Centres.
8. Auto Washes/Products/Equipment.
9. Automotive Products/Services.
10. Beauty and Slendering Salons.

11. Building and Construction.
12. Business Aids/Services.
13. Campgrounds.
14. Catalogue Sales.
15. Chemical Maintenance Products.
16. Children's Products/Services.
17. Cleaning/Maintenance/Sanitation Services.
18. Cosmetics.
19. Credit/Collection Services.
20. Dance Studios.
21. Dispensing Equipment (Food and Beverages).
22. Domestic Services.
23. Employment and Temporary Help Services.
24. Entertainment.
25. Food Operations. This category is broken down into nineteen types of operation:
    Barbecue
    Cantonese
    Chicken
    Donuts
    Fast-Foods
    Full Menu
    Hamburgers/Frankfurters
    Italian
    Mexican
    Mobile Units
    Pancakes/Waffles
    Pizza
    Roast Beef
    Sandwiches
    Seafood
    Smorgasbord
    Speciality
    Steaks
    Miscellaneous Food Operations (e.g. Bakery routes).
26. Fund Raising.
27. Glass Tinting.
28. Health Aids/Services.
29. Health Clubs.
30. Hearing Aids.
31. Home Improvement.

32. Industrial Supplies/Services.
33. Lawn and Garden Care.
34. Marketing Sales Promotion.
35. Motels.
36. Nursing Homes.
37. Office Machines/Systems.
38. Paint/Chemical Coatings.
39. Paint Stripping.
40. Pest Control.
41. Pet Shops and Services.
42. Physical Conditioning Equipment.
43. Printing/Duplicating Services.
44. Publishing.
45. Rack Merchandising.
46. Rentals and Leasing (General Equipment).
47. Safety Systems.
48. Sales Training.
49. Schools/Instruction.
50. Scientific Social Introductions.
51. Sewer Cleaning.
52. Signs.
53. Sport/Recreation.
54. Stores (Retail). These include such stores as: dry cleaners; shoe and heel bars; ice cream; bridal salons; jewellers; gift shops; and coin-operated laundries.
55. Swimming Pools.
56. Telecopy Systems.
57. Television Systems.
58. Travel Agencies.
59. Tree Services.
60. Vending Operations.
61. Vinyl/Plastic Repair.
62. Water Conditioning Systems.
63. Weight Control.
64. Wigs/Hairpieces.
65. Miscellaneous Products and Services.

Now six years old and still relatively young with, at the time of writing, fifty members, the British Franchise Association's membership already covers the following twenty-four business classifications. These classifications also incorporate the twenty-four businesses which are listed in the B.F.A. register (see explanation in Chapter 15):

1. Motor Vehicle Services.
   (a) Rustproofing.
   (b) Car-tuning Service.
   (c) Motor Accessories; Cycles; Cycle Accessories; Camping; Caravanning and Leisure Goods.
   (d) 24-hour Mobile Windscreen Replacement Service.
   (e) Exhaust System Replacement.
   (f) Vehicle Security System.
2. Brewers.
3. Car Hire.
4. Drain and Pipe Cleaning.
5. Print Shops.
6. Fast-Food.
   (a) Fried Chicken.
   (b) Hamburgers.
   (c) Ice Cream Parlours.
   (d) Restaurant/Snack Bars.
   (e) Pizza.
   (f) Coffee Shops.
   (g) Baked Potato Shops.
7. Hotels.
8. Central Heating and Air Conditioning.
9. Repairing and Recolouring of Vinyl and General Upholstery Services.
10. Soft Drinks.
11. Hairdressers.
12. Window Blinds.
13. Same Day/Overnight Parcel Delivery Services.
14. Formal Wear Hire Service for Men.
15. Carpet, Curtain Cleaning, etc.
16. Driving Schools.
17. Industrial and Office Cleaning.
18. Accounting Services.
19. Miscellaneous Retail.
    (a) Bridal Attire.
    (b) Kitchen Equipment: cutlery, crockery, etc.
    (c) Perfume.
    (d) Confectionery.

(e) Health Foods.

(f) Home Security.

20. Building Maintenance.
21. Home Decoration Design Services.
22. Travel Agent.
23. Dry Cleaning.
24. Advertising Services.
    (a) Estate Agents' Signs.
    (b) In Store Display Units.

A selection of the franchises listed by the United States Department of Commerce, *Franchise Opportunities Handbook*, results in the list which is contained in Appendix A. The list follows the business-type classification in the handbook and comprises some forty-one categories (up from thirty-eight two years ago) compared with the sixty-five shown on pages 36–38.

It will be seen from this selection how widely franchising has been applied in practice and how limitless the scope appears to be. There has also proved to be room for more than one similar type of business within each classification.

In assessing whether a business may be franchised the following criteria should be established:

1. The concept must be proved in practice to have demonstrated its success.
2. It should be distinctive both in its public image and in its system and methods.
3. The system and methods must be capable of being passed on successfully to others.
4. The financial returns from the operation of the franchised unit must be sufficient:

   (a) to enable the franchisee to obtain a reasonable return on the assets employed in the business;
   (b) to enable the franchise to earn a reasonable if not good reward for his labours; and
   (c) to enable the franchisee to make payment to the franchisor of a reasonable fee for the services which he will continue to supply to the franchisee.

There is a word of caution, however; a prospective franchisee must decide whether he is being offered a franchise at all. A franchise scheme must contain the elements of a franchise as described in the first chapter to qualify as a business format franchise.

A number of business opportunities offered in good faith are often loosely described as "franchise opportunities". Examination of the elements of the transaction by reference to the principles contained in Chapter 1 will assist in reaching a conclusion as to whether or not it is a franchise. The types of business that are likely to be within this category are area distributorships, agencies, and dealerships, as described earlier in this chapter. These have certain elements of a franchise, but usually a vital element such as the continuing relationship is almost completely lacking. While these other types of businesses do not amount to a business format franchise they are frequently conceived and developed by the application of the principles upon which such a franchise is based.

New schemes amending and adapting these principles will arise from time to time. This is only natural. It is, however, important that any prospective franchisee should recognise the extent of the services and facilities being offered to him. The fact that a particular business on offer does not amount to a business format franchise does not of itself mean that it is not worthwhile.

The ingenuity of the businessman has fully demonstrated the versatility of franchising as a business method.

The ingenuity of the modern businessman unfortunately has not been limited to the pursuit of legitimate ethical franchising. Indeed, franchising offers scope for the fraudulent as the transaction involves a continuing relationship. If, therefore, the initial franchise fee is set too high, allegedly to cover some of the continuing services which are never intended to be provided, the scope for fraud is obvious. There developed what has become known as the "pyramid selling" scheme which is also sometimes described as a multi-level marketing scheme.

These schemes involve the sale of distributorships to purchasers who may divide and subdivide them and sell them on to those whom they recruit as sub-distributors. Expansion of these enterprises takes place on the chain-letter principle. The ostensible object is to build up a sales force which will sell the company's products or services from door to door. In fact, selling the goods or services is difficult; they are usually expensive, and areas are often saturated with other distributors. Selling distributors is much more lucrative and becomes, effectively, the company's business.

There is a very good description of a pyramid selling scheme in a 1972 case in which the Secretary of State for Trade and Industry brought proceedings to wind up two companies which were engaged in a pyramid selling scheme.

The case was heard by Mr. Justice Megarry (as he then was) who described the scheme in that case in the following terms:

The sale of cosmetics is conducted through a hierarchy of individuals. At the lowest level there are "Beauty Advisors", who sell the company's products direct to members of the public. Above them there are the "Supervisors", who not only themselves sell to members of the public, but also each recruits and supervises a team of beauty advisors. Above the supervisors are the "Distributors", who constitute the top rung outside the company, and may have a team of supervisors under them. As I have indicated, the rights that go with the position of distributor or supervisor are embraced by the term "franchise". The company allows a discount of 60 per cent on its products, and when a beauty adviser makes a sale, he or she received half that discount, and the other half is shared equally between the supervisor and distributor above the beauty adviser in the chain. On direct sales by a supervisor, the supervisor receives a commission of 45 per cent, and a commission of 15 per cent goes to his distributor. On direct sales by the distributor, the full 60 per cent commission goes to the distributor.

In addition to any profit that the company makes on the sale of cosmetics, the company has the other source of income that I have mentioned. A distributor has to pay £1,500 to the company for his position. If he has been recruited by another distributor, that distributor receives a commission of £795 from the company, the company keeping the balance of £705. On the other hand, the supervisor pays the company £700 for his position, and for his recruitment the company pays a commission of £245 keeping the balance of £455. If the new supervisor has been recruited by a distributor the distributor keeps the whole of the commission. If the new supervisor has been recruited by another supervisor, the commission is in effect split between that supervisor and his distributor, the supervisor receiving £140 and the distributor the remaining £105.

After a supervisor has been appointed, he may secure his promotion to distributor on paying a further £800 to the company, this sum bringing his initial £700 up to the requisite £1,500. On such a promotion occurring, the distributor who originally recruited the new distributor, or whose superior recruited him, receives a commission of £550, the company keeping the remaining £250 out of the additional £800.

The financial incentive to recruit distributors or other participants in the scheme is self-evident. The lack of incentive to sell products was reflected in the evidence, from which it emerged that average sales of products during the period July 1971 to January 1972 at a peak reached between £8 and £9 per week per participant. On the other hand, one distributor had received £5,625 for the sale of the right to participate.

The main emphasis by the companies in marketing the scheme was placed upon the money which could be earned by the recruitment of distributors and supervisors. The rewards could be considerable. If a distributor could each month promote one supervisor to be a distributor and the supervisor appoint another to take his place, the distributor would earn £10,800 in a year. The company, of course, would have been paid £13,920. There is no mention of the income to be generated by sale of products.

Evidence was given by the Government Actuary that if each distributor achieved the targets indicated in the manual, after two years there would be over 16 million distributors. If, on the other hand, each distributor achieved as encouraged in the manual, double the rate, there would be 16 million distributors after one year, over 66 million after thirteen months and over 280 billion in two years.

The judge concluded that the projected figures in the manual were "utterly devoid of reality".

The fundamental difference between franchising and pyramid selling lies in the objective of the participant which, when fulfilled, will earn him profit.

The franchisee intends to and can only make his profit from conducting his fast food restaurant, mobile service or other business.

The pyramid participant gets his main profit from recruiting equal or lower status participants. Supplying goods or services to consumers is incidental and may be of so little advantage that the participant does not bother with it.

A franchisee gets nothing from recruiting others. A pyramid participant (except at the lowest level) gets practically nothing from anything else.

These pyramid schemes have been recognised as containing elements which are dishonest and, accordingly, the Fair Trading Act 1973 contains provisions which define pyramid-type schemes. The Act also contains provisions which permit the making of regulations (which have been made):

(a) to control or prohibit the issue, circulation, or distribution of documents circulars, notices, advertisements and announcements which contain invitations to persons to participate in a scheme; and

(b) prohibiting the promoter of a scheme from performing functions which are vital to the operation of such a scheme:
  (i) a limit of £25 on the value of goods to be supplied to a participant in a scheme unless advised in writing;
  (ii) the prohibition of non-returnable deposits;
  (iii) the prohibition of charging for the provision of training or other services to a participant.

One of the basic weaknesses of the regulations is that they do nothing to restrict statements made orally at sales meetings held by those who promote pyramid or other multi distributorships. These meetings were the technique employed for selling pyramid schemes and were used to generate a high level of infectious enthusiasm which lowered the guard of those attending and played upon their greed for making money. The regulations do nothing to control or prohibit the use of this technique.

It is vitally important to be able to recognise involvement with a pyramid-type scheme. And obviously before signing any contract or parting with money one should take proper professional advice. But it is a matter for suspicion if one is offered or told that there will be a reward (i.e. payment, supply of cheaper products, or any other disguised benefit) for doing something totally unrelated to the sale of the basic product or service with which the scheme is involved. For example, one may be offered a percentage payment of any sum paid to the promoter of the scheme for recruiting another participant, or for persuading such participant to purchase a higher position in the scheme. Other rewards could include a profit or commission on sales, or the provision of services or training to other participants in the scheme, or a commission on sales effected by other participants in the scheme. Attendance at meetings of the nature described above should be avoided, but if one is tempted to join such a meeting the temptation to sign up on the spot must be avoided. If tempted, one should take away any paperwork which is presented so that appropriate professional advice can be taken. If one is not permitted to remove the documents one should not pursue the proposition further.

Pyramid-selling schemes have cost, for some unsuspecting people, a great deal of money; there are may legitimate franchises in which to invest without becoming involved in pyramid schemes. No legitimate franchise will do what the pyramid schemes do, and that is to promise rich rewards quickly and without hard work. Whatever is being franchised legitimately will offer reasonable prospects of good rewards in return for the hard work and application which is the lot of all successful self-employed businessmen.

CHAPTER 6

Setting Up a Franchise

THERE are seven basic elements involved in setting up a franchise which break down as follows:

1. Business concept.
2. Pilot operations.
3. Developing the franchise package.
4. Developing the operational manual.
5. Marketing the franchise package.
6. Selecting franchisees.
7. Developing the franchisor's organisation.

We shall consider each in turn.

1. Business Concept

The move into franchising can arise in two sets of circumstances. The first is when it is decided to expand an existing business by means of the franchise system. The second, which is more rare, is when a positive attempt is made to set up and establish a business for franchising from day one.

The latter case is not to be recommended for the beginner, and although an experienced franchisor may be able to proceed in this way, significantly few have succeeded.

Indeed, one can go further; only very few successful franchisors have been able to expand their activities into the development of another franchise.

The more usual course is for the proprietor of an existing business, which has scope for a more rapid expansion rate than its capital and staff resources would permit, to turn to franchising as the means to exploit that scope to the full.

There are also some companies which see franchising as an additional way of expanding their retail network without requiring additional capital or manpower.

It is essential if one is intending to franchise to keep the business system simple. Others with have to be taught to operate it as successfully as the innovator, and the more complex it is the more difficult it will be to recruit, train and sustain franchisees. So basically the scope must deliberately be limited to a framework which is manageable by others.

It is also important that the business is easy to set up in terms of shopfitting and installation of equipment. Let us look at a fast food operation as an example—a large number of franchised operations have been built up in this field. The more simple the design and layout of the kitchen and preparation areas, the more standardised the decor, design and layout of the take-out and/or restaurant area, the easier it will be to adapt premises to the design and the more quickly one can cope with the establishment of each operation. There is also the paramount need to keep the menu simple. This reduces the inventory requirements and makes it possible to keep the preparation and serving of the food simple, quick and efficient. Also one is more likely, with a simple and limited menu, to limit the amount of equipment to be employed and thus reduce the requirements of the business in terms of space, initial cash and maintenance.

The overall aim should be to simplify control, reduce paperwork, and make the system as foolproof as possible.

A retail outlet is another example of the extent to which the franchisor must go to try to achieve simplicity. Apart from the design, decor, and layout, which are all vital, there is the question of the stock inventory. The more extensive it is, the more complex is the task of all who will have to deal with it, and the greater likelihood of financial loss through mismanagement.

A classic example of good stock management is that of the American and International 7-Eleven Convenience Stores, which carry a very large range of stock as well as an extensive inventory. These stores are in reality what, in England, are called the "corner shop" or the comprehensively-stocked "village store". 7-Eleven keeps a rigid degree of control of its franchisees over their stock and produces two or three times a week, via its computer, detailed inventories of stock.

This may be an extreme case, but it does illustrate the degree of care taken in developing their particular concept, recognising as it does the problems of a wide ranging and extensive stock inventory. The result of this care in development, tempered by the franchisor's experience, has been to provide franchisees with a back-up service and information which no single trader in a business with highly aggressive, low margin competitors working on large volume could ever hope to achieve or expect to match.

Thus we see that the development of the concept requires meticulous planning and anticipation of needs and problem areas.

It is also important that one defines clearly the market at which one is intending to aim the business. There is little point in having a good idea and a great business prospect if, for example, as can be the case in the motor trade, one is dependent upon others in the trade who do not see the need to deal with the business being established, or who are already coping with the aspect of the business in which one is interested. Nor is there much point in aiming oneself at the ultimate customer if that customer is, through common practice or prior business contact, likely to go to the established trade first. This could arise if one is intending to provide a specialist service which may be part of the total service which existing motor traders or service stations provide. This does not mean that one cannot seek to innovate and attempt to break in, but there is a vast difference between taking the risk inherent in taking such steps for oneself and selling to others the right to take those risks.

There are five important facets to the question, "Is one aiming at the right market?" These are:

1. Franchisees with finance—will the franchisor be able to attract franchisees with, or able to acquire, sufficient finance?
2. Staff skills—will the franchisor and the franchisee be able to attract staff with adequate skills, or can the skills easily be taught?
3. Property—can sufficient suitable property be found and afforded?
4. Consumer demand—is there, or will there be, sufficient market demand for the product or service?
5. Will the business have staying power or is it merely pandering to a temporary fad or fashion?

A principal aim should be to make the business distinctive in its image. Each franchised business which is successful has its own innovative concept, which sets it apart from other businesses of the same type. This is what makes people choose to patronise that business as well as, or instead of, others in the same category. The existence of competitors can often be very healthy. It can help to develop and enlarge the overall market and act as a stimulant to both franchisor and franchisee alike.

Do not copy or imitate others. In the long run it will not be profitable. They may have legal sanctions which they can bring, but even if they have not they are probably already working out how to update and improve upon what they are presently doing. They will no doubt, through the development of their business and their longer experience, always keep one step ahead.

In order properly to protect the distinctiveness of one's business image it is best, if at all possible, to structure it around a trade mark registration. It should be noted that trade marks in England can only be registered in respect of goods. The Government have accepted the principle of introducing service mark registration—that is, trade marks in respect of the provision of services—and it is hoped that these will be introduced in the near future*. This will make life somewhat easier for the franchisor of a service and enhance his ability to protect his name. In selecting a trade mark or trade name there are some basic principles which experience and market research have shown to be wise:

1. It should be easily pronouncible—compact and roll easily off the tongue.
2. It should not be capable of being translated. What sounds good in English may be offensive when translated into a foreign language.
3. It should be an invented, or coined work, which is more readily registered as a trade mark.

Remember that the franchisee's business will not only have to provide sufficient profits to enable the franchisee to obtain an acceptable return on capital and salary, but it must also provide sufficient to enable the franchisee to pay a fee or royalty to the franchisor for the provision of all the continuing services which will be available. Unless the business can generate sufficient profitability for these purposes one will have to think again.

It is essential before commencing franchising to have proved by experience in actual operations in the market place that the business is clearly a success. Success in the franchising phase will also need:

1. Good timing for its market introduction.
2. A climate of confidence in the business which has been developed.
3. A supply of franchise prospects with adequate financial resources.

* An Act has now been passed to introduce Service Mark registration by October 1987.

Having established the business with a distinctive name, image and system, the next step is to set up and experiment with a pilot operation.

2. The Pilot Operation

It is essential that at least one and probably in many cases a number of pilot operations should be established. It may be necessary to set up more than one pilot operation so that one can demonstrate that the success of the business is not dependent on what might be considered a unique or a typical location. The business must be able to achieve a universal acceptance and be demonstrably capable of that achievement.

It has been suggested that a pilot operation is not always possible or relevant, and that the franchisor can overcome the lack of a proven pilot scheme by giving to the franchisee a guarantee of his money back in the event of failure.

In the author's view this is a dangerous attitude and one which negates the fundamentals upon which business format franchising is established. Fundamentally and essentially the franchisor is selling a sophisticated package of know-how. If the franchisor has not proved the ability to operate that package with success, putting his own money at risk, he has no right to market the franchise. Nor indeed will he have established the goodwill, reputation and identity of the name which is associated with that package.

It is irresponsible to seek to establish a franchise by the trial and error of the initial franchisees. It is also the path chosen in the past by those who have perpetrated frauds upon the unsuspecting. A guarantee of money back is no substitute for a lost business or a lost opportunity. Anyway, how with an untried and untested concept does one ensure that the franchisor will be there with adequate money to pay back to those who claim. Even if the franchisor and the money are there, inevitably there will be disputes about whether the failure was that of the "franchisor's" concept or of the franchisee's failure to comply with the franchisor's guidelines. There can also be disputes about the extent of losses. Is it loss of capital or trading losses or both?

One cannot emphasise too much the great responsibility borne by a franchisor to his franchisees. These franchisees will be invited to part with their life savings, change their whole way of life and, to a great extent, become dependent upon the franchisor and the concept for the welfare of themselves and their families.

Apart from these justifications for the pilot operation it will fulfil the following functions:

(a) The viability of the concept in practice will be developed and established as acceptable and exclusive in the minds and eye of the general public.

(b) It will identify problem areas in relation to:

    (i) marketing,
    (ii) acceptability of product or service,
    (iii) methods of marketing,
    (iv) local By-laws (e.g. building regulations),
    (v) fire regulations,
    (vi) health and safety at work,
    (vii) wages council regulations (if applicable),
    (viii) planning requirements,
    (ix) staff availability and training requirements,
    (x) taxation, including V.A.T.,

and the other similar aspects which are relevant to the particular type of business.

(c) It will enable the franchisor to experiment with layout (see below) so as to discover the best combination of equipment and the decor and design of interior and exterior.

(d) The actual trading experience and potential of different types of locations can be obtained. This will include experimenting with opening hours to discover what are the optimum hours during which the business should be operating. It should be borne in mind that in deciding the trading hours during which the business will be open one must give consideration to staff hours and a shift system. It could be that the ongoing costs of opening at certain times might make it uneconomic to be open owing to the need to introduce additional staff.

(e) It will be appreciated that as training in the operational side of the business is necessary so, of course, is training in the business management and accounting aspects. In developing the pilot operation particular attention should be paid to the introduction of simple and effective systems of accounting, stocktaking and controls (e.g. in a food operation, portion and quality controls).

(f) Bearing in mind the need for an operations manual, there should be developed detailed job descriptions outlining the specific duties of each member of staff and the manner in which they are to be performed.

So far as the layout of the premises is concerned, the requirements will obviously differ from case to case. Some businesses are very dependent upon the way in which goods are merchandised, others will not be. In other cases the way in which the staff conduct themselves and the way their time and activity is organised can be of great importance. This point is best illustrated by reference to the fast food business. These will either have a separate kitchen or a "call bar"; in both cases the layout will have to be carefully planned so that the preparation is progressed by logical steps without the need, so far as possible, to retrace one's steps. The whole operation of preparation will, in all probability, be timed, and if the layout is such that a few unnecessary seconds per operation are inevitably required this could add up to an additional employee. This would reduce the profitability of the operation and is illustrative of the sort of costing which could stand between a scheme which could be franchised and one which could not. One of the features for which the franchisee could be paying is the "fine tuning" which lead to these economies of operation. In a "call bar" situation the availability within easy reach of what is required is essential if staff are not continually to be getting in each other's way.

Having proved the concept with the pilot operation, this does not mean that the need for continuous "pilot" operations ceases. The need, in fact, is greater, except that from being called "pilot" operations they are now company-owned stores. The franchisor has to remain ahead of the game; he must be continually experimenting and developing, and by being in the field, in the market place, he can put his experiments and developments into practice. He will know that what he suggests to the franchisee is proved and tested and will be able to demonstrate that to franchisees. It is just as important that the continuing developments are proved and tested as it was to prove and test the initial concept by the establishment of the pilot operation.

A franchisee may at some time need to be persuaded that his store needs refurbishment, that equipment should be replaced and that he must update the appearance of his store. What better way is there to persuade him than to be able to demonstrate by the experience obtained in a company-owned store just what can be achieved.

3. Developing the Franchise Package

The experience obtained in setting up and running the pilot operations will provide the basis upon which the elements in the package are structured. The package involves bringing together the accumulation of the total experience in a transmittable form.

It might be considered appropriate at this stage to consider employing the services of a consultant. Certainly there are some who offer franchise consultancy services, and the considerations which arise in employing a consultant are dealt with in Chapter 14.

The franchisor will have to know where one can establish a unit and the criteria by which the site can be judged. It will be appreciated that the factors which follow will not necessarily apply in all cases. Some franchise operations are dependent upon the specific location from which trading is to be carried out, others, mainly mobile operations, may depend upon advertising and marketing followed by telephone contact. Retail and fast food franchises are typically in the former category, while such franchises as Dyno-Rod and ServiceMaster are in the latter. Furthermore, experience with the pilot operations should have indicated when custom is likely to arise and what time of day or week is likely to produce peaks of business activity.

It is suggested that the following considerations, which are not unique to franchising, should be taken into account in assessing the degree of business activity a particular site may be capable of generating. The requirements will differ in some cases and so may the conclusions to be drawn from the information revealed by enquiries.

(a) Type of street:

    (i) dual carriageway—is there a centre barrier?;

    (ii) local road or trunk road;

    (iii) motorways are very expensive and services on motorways are very restricted;

    (iv) is car parking available?;

    (v) is there a traffic hazard inherent in the site?;

    (vi) do not be misled by the existence of a pedestrian crossing. These crossings take people away as well as bring them towards a site. If the crossing is leading to a town centre or shopping area it could place the site just out of the main flow of pedestrian traffic.

(b) The environment:

This is an increasingly important factor in assessing the suitability of sites and the appropriateness of the type of business.

(c) Foot and/or road traffic volumes:

The volume of traffic must not be permitted to mislead. For example: Road traffic may not stop if it is travelling too quickly or if there is too much congestion or risk of congestion. Similarly, foot traffic can be quite large but disinterested for various reasons; such as, commuter foot traffic at a London Railway Terminus Station; there people are invariably in a great hurry in the morning to get to work and in the evening to catch a train and will only stop for a quick, maybe impulse, purchase.

(d) The degree of identification to which the premises are exposed:

This will depend for its importance on the specific franchise involved, but clearly the better exposure to public gaze the greater the prospects of business.

(e) Landmarks and the business they generate:

    (i) museums;
    (ii) schools;
    (iii) cinemas, pubs, dance halls;
    (iv) youth clubs;
    (v) certain multiple stores in a High Street or shopping centre, e.g. Marks and Spencer or Sainsbury's;
    (vi) office blocks;
    (vii) sports facilities (which may provide evening and weekend business);
    (viii) travel facilities, e.g. railway stations, (in London) tube stations, coach depots, car parks;
    (ix) tourist attractions;
    (x) post offices;
    (xi) banks.

Having decided that the particular location is acceptable by the relevant criteria, one also has to assess the premises for their suitability for the purposes of the specific business. This also would be the case, of course, regardless of the fact that there will be a franchise involved. The factors to be considered and the effect they have on the business would include:

(a) The size of the premises and whether one can fit into them all the necessary fixtures and fittings and equipment (if any) and selling space.

(b) The suitability or otherwise of the premises for conversion into whatever sort of end product at which one is aiming. This must take into account the ventilation, sanitation and health requirements so far as may be appropriate.

(c) The availability or otherwise of the necessary services at the premises.

(d) The amount of rent and rates.

(e) The terms upon which the lease will be granted.

(f) And then in particular drawing on the experience gained in running the pilot operation assessing the cost of:

    (i) obtaining the necessary Planning Consents as well as the likelihood that they will be forthcoming;

    (ii) complying with Building By-laws and Fire Regulations; and

    (iii) complying with any other Statutory or Local Authority By-law requirements.

In the case of a mobile franchise these considerations are not relevant. Examples of mobile franchises include ServiceMaster and Dyno-Rod, whose case studies are featured in Chapter 13. Other examples include Home Tune, the mobile care tuning service, whose franchisees tune motor cars at the home or the business premises of the customer; Snap on Tools which provides for the sale of tools at their place of work to those who use them; and Identicar which provides for the marking of vehicles as a theft deterrent.

In the case of a mobile franchise it is the assessment and selection of the area of operations which is important; the location of trading premises is a very secondary factor, and in many cases, certainly in the early stages, the franchisee can run the business from his home.

The need to be visible and uniform in appearance is achieved by the use of the same type of vehicle which is decorated in a distinctive livery so that each operational unit is a moving advertisement for the franchise and the franchisees' business.

Marketing of these sort of operations is calculated to ensure that potential customers are aware of the service being offered, and when they require that type of service will think of the trade name of the franchisee: use by consumers of these services is invariably on "an occasional as the need arises basis" and the most frequent point of contact is the telephone. These schemes tend, therefore, to market their telephone numbers in association with their name and to be heavy users of Yellow Pages and other telephone directories and guides. In a number of these cases, control by the franchisor of the telephone number's association with the trade name is essential, and the franchisor will tend either to become the subscriber or to require that on termination of the franchise agreement the franchisee will surrender the use of the number, preferably by transfer to the franchisor.

The experience obtained in running the pilot operation will enable the franchisor to prepare standardised packages which can be varied and amended so as to fit in with the requirements of a particular site. The basic requirements in terms of fixtures and fittings and equipment will have been established, as will the correct layout. This may have to be amended to fit into the particular premises which have been obtained, and the franchisor should set up arrangements to enable this service to be provided. The franchisor will also direct the franchisee to ensure that the decor of the store reflects the established brand image.

It should also be possible with the information available to the franchisor to streamline the preparation of any applications which are necessary for Planning and By-laws and to anticipate the problems which may have to be faced.

The franchisor will also prepare operational manuals which will provide the franchisee with all the information he will require in connection with operation of the franchised business. The manual will invariably be used in training, and then while the franchisee is running his business he should have it available to him at all times so that he can obtain guidance or refresh his memory on any aspect of the business. Most manuals contain very detailed guidance on even the tasks to be performed by each individual member of the staff of the franchisee. The manual is an essential part of the process whereby the franchisor transfers to the franchisee his know-how relating to the running of the franchised business.

The franchisor frequently will make arrangements with suppliers of the basic material or goods in which the franchised business deals for their sale to the franchisees at competitive prices. These arrangements may extend to suppliers of any bags, boxes or other materials which are utilised at the point of sale. It will also usually be arranged that these materials will bear the franchisor's trade mark or trade name.

Arrangements will have to be made with equipment suppliers so that proper supplies are available to meet the franchisee's demand for equipment and spare parts and any necessary service facilities are available. Systems of work will have to be reduced to writing. Job descriptions will have to be prepared explaining the scope and all the facets of each employee's activities so as to fit in with the overall scheme.

Promotional literature, including point of sale material, will have to be prepared, as will any common format literature and note paper.

The franchisor will have to set up training schedules and training facilities for franchisees and their staff, where this is appropriate, for the particular type of business. The franchisor will have to prepare accounting procedures and business systems which are to be operated by the franchisee. The franchisee will have to be trained in these systems and methods which will operate to fulfil two purposes. Firstly, to ensure the franchisee has the maximum amount of information available to enable him to see where his operation is going wrong or, if it is going right, that it is in fact going right. Secondly, to provide the franchisor with the maximum information to enable him to keep control of the business in so far as it may be necessary for the purpose of carrying out his trouble shooting and follow-up service. It will also provide the franchisor with information which he will need to have readily available for the purposes of selling franchises.

The franchisor will also be developing the necessary information and skills in order to enable him to give advice to the franchisee in connection with the leasing of premises or equipment and other contracts into which the franchisee may have to enter with suppliers and with those who provide maintenance services generally in or about the conduct of the franchise business.

The franchisor will also no doubt have made arrangements with sources of finance so that assistance can be given to franchisees who require loans or hire purchase for the purpose of financing the acquisition, the initial equipment package and for paying for any of the necessary shopfitting and equipment which is also required for the franchisee to open his business.

In the last two years the Banks have become increasingly involved in the financing of franchise operations, and this development is examined at length in Chapter 14.

There is a clear need for the franchisor to have early consultation with his solicitor to discuss the contract. Franchise contracts are discussed later (see Chapter 10), but at the early stages of the preparation of the package it is sensible to be in contact with one's solicitor. A franchise contract is complex and invariably carries a range of legal topics which are not often seen in one transaction. It is not a document which should be prepared by a layman, as there are too many potentially difficult legal aspects for this approach to be successful except by accident. The contract should reflect one's business practices, methods and systems, and it is as well to ensure that what is proposed in structuring the package is capable of achievement in legal terms. The contract is also part of the franchisor's sales literature and should be written in an uncomplicated style.

However, it is wise to take advice about trade marks, trade names, copyright and trade secrets at the earliest possible time; possibly even before establishing the pilot operation. Solicitors should be able to give the necessary advice and may also consult with a trade mark agent. At the same time advice should be taken to ensure that, whatever industrial and intellectual property rights are being developed, nothing is done innocently which might put them at risk.

In any event, before the package can be sold the form of contract must be finalised.

All these aspects are brought together into what is called the franchise package, and it is this package which contains all these diverse but essential elements which are necessary to establish the franchisee in his business.

4. Developing the Operational Manual

The need for an operational manual (or manuals) has already been pointed out. In practice the franchisee will first have contact with the manual when he attends for his training, and then it will be retained by him as his continuing guide to the conduct of his business.

The manual will contain in written form the complete method for conducting the franchised business. It will probably have the benefit of copyright protection which a spoken explanation, not supported by a written script, could not have. It thus forms an essential part of the legal methods by which a franchisor protects his ideas, know-how and trade secrets.

It will be appreciated that the manual should be extremely comprehensive and cover in detail all aspects of the day-to-day running of the franchisor's business not only to provide the business guidance but also in an endeavour to secure the best legal protection. It is not practicable to deal with all types of franchise operation. It is therefore necessary to confine comments to what one might expect to be basic in any franchise operation. There are also some specific suggestions which may be appropriate for the particular types of franchise operation mentioned.

Introduction. Each manual should contain some introductory remarks explaining the basic nature of the operation and the business philosophy which underlies it. The introduction should spell out in broad terms what the franchisor will expect from the franchisee and what the franchisee should expect from the franchisor.

Operational system. There should then follow a detailed description of the operational system, explaining how the operation is set up and how and why the various constituent elements dovetail with each other.

Detailed operational methods. This section should deal with the equipment which is required for the operation of the business. It should provide a detailed explanation of what the equipment is, what is its function and how to operate it. Guidance should also be given on how to "trouble-shoot" basic and common faults which are likely to develop. There will be a directory of telephone numbers in the manual (see below) and this will include the telephone numbers of supply and service centres for the equipment.

Operating instructions. This section will probably be broken down into a number of sub-sections. The following are suggested:
  (a) *Opening hours/days.*
  (b) *Trading patterns.*
  (c) *Staff schedules and rotas.*
  (d) *Use of standard forms and procedures.*
  (e) *Requirements as to staff appearance* (e.g. use of uniforms).
  (f) *Staff training procedures.*
  (g) *Procedure for employing staff* and guidance on statutory obligations in this regard.
  (h) *Procedure for disciplining staff* and the statutory obligations imposed on the franchisee as an employer.
  (i) *Procedure for dismissing staff* bearing in mind the Employment Protection Laws.
  (j) *Pricing policies.*
  (k) *Purchasing policies.*
  (l) *Products standards* (quality and quantity).
  (m) *Service standards.*
  (n) *Staff duties.* A detailed job description for each member of staff should be included, setting out not merely the nature and extent of the duties, but also the methods and procedures to be adopted in performing them.

(o) *Payment of franchise fees.* The detailed procedure for calculating and accounting for franchise fees with specimens of the appropriate forms.

(p) *Accountancy.* The specified accounting methods to be employed by the franchisee and the flow of information to be provided to the franchisor to assist him in the provision of guidance to the franchisee. Advice on V.A.T. requirements and P.A.Y.E. and how to complete the necessary paperwork. Examples of the forms to be used in the operation of the accounting method and system and how to complete them should also be featured in the manual.

(q) *Advertising and marketing.* Basic guidance on standard point of sale advertising and marketing technique to be employed—also a list of "dont's".

(r) *Trade name/trade mark control.*

(s) *Insurance.* Details of cover recommended and any schemes offered by or through the franchisor. Alternatively guidance on how to go about getting the cover required.

Standard forms. There will be a section devoted to standard forms which will include all those referred to above in relation to specific sections. Additionally there could be:

(i) Contracts of employment under the Employment Protection Act.

(ii) Agreements with managers and/or staff requiring them to keep the franchisor's trade secrets, methods, etc., secret and not to use or disclose them for any purpose except in the discharge of their responsibilities as employees.

(iii) Contract forms used in the course of the conduct of the franchised business.

(iv) Standard work sheets operating as check lists or for customer's information.

Technical supplement. This would contain more detailed technical information about equipment than is contained in the section dealing with detailed operational methods. It is not uncommon to see manufacturer's explanatory literature supplemented by those prepared by the technical management of the franchisor's organisation.

Franchisor's directory. A directory of Who's Who in the franchisor's organisation and whom to contact in relation to particular aspects of the franchised business.

Telephone directory. A directory of all useful telephone numbers such as service centres, suppliers, etc.

This basically then is what one would expect to find in most manuals whatever the business; with, or course, certain variations from business to business. In appropriate cases, of which two are offered as examples, one would expect to find the following sections, as well as some consequential variation of the sections previously mentioned.

Fast Food

—Recipes.
—Methods of preparation of food.
—Kitchen procedures, including kitchen layout.
—Time for cooking preparation, holding and serving of each menu item.
—Portion quantities, including how many portions one might expect from a given quantity of ingredients.
—Stock requirements.
—Display and merchandising techniques.
—Local advertising, promotion and public relations.
—Menu content and variations according to time of day.
—Customer complaints procedures.
—Legal/neighbourhood requirements—planning, by-laws, statutory requirements, hygiene, litter, night operations, noise, parking.
—V.A.T. (take-away or not), work permits for foreign staff.

Retail Outlet

—Stock requirements in terms of quality, quantities and range.
—Store layout.
—Display, including window displays and merchandising techniques, including discounting.
—Customer relations.
—Guarantee and customer complaints procedures.

The list could be almost endless as one looks at the variety of franchise offers—Dyno-Rod, Zeibart, Budget Rent a Car, Holiday Inns, Pronuptia and Home Tune are but a few examples. The specific manual requirements of each could well form the subject of a separate study and their differing requirements are obvious.

All franchisors should be conscious of the need constantly to keep their methods under review and to introduce change and variety so that their operation is at the forefront of its market. Such changes and variations should be reflected in supplements and amendments to the manual or manuals so that the franchisee is constantly kept informed and up to date. This is likely to apply particularly to the marketing, advertising and promotional section of the manual. For this reason this section is often produced as a separate volume more readily to facilitate the updating process.

5. Marketing the Franchise Package

It may seem obvious, but the best way of marketing the franchise package is to demonstrate success. The best franchises sell themselves; in franchising the "hard sell" should not be necessary. Company-owned pilot units will have been established to prove the concept in practice. If these units are able to demonstrate success (without which, of course, there is little, if anything, to franchise), this in itself will be the very best "marketing tool" in the launch of the franchise.

Many franchisors deliberately maintain a low profile in the marketing of the initial franchise. Many have found that editorial matter in the media is very effective. This can, of course, only be achieved if the franchise or someone connected with it can present to the media a newsworthy feature which is attractive. There is also luck to be taken into account, since even newsworthy features get dropped if something better turns up. One can employ public relations consultants, but this is usually a greater expense than most franchisors can afford at such an early stage of their development.

It is worth appreciating that most franchisors in the end make contact with their franchisees in one of the following four ways.

1. The franchisee will be attracted by a friend who has taken up a franchise or by talking to an existing franchisee.
2. The franchisee will respond to a feature in a newspaper or magazine mentioning the franchise.
3. The franchisee will have seen an advertisement in *Franchise World Magazine* or the business opportunities column of a newspaper.
4. Now that franchising has become better known it is not uncommon to hear of owners of attractive looking businesses (who may or may not be considering the franchise route) to be approached by those who seek to obtain a franchise.

Obviously the first of these four ways will not be applicable, with its pitfalls, but there is no reason why one cannot attempt to achieve the second or spend the money on the advertisements referred to in the third.

Some franchisors feel that one of the best methods of achieving the second is to have a gala, or grand opening of one or more of the company outlets, but only once the concept has already been proved successful in prior pilot operations. The trade, national or local press would normally be invited to a press party at the premises, customers attracted by means of discount offers/small gifts and perhaps a personality to perform the opening ceremony plus some attractive young ladies to distribute leaflets and beam smiles in all directions. The main aim is to create a public event, and this can be achieved for a relatively modest cost; but it does take time to organise. Attention to detail is essential, for little credit will be given when the only spectacular feature of a launch is the failure of the arrangements which have been made. One's suppliers can often be persuaded to provide products at specially discounted prices and/or to take the advertising space in a special feature in a local paper.

Having achieved some measure of public awareness through the visible success of the company or pilot units, the next course is to make public the decision to expand by the franchise route.

Again the best possible marketing technique is that of demonstrated success brought visibly to the notice of potential franchisees.

It is therefore crucial that the early franchisees and locations or territories should carefully be chosen. At all costs the franchising operation must avoid a false start.

The financial terms (i.e. initial franchise fee plus ongoing royalty or mark-up on supplies) will have been worked out to ensure that the franchisee will obtain a reasonable return on his capital and an appropriate income for his labours.

The success of the company operations will doubtless have produced some franchise enquiries, particularly if publicity has been achieved in the trade and/or national press.

The opening of the first franchised unit may be approached in the same gala/grand manner as a company store as described above.

It is useful to provide the press with thumbnail life stories of the franchisee so that human interest and personal finance/investment stories can be written together with appropriate career details of the franchisors and results to date.

All the facts and data provided must be truthful and accurate, of course, and must be presented in a direct, positive manner which can be easily assimilated.

It is likely that the opening will be busy and well attended and that there will be little time for lengthy explanations of any complex details; this makes the written material which is available so important. It will certainly form the basis of most editorial comment which will be made.

This aggressive approach does not appeal to all, nor indeed is it necessarily the right approach in each case. However, one factor which is undoubtedly essential is that the franchisor *must be patient* at this crucial stage. He must not try to expand faster than his capacity to service his franchisees.

In the end this policy will pay off for (and this brings us to the third way) the visible success of both the company and the franchise units will produce more enquiries from prospective franchisees. This source and word-of-mouth recommendation from existing franchisees who are satisfied with their investment are the best possible means of attracting franchisees.

Other means which can be used to supplement the above methods are:

1. Trade press stories and advertising.
2. Advertising in business opportunities columns.
3. Trade and business exhibitions.
4. Business and investment publications.
5. Advertising in *Franchise World Magazine.*
6. And don't forget consumer advertising. Your outlets/operations will be advertising for customers for their products/services. This activity in itself will generate enquiries from prospective franchisees.

Avoid being let down by gaining massive publicity and then, in response to franchise enquiries, produce a "tatty" piece of paper with some inadequate explanation of the franchise scheme which is on offer.

The material which will be supplied in response to these enquiries will be part of your "shop window" display. It will pay to prepare a set of literature which explains who are the people involved in the franchise and their experience. The history of the business to be franchised should be given and a description included of the franchisor's services. Pictures of the business and the people are a good idea for such presentation.

By this stage the franchisor should have a business of which he is proud and which he will be pleased to explain to others. Many franchisors follow a logical procedure when marketing the franchise. Remember, out of every hundred enquiries, eighty will probably never get beyond the initial communication, ten will on submission of personal details be unsuitable, ten may be worth meeting with and discussing the proposition, and two or three may ultimately be considered suitable and sign up. Marketing the franchise requires considerable patience (no apology for repetition—it is important). No franchisee worth having is waiting with pen poised to sign your contract. The franchisor has the patient and sometimes long task of explaining the contract and the reasoning behind the provisions. Just remember that for the franchisee this is one of the big decisions in life; also the selection of each franchisee is a big decision for the franchisor. Many prospective franchisees whom a franchisor would consider ideal will not do a deal with him.

What then is this procedure? It is very important to get this right. First impressions count a lot, and the written presentation will tell a lot about the franchisor and how businesslike he is.

1. Normally the franchisor will receive a letter or telephone call from the prospect. He will respond by sending out a glossy presentation describing the franchise company and its success story. Often this is presented in a question-and-answer form. Some companies explain briefly what franchising is. It may also be sensible at some stage to send prospects a copy of one or more of the publications or articles on franchising which are available. Some companies do, and find it assists in putting franchising into perspective for franchisees and their professional advisers, who may never previously have had contact with franchising.

2. The presentation is often accompanied by an explanation of what the franchisor does for his franchisees in terms of setting them up and in continuing to service their needs and requirements later.

3. Financial projections are also usually despatched with the initial material. These are very rarely presented as suggestions of what one WILL ACHIEVE. Rather they illustrate what profits MAY be achieved IF certain levels of business ARE reached.

4. The franchisee will also be invited to complete an information sheet providing the franchisor with sufficient details about the franchisee to enable the franchisor to find out whether the franchisee is a suitable person with whom to proceed further.

5. This will all be accompanied by a letter inviting the prospective franchisee to contact the franchisor to discuss the matter further.

In some cases franchisors do follow up with contacts by letter or telephone to see whether there is further interest.

At the end of the day the key to marketing the franchise package is that of the visible and demonstrated success of both the company and franchisee operations. In other words, it should sell itself.

6. Selecting Franchisees

This is not an easy subject on which to give advice. The selection of suitable franchisees is of crucial importance, particularly in the early days of the franchise. However, the skill of choosing the right people is, of necessity, developed with experience.

Regard should be had to the following considerations.

Special Deals

One of the most common mistakes which is made by the new franchisor is to be too ready and willing to accept the initial few applicants for franchises and to give them special deals. This is quite understandable, since at that point the franchisor has spent a great deal of money on establishing his franchise and in running his pilot schemes. He wants to expand quickly and establish a return on his investment as soon as possible. He is at the point of maximum vulnerability just when he requires the strongest nerve. It is a great mistake to accept as a franchisee someone who is willing to buy a franchise UNLESS he matches up to the franchisor's requirements IN EVERY RESPECT. The author knows of many franchisors who, having become established, express a wish that they could be rid of some of the earlier franchisees whom they accepted because they were available and not because they matched up to the franchisor's requirements. They would not qualify for acceptance now, because the franchisor is established and can afford to be more selective, not necessarily because his ideas of who should be a franchisee have changed. Would one set up a pilot operation in a totally wrong location merely because it was available or would one wait patiently for the right site? Of course one would wait for the right site. So one must be patient with the selection of the first few franchisees and wait for the right person. It will pay dividends in the long run.

Then we have the franchisors who will give special deals to initial franchisees to lure them in, again as a means of starting up quickly.

This is also a mistake and, as experience shows, on the whole it builds up problems later in exercising control over such a franchisee who still rates himself a "special case" and thus entitled to "special treatment". Additionally, franchisees do talk to each other and special deals cause ill feelings among later franchisees with the attendant difficulties for the franchisor.

Franchise Profile

Many franchisors develop what they call a "franchisee profile" as the number of franchisees increases. This is the average of the qualities and qualifications of the franchisees which they have. As an example, a franchisor may be able to say that his franchisee is most likely to be: a married man aged 39–45 with two children, a successful career in middle management, fed up with the lack of prospects and stifled by company policies. Keen and anxious to be his own boss, supported by his wife in his ambitions, no previous experience in the type of franchised business on offer. Adequate finances and with a fairly good equity in his house on which he can borrow.

Financial Resources

It is important that the prospective franchisee has enough money to get started—but possibly not much more. While the franchisee may have to borrow some of the funds, the rest should be his own cash. Any borrowing should be arranged with an ethical source of funds, e.g. a reputable bank, finance house or insurance company, and over a reasonable length of time to enable the business to repay the borrowed funds, and the interest thereon, while leaving sufficient for the franchisee on which to live. Five-to-ten-year money should be satisfactory for most purposes.

It is as well to remember that if the franchisee has put in no funds of his own, then he may well be tempted to walk away from the franchised operation if difficulties are encountered, rather than work his way through them. An appropriate financial commitment is a considerable incentive and is usually regarded as an essential feature of a franchise transaction.

Individual Franchisees

The ambitious individual is then the archetype of the successful franchisee. However, in some cases companies have made good franchisees, and there are some very successful multiple franchisees, notably in the hotel and fast food businesses. Also in some cases, such as hotel or fast food, the cost of setting up is so high that "investors" are attracted or are required. Some franchisors feel that the only way for a multiple or investor franchisee to succeed is for him to insist that his managers are required to have equity participation for which the manager has to pay. There is a tendency for large companies to become franchisees. It enables them to acquire know-how more effectively and thus make better use of their resources. In such cases one finds that a franchisor will require that a special division or subsidiary of the company is established to run the franchised business under the control of a General Manager or Managing Director who is trained and approved by the franchisor. The more common relationship is basically between the franchisor and the individual franchisee and is a very personal relationship. The success of the personal relationship is indeed the key to the successful growth of the whole operation.

Health

An individual franchisee must be healthy and vigorous enough to withstand considerable physical and nervous strain. The hours will undoubtedly be long and unsocial; there will be fetching and carrying and he may be on his feet for extended periods. The nervous strain can come from the entirely novel experience of having his total wealth and livelihood at stake in the franchised venture. He cannot hold out his hand for wages at the end of the week to anyone but himself.

It is important from the customers' point of view that the franchisee looks healthy, clean and tidy, particularly in any operation where he is handling or serving food. The franchisee who is clean, tidy and healthy himself is likely to keep his operation looking the same way.

Experience

Most franchise companies do not require their franchisees to have prior experience of their particular trade as full training will normally be provided. Indeed, some franchisors believe the previously experienced person will be more difficult to train in the franchise company's particular methods. On the other hand, there is the minority view that a sprinkling of franchisees with prior experience in the trade can help develop the franchise and produce a two-way dialogue leading to the introduction of new methods, products or services.

Age

Age is relatively unimportant in many cases so long as the prospective franchisee is old enough to be responsible and mature, and young enough to be vigorous and hard-working.

Most prospective franchisees will be in the age range of 35 to 50, but the author has heard of successful franchisees as young as 18 or as mature as 66.

Marital Status

This is an important subject, as experience shows that most prospective franchisees will be married. However, the most important facet of the marriage question is, does the spouse support the prospective franchisee in his or her intended venture? In some franchises the husband and wife team is an ideal combination, with both partners active in the business. Even where this is not required, it is important that the prospective franchisee has the full moral support of his spouse. There will be telephone messages to be taken and relayed at peculiar times of night and day, normal mealtimes will continually be missed and there will be widespread disruption of any normal social or domestic life. It is important also to have at least one meeting with the franchise prospect and his wife in their own home. Seeing them together and the way in which they live and keep and maintain their home can tell a lot about them. Those who live like slobs are likely to run their business in the same sloppy way. Don't find out too late.

Independence

The prospective franchisee must be independent enough to be able to manage a business on his own, to be a self-starter, indeed to make the decision to take up the franchise. However, he must not be so independent that he will not want to remain within the rules of your franchise and not continually be wanting to break away.

Trust

It is essential, in view of the relationship which exists in a franchise, for the franchisor and franchisee to have mutual trust and respect. The franchisor must be certain that the franchisee is someone whom he can trust with his name and goodwill. Will he be honest in his financial returns on which the franchisor's fee income will depend? Will he give his staff and customers honest and fair treatment? THE FRANCHISOR MUST BE ABLE TO TRUST HIM; on the other hand, *he must be able to trust the franchisor* and the franchisor must deserve and earn that trust. The franchisor must demonstrate a successful record in ethical business conduct.

Organising ability

Can he organise himself enough to run his own business, probably for the first time albeit according to the franchisor's system. The first couple of meetings should provide some indication whether he has ability, as will the visit to his home. One should be able to tell if he is serious in his approach by the way he asks questions about the operation and the effort he puts into visiting outlets and generally vetting the proposition. Will he be receptive to the training and guidance which he will be given? Does he have the capacity to cope with the assimilation of information and the confidence to apply it in practice to his own situation?

Compatibility

Is he likeable? Since the franchisor and franchisee will undoubtedly see (and hear) a lot of one another and are mutually dependent, it is most important that they can get on with each other and have mutual respect. After all, they will both be working considerable hours for the same end—the success of the franchise. They really do need each other to be successful. The franchisor's own success and that of the franchisee will be inextricably interwoven.

Final Decision

Essentially if any error is to be made in the selection of franchisees it should be to err on the side of caution. The franchisor must never sign up the first warm body which comes through the door with the franchise fee in hand. All applicants should be weighed up very carefully. The ultimate decision about the acceptability of the franchisee must be made by the proprietor of the franchising company.

If one wishes to consider making use of the services of a consultant in the recruitment of your franchisees the guidance contained in Chapter 14 must be borne in mind.

Summary

In summary, therefore, the best advice is that franchisees should be selected deliberately, cautiously and with sufficient time allocated to do it properly and thoroughly. Remember it is a crucial decision for both franchisee and franchisor. For the franchisee, his whole life savings and lifestyle will often be at stake. For the franchisor, the reputation of his business, his future income and his ability to sell franchises in the future are at stake.

7. Developing the Franchisor's Organisation

We now examine the organisation which the franchisor will require in order to handle his franchising activity as it grows.

As in any business, it is sensible to set up and expand the organisation gradually with the development of the business. It would not be financially sensible to take on too many additional people initially when there are as yet no franchisees. On the other hand, it is essential that all the franchisees (especially the early ones) are fully serviced; therefore, the franchisor must have properly trained staff available to deal with this requirement and not leave the hiring of these people until too late. So it is a matter of timing and judgement on the part of the franchisor to ensure that he has sufficient staff resources to cover the franchising requirement.

This requirement needs to be carefully analysed, as it will impose financial demands on the organisation. There are definitely going to be expenses incurred in establishing and running new franchising activity before there is any income. It is very likely, and indeed invariably, the experience that franchising activity produces a net loss in the first couple of years.

There will be unavoidable expenses of trade mark registration, brochure production, staff salaries, office expenditure, travel, franchise agreement, etc., while the franchisees become established and the royalties or management services fees on turnover or profits on the supply of goods begin to flow to the franchisor.

Furthermore, it is not a solution in the author's view to charge unrealistically high initial franchise fees. This is not a good practice and has certainly led to abuse in the past and has damaged the good name of franchising.

In the author's view, the franchisor must take the majority of his income from the ongoing and successful operation of the business by the franchisee. The initial franchise fee should be a fairly modest sum of money and provide a contribution towards the expenses incurred by the franchisor on site and franchisee evaluation, training and supervision.

Franchise Fees

Franchise fees are discussed in detail in Chapter 7. They, of course, provide the franchisor with the gross revenue from the operation of his franchise out of which he has to cover his expenses, return on capital and make a profit.

Source of Income

Each franchisee should represent a secure and growing source of gross income to the franchisor, provided that the franchise is a good viable system, and is kept that way by the sensible management of the franchisor. Furthermore, successful existing franchisees will provide a source of additional expansion for the franchise as they seek to re-invest their profits by opening further units or expanding their territories. It is not uncommon, in the fast food industry, to find that existing franchisees open a significant number of new units.

The long-term nature of the franchise contract, with its secure payments, is a major advantage over the normal sales operation where, say, packets of tea have to be sold to the same grocer every few weeks. That type of operation needs a large sales force, heavy continuous advertising and can always be replaced by a competitive product.

These factors have an impact on the type of organisation which the franchisor should develop. Basically, he will need few, but good, competent, people who are flexible and hard working. "Hard working" is not lightly said, since the franchisees will generally be working long hours, seven days a week, and having invested their life savings in your idea will generally expect to be able to talk to the franchisor whenever they feel the need. Certainly, there is no doubt that running a franchise involves a great deal of personal time and effort.

Breadth of experience is also important as the franchisee will want answers on all sorts of subjects and will prefer to cover them all in the one conversation with the particular person to whom he is talking, or with whom he is accustomed to dealing.

The functions most companies need to cover are finance (accounting), marketing, franchise sales and operations (including innovation). Let us examine each in turn.

Finance—Accounting

For the new franchisor, the finance field will need to be covered by his existing staff who will be looking after his own company operations.

They must be able to devise and develop a simple book-keeping system for the franchisee and give advice on this. Regular returns and accounts will be required from the franchisee, and it is vital that the franchisee understands exactly what is required in this respect from the outset. It is also important to enforce compliance and to evaluate information being received.

The existing finance and administration department should also provide advice and a brief guide on matters such as the payment of wages, employment laws and regulations, V.A.T. returns, and on the need for auditors and how to go about raising finance. These requirements mean that the franchisor's accounting staff will need to be widely experienced and, above all, interested in the business.

In time, it may be necessary to have additional accounting staff for the franchise side of the business, but certainly not initially. Indeed there is much to gain by using the existing staff. They will be able to advise from a basis of knowledge and experience and also they will doubtless deepen their own understanding of the company's business in the process. When it comes to talking to the professional advisers of the franchisees—auditors, lawyers, bankers, etc.—this should be handled at a very senior executive level in the franchisor's organisation. The expertise thus displayed will assist in the marketing and in promoting confidence in the franchisor's ability to cope with ongoing problems which may arise.

Some franchise companies develop in-house computer systems and provide an accounting service to franchisees. The systems and services provide a greater ability, both to the franchisor and franchisee, to monitor and control the franchisee's business.

Franchise Sales

On the sales side, the proprietor of the business will initially have to do the selling or marketing of the franchise. Selling is not necessarily an appropriate word in the normal sense. It is much more a case of explaining the proposition and services offered, and of visiting existing units with franchisee prospects.

The proprietor of the business is the appropriate person, as he will fully understand the motivation and worries of the nervous prospective franchisee about to go into business on his own.

Recruiting a specialist salesman from the outside is potentially dangerous in these delicate early stages—he will not know the business and you do not know him well enough to rely on his judgement and his ethics when it comes effectively to parting people from their life savings. While outside consultants may well offer useful advice on setting up the franchise package, it is not, in the author's opinion, sensible exclusively to rely on them to sell the package, since they may not be around later if and when any problems arise. At this point of time in England there are precious few consultants with the experience, skill and ability which is necessary. If you decide to use consultant services, take the greatest care to ensure that the consultant whom you chose has a successful track record either in direct employment or as consultant to other franchise companies. (See Chapter 14 for a full discussion of Consultancy Services.)

When extra help is required on the sales side, the people concerned should be taken on one at a time, very carefully screened, thoroughly trained, and they should have impeccable references from previous employers. Alternatively, you should consider transferring someone from your own internal operations organisation to assist you on the sales side. The advantage of internal candidates is that they have the product knowledge and you know their integrity. An over-zealous franchise sales department can render the franchisor vulnerable to claims by franchisees for the misrepresentation of the franchise and its financial performance.

Mention has been made of the proprietor carrying out the sales function, on the assumption that it is a proprietorial company. Where this is not so, e.g. where the operation to be franchised is part of a large organisation, then the head of that division—the director in charge, or the managing director of the subsidiary company—should similarly personally devote himself to the initial selling effort.

Any individual specialising in this activity should be paid a good salary, with regular reviews, and good conditions of service. Never link his earnings to the number of franchises sold or the objective approach, which is so essential, will be lost. Saying "no" should not affect his own pocket and thus his judgement. The aim is to attract and retain a career-minded, long service individual who will produce a steady flow of high quality results. He provides an essential link with franchisees, who will often consult him as an "uncle" figure when problems arise.

Ethical franchising is not a foot in the door, immediate performance, high bonus, or "you're out" type of selling operation and such pay scales are inappropriate.

Marketing the Product or Service

In the early days of franchising activity it is unlikely that any additional specialist marketing staff will be needed. If there already is a marketing department for company operations, they should obviously be used and will be a great help. If there is an existing advertising agency, they should also be briefed on the franchising plans. If there is not an advertising agency, it is recommended that one should be appointed, although the developing operation may find it difficult to interest one as it may be considered too small.

Expenses in this area have to be carefully watched, especially in the early stages when little can be afforded.

However, good design work to establish the image will be needed. Some of this may already exist, but in switching to a franchise it may be wise to take another look and perhaps ensure greater distinctiveness. There are specialist design firms who offer such a service.

There will be advertisements to be placed and P.R. events/releases to be handled. All these items should be carefully considered and it is best to start with a modest programme to save unnecessary expense. At that stage, more than any other, it is vital to obtain full value for money.

Although these specialist agencies exist, as the franchisor's organisation grows, so too will the capacity to do a great deal of promotional and design work in-house. There should be those on the staff of the franchisor who specialise in promotion and design work. Liaison with the specialist agencies and with the franchisees in the field will have to be established. There will be considerable advantage to be gained from discussions with franchisees about various marketing and promotional ideas. Point-of-sale material is often worth trying with selected franchisees before introducing it throughout the operation.

A continuous and positive approach to marketing and promotion from within the franchisor's organisation is also good for the morale of franchisees and demonstrates in practice the franchisor's concerned involvement in the success of their businesses.

Operations—including Innovations

Here the franchisor will definitely need staff help, as franchisees will require a lot of detailed help to discuss and implement their new venture. The franchisor will have the obligation to continue to monitor and advise the franchisee and if necessary control him after he is established in business.

The obvious source for candidates will be the internal company operations team. To begin with, it should be just one person, an experienced all-rounder, particularly good in practice. He must be able personally to perform all the tasks necessary and be prepared to roll up his sleeves and actually work alongside the franchisee in the early days.

The operations manual will need to be written, and this individual should be made responsible for that task. He will need to cover the shopfitting and equipping of the new outlets, so he must have first-hand experience of these functions. He will need to keep on good terms with the franchisor's own operational staff to obtain help and advice for himself and training for the new franchisees.

In the early days, this training will be carried out at the company-owned locations by one of the experienced operational unit managers, using the manual which has been written. If the company already has a training officer, all well and good, but most new franchisors will not be so well blessed and will need to use the limited number of existing operational staff and facilities.

The next stage in development would be the addition of a classroom and possibly dummy-run equipment. This will often be sited conveniently on the floor above, or in space behind, an existing company shop/location. The staff involved in operations will expand with the growth of the business and the operational side of the franchise business will develop along a number of paths.

(a) There will be the training of new franchisees and staff.
(b) There will be the continuing retraining of franchisees and staff. This will mainly be done at the franchisees' premises. Its purpose will be to work out operational flaws, or bad habits developed by the franchisee, or to introduce new methods.
(c) There will be the team in the field offering trouble-shooting advice.
(d) There will be a section dealing with product or service innovations and experimental ideas. (Initially these should always be tried out in the franchisor's company-owned units.)

The size and degree of sophistication of any of these "units" will depend on the nature and extent of the franchised business and operation.

A good example of an organisational structure is that set out in relation to the Zockoll Group in Chapter 13 (see pages 135–142). The Zockoll group structure is that which exists in a company which has been established for many years. A new company will not have such extensive requirements.

In addition to internal assistance, help will be required from the company's bankers, accountants and solicitors. The franchising project should be fully explained to them at an early stage, as it is possible that they may not know too much about the subject.

The company's bankers may be helpful in providing partial finance for the franchisees, either directly or through an associated finance house. It is not generally sensible for the company to be involved in financing franchisees itself, either by lending funds or by guarantee, and the function of the company should be to introduce the franchisee to the source of finance and provide any necessary information to the bank/finance house.

The company's accountants should be asked to advise on the methods selected to monitor the franchisee's performance and the receipt and recording of income and expenses. The solicitors will need to review any franchise literature and also draw up the franchise agreement.

One can sum up the initial organisational requirements for the new franchisor in the following way:

Franchise selling—
    Proprietor himself, plus a good secretary.
Marketing of the product or service—
    Proprietor himself, plus a good secretary, plus an advertising agency.
Operations—
    One person transferred from existing company operations.
Shopfitting and equipment—
    The operations person as above, plus outside suppliers/shopfitters.
Training—
    Existing company operations management.
Finance and administration—
    Existing company department, plus help from company's bankers, accountants and solicitors.

The basic principles to be borne in mind in the early stages are:

1. The owner of the franchise personally must be fully involved,

since he must be prepared to demonstrate his faith in his business and in franchising; and

2. The maximum use should be made of existing company staff for reasons not only of economy, but also knowledge, experience and dependability. The choice of initial supporting staff is absolutely vital.

CHAPTER 7

How the Franchisor Obtains
His Income

CLEARLY the franchisor expects to receive payment for the package which he is selling to the franchisee and for the continuing services which he will be providing to the franchisee.

The franchisor, when setting up his franchise scheme, will have to decide how much he requires by way of franchise fees in order to finance the provision of his services, give him a reasonable return on his capital, and show a reasonable profit. The franchisee, on the other hand, wants to know how much money will be taken out of his business by the franchisor. While in practice there is little the franchisee can do to negotiate a franchise fee, he must ascertain the sources of the franchisor's income. He must know the manner in which the franchise fees are to be calculated so that he can judge whether the franchisor's fees are fair to both parties. The franchisor's approach to franchise fees, their extent and method of calculation, can also provide an interesting insight into the nature and attitudes of the franchisor. There are a number of different ways in which a franchise fee may be charged, and it is possible that franchise fees will be payable in more than one of the ways described.

The various methods by which a franchise fee is taken are as follows.

1. An Initial Franchise Fee

In some franchise schemes an initial franchise fee is payable on the signing of the franchise contract or on opening for business. In some cases, where the fee is sizeable, payment by instalments may be allowed, but usually the whole fee will be payable on or before the franchisee opens for business.

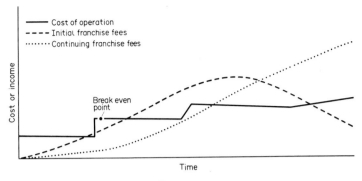

FIG. 7.1.

It is difficult to be specific over rates of fee in a general work of this nature. The basic principles and an indication of the experience of others are a useful guide. Franchise fees of whatever description provide the franchisor with his gross income. In the early stages the income from franchise fees is the major source, but as the network becomes more mature it is replaced in importance by the continuing fees. If the network is to grow to full maturity, it will have to be on the basis of a good flow of continuing fee income.

Any top heavy fee arrangement with large front end fees and small continuing fees is suspect. Front end fees dwindle as the territory available is taken up by franchisees, and low continuing fees would not provide the franchisor with the income needed to sustain growth. It should be noted that heavy front end fees with low continuing fees may indicate a fraudulent purpose.

Figure 7.1. gives an illustration of the sort of trend one might expect to find in the development of a franchise network.

The figure shows the initial fee income as providing the main source of income in the early stages and then being caught up and overtaken by continuing franchise fees.

The figure also illustrates the way in which the expense of running the franchisor's organisation grows in steps. Each step prepares it to cope with the expansion which follows, to the point where the organisation is developed and the rising continuing fees result in an increasing profitability. The staff required to cope with five franchisees may well be able to cope with twenty-five to fifty franchisees. The figure makes clear the need in the early stages for the franchisor to provide adequate working capital to finance the initial deficits. It ignores any profitability from pilot or company-owned stores.

If one examines the level of front end franchise fees the average seems to fall within the range of 5–10% of the total cost of the franchise package, i.e. the total investment costs to the franchisee of getting into business and opening. Therefore, with an investment level of £20,000 to £30,000, an initial fee in the range of £1,000 to £3,000 seems to cover the current average. In the case of the smaller and less expensive packages, e.g. ServiceMaster and Home Tune, the percentage fee can, of course, exceed the 5–10% level.

As the initial investment grows, the percentage fee in cash terms may be too high in relation to the initial supply of services. Thus a fee of £5,000 rather than £10,000 might be charged for a franchise package involving investment in the region of, say, £100,000, although it will be noted that this is still within the 5–10% range.

The franchisor should in essence relate the amount of the initial franchise fee to the expense incurred by him in selecting, assisting and preparing the franchisee in the establishment of his business.

It may be possible to raise the initial franchise fee in the course of time to reflect the growing strength and success of the franchise. In some cases membership of the network in itself is of great value. It would also be prudent to review the fee to reflect inflationary pressures on overhead expenses. The franchisor would do well to remember that his success will, in the long run, be dependent upon his ability to help the franchisee make the most of his money. The objective can be assisted by keeping the initial investment level as modest as possible; there are more potential franchisees with £25,000 to invest than there are with £50,000 or more.

It would be very unusual for the initial franchise fee to be the only fee the franchisor will ever receive, otherwise he would have no capacity to finance the continuing relationship. While such a fee is often taken, it is invariably tied to one or other of the fees which are described below.

2. Sale of Initial Franchise Package

Many franchise schemes involve the purchase by the franchisee of a franchise package. This package will comprise a number of different elements, the sum total of which will equip the franchisee by means of training, pre-opening services, supplies and equipment to be ready to open for business. The equipment and supplies element of the package will have been gathered together by the franchisor from various suppliers, no doubt at a discount below the normal retail price. The franchisor will mark up the items included in the package to show himself a profit to cover the cost of getting the package together and for getting the franchisee into business. This mark-up would contain a sufficient margin to allow for a contribution from this particular package sale to the general costs of running the franchisor's head office organisation. This may be in addition to the initial franchise fee payable, or that fee may be included in the package price.

3. Sale of Equipment

(a) Invariably there will be a sale of equipment included in the initial package as mentioned above. What one must guard against, as a franchisee, is the possibility that what is being sold as a franchise is in effect a disguised sale of equipment. Some describe as a franchise what is in essence a distributorship or agency in respect of goods with a minimum stock requirement. This is not necessarily wrong. Indeed many distributorships and agencies exist, but the transaction must be recognised for what it is. Some try to cloak the distributorship or agency with the appearance of a franchise so as to be able to charge a franchise fee in return for granting alleged territorial selling rights. It will often be linked with an obligation to purchase from the seller (franchisor) material to be used with the equipment. If one can establish the correct nature of the transaction it can be placed into perspective and be properly assessed, as can the value (if any) of the rights offered.

(b) In some cases there may be an obligation imposed upon the franchisee to purchase future supplies of novel or essential equipment from the franchisor. Such sale will undoubtedly include a profit element for the franchisor. In a franchise which is dependent upon a specialised piece of equipment, the obligation may extend to the purchase and use of later and improved versions of the equipment. In such a case the franchisee would be satisfied about two aspects: first, that new equipment cannot be imposed upon him when the existing item of equipment is doing the job perfectly well, whatever refinements the newer equipment may have; and second, that the franchisor cannot overcharge the franchisee by unreasonably increasing the mark-up.

4. Leasing of Premises

This is a complex aspect of franchising with problems which arise, not only from the legal implications but also the attitudes and practices which are prevalent in the property market.

(a) Sometimes the franchisor will be able to negotiate terms for leasing a suitable site at extremely good terms in view of the covenant which the franchisor is able to offer the landlord. (See Chapter 13, page 161, in relation to Wimpy.) The franchisor may decide to sublet these premises to the franchisee at a higher rent, thus showing a profit rental for himself.

(b) The franchisor may, in some cases, own the freehold of the premises from which the franchisee is to trade and will grant a lease to the franchisee.

(c) In both cases the franchisee should take care to ensure that the terms contained in the lease are those which obtain in the market, allowance being made for the risks taken and with support given by the franchisor. Care must also be taken to ensure that the franchisor does not use the lease to impose unreasonable conditions which he would not feel able to insert into the franchise contract.

5. Financing Arrangements

The franchisor may make arrangements with a finance company for a commission to be paid to him on the introduction of franchisees to the finance company. The franchisor may also set up his own finance company and make a profit on financing the requirements of franchisees.

6. Leasing of Equipment

Some franchisors arrange for the leasing of equipment to the franchisee rather than a sale, so as to reduce the cost of the initial package. The franchisor may receive a commission from the leasing company. Alternatively, but less frequently, the franchisor will lease the equipment direct to the franchisee and take his profit on that transaction. Indeed, in some cases where the franchisor's scheme involves the use of specialised patented equipment, it is only possible for a franchisee to arrange to lease that equipment, the franchisor being reluctant to sell it. With the increasing cost of financing a new business, finance packages which are prepared will often include leases of equipment. Rental of equipment can also often be arranged with suppliers. What the franchisee must know is the extent to which the franchisor can add to his cost of running his business by taking commissions on introducing the franchisee to such financial assistance where such benefits may otherwise be available to the franchisees.

7. Continuing Fees

(a) *Management Services Fees.* The franchisor may charge a straight percentage fee on the gross sales of the franchisee. This may involve a minimum fee, although this is not frequently done. The British Franchise Association do not recommend minimum fees. There are some who consider that the percentage fee is the best way, as the franchisee knows precisely how much he has to pay up; he knows precisely how to calculate it and he knows that the franchisor will not be taking fees in any other way. The other view held by many is that this is not a good way to charge a franchise fee. The view is that psychologically the franchisee will not like parting with his money to somebody else. It can be painful visibly and frequently parting with a slice of hard-earned cash. Further, as the franchisee feels a degree of independence of the franchisor, which is a feeling which many successful franchisees do develop, he will become more reluctant to pay the franchise fee and more aware of the drain from his pocket.

There are many good franchises which operate on the percentage fee basis and there are some good franchises which operate on a different basis. Certainly, from the franchisor's point of view it is a safer and more reliable method. In the U.S.A., with its much more stringent anti-trust laws and other laws affecting franchising, the percentage fee method seems to be much the better system. One is inclined to the view that it is also in the long term the best method to employ in the U.K.

One common error is to apply the misnomer of "royalty" to franchise fees. The error usually arises because franchise fees are invariably calculated as a percentage of the gross income of the franchisee rather in the same way as one calculates royalties. Royalties are usually passive income; that is to say, an income earned for the use of an asset rather than an income earned in exchange for services or goods. The common examples are royalties for the use of a patent or a copyright royalty. Franchise fees are a payment by the franchisee in return for the continuing services with which the franchisor will provide the franchisees.

(b) *Sale of Products.* In some franchises, particularly those where trade marked goods are involved, the agreement compels the franchisee to buy goods from the franchisor or a nominated supplier of the franchisor. The franchisor obtains his fee by marking up the goods so that he receives, in fact, a franchise fee by taking a larger gross profit for the goods than he would otherwsie have obtained. Where a nominated supplier is used, the franchisor can obtain income by receiving a commission from the supplier.

One of the difficulties which can arise with this method of charging a franchise fee is that the franchisee can be at the mercy of an unscrupulous franchisor. There are undoubtedly very many companies which operate this system fairly and properly, often delaying price increases to the last possible moment. It is, nevertheless, a method of payment of a franchise fee which should be carefully scrutinised by the franchisee. The franchisee should satisfy himself that the franchisor is not taking and cannot take advantage of him and that there are forms of protection upon which he can rely.

It is essential for the franchisor to consider the alternatives available. Very often it is fairer for both parties to have the percentage fee payable rather than the mark-up on goods. If the franchisor contrasts his income calculated as a mark-up on the goods with his income calculated as a reasonable percentage of the franchisees' gross income he will often find that he is no worse off. The franchisee can look at a relatively modest percentage fee in the confident knowledge that the franchisor will not be able unreasonably to increase the margin for himself at the franchisee's expense.

Two factors clearly emerge from the above: firstly, so far as the franchisor is concerned he must make a policy decision at the very earliest moment on the manner in which he will take his franchise fees. He must budget to ensure that the flow of fees which he receives from the various sources are sufficient to show him the return which he needs to cover his overheads and to make a reasonable profit. Secondly, so far as the franchisee is concerned he must ascertain the sources of the franchisor's income. He must satisfy himself that the franchisor will not be in a position unfairly to take advantage of him.

Advertising Funds

Most franchise schemes provide for expenditure on advertising and promotion by both franchisor and franchisee. Where the franchisor undertakes the obligation to advertise and promote, there are three alternative methods of dealing with the expense:

(i) The franchisor charges the franchisee a sum calculated as a percentage of the franchisee's gross income rather in the same way as the continuing franchise fee (management services fee) is calculated. The sums so received by the franchisor are placed into a fund to be disbursed by the franchisor on advertising and promotion. Most franchisors will want to have complete control over the advertising and promotional activities upon which the sums in the fund are spent.

(ii) The franchisor includes the advertising expense within the continuing franchise fee and undertakes to spend not less than a minimum percentage of such fees on advertising and promotion. Again most franchisors will wish to have the same degree of control over expenditure as above.

(iii) The franchisor undertakes to do such advertising and promotion as he thinks fit without collecting a contribution for allocating a fixed sum for the purpose. This approach is often used when the franchisor is already a substantial advertiser on his own account and the franchisee will inevitably benefit.

Apart from these cases there are franchise operations in which it is considered better to concentrate on local advertising and promotion than on a national basis when the franchisor will probably adopt the approach outlined in (iii) above.

In all cases, both national and local, the franchisor will insist on control of the form and content of all advertisements and promotional material, since it is his name and system which is being advertised.

CHAPTER 8

The Franchisor's Initial Services to the Franchisee

THE following services will have to be provided by a franchisor to a franchisee before the franchisee is in a position to open for business. It is difficult to place these items in order of importance as most of them are equally important, but in different ways.

There are, however, some which are very basic, and one absolutely fundamental service which should be provided by a franchisor is training. Training should cover two aspects of the business.

Firstly, there is the basic business training which has to be given to the franchisee. This will include training in book-keeping skills, staff selection, staff management, business procedures and documentary systems necessary for the purposes of controlling the operation, and elementary business training which will enable the franchisee to do basic trouble shooting of his own. It should not be thought that this training will be so detailed that the franchisor will, in effect, be running a small business management college. The training will be limited in its application to providing the franchisee with the basic skills which are necessary for the purposes of the particular operation with which he is concerned.

The book-keeping system which will have been set up will have been so arranged as to provide the minimum of work and effort for the franchisee but the maximum of vital information. It will be geared to produce without too much difficulty the vital flow of financial management information which is necessary for the franchisee to see where he stands at all times. The value of up-to-date meaningful financial information cannot be emphasised too much. It should show trends, stresses and strains which, if correctly interpreted, should enable appropriate remedial action to be taken in relation to the business at the earliest possible moment.

The staff selection and staff management training the franchisee will receive will give him the basic skills which he requires for interviewing staff, assessing their capabilities, and training them in the work which they will have to do. Handling people is largely a matter of experience, but there are nevertheless guidelines which can be given to help the inexperienced. The franchisee will, when he allies practical experience to the principles which have been laid down for him, find that he is achieving far more than he would otherwise have been capable of.

The franchisor may design and prepare certain forms which the franchisee will have to complete. These forms will be designed to show the performance of the operation and demonstrate to the franchisor and franchisee the areas in which the franchisee needs to improve his performance. There should be a sound reason for any documents which the franchisee is compelled by the franchisor to complete. It is not the franchisee's function merely to operate as a source of useless information.

The franchisee should be trained so that he is able to detect problems as they arise in his business and thus be in a position to take remedial action without waiting for the franchisor's trouble shooters to call upon him and diagnose that trouble is brewing.

The training which will be given to the franchisee will not be as wide ranging and thorough as it would have to be if he were preparing to cope with the unknown; he is only prepared to cope with the business which is being franchised to him. His training will therefore be limited in this way.

The second area in which training will be given to the franchisee relates to the operational details of the business.

In a food franchise, for example, the franchisee will be taught portion control, quality control, preparation methods, any particular recipes, and any particular processes which will have to be applied to the food before it is passed on to the consumer.

The franchisee may be required to attend a special training school to be trained in these aspects. Above all, one thing must occur, whether or not there is a training school, and that is that the franchisee must, after he completes his training, be capable of stepping into his own business and opening and running it without pausing to scratch his head and wonder where his next piece of inspiration will come from.

Apart from these areas of training the franchisor should perform other functions.

The franchisor will, with the criteria for site selection which he has established, investigate and evaluate sites for the franchisee. He will advise whether or not the sites come within his accepted standards and what sort of performance can be expected of them. This is a very critical area of the franchisor's functions. One franchise company has instructed its site finders that unless the site which they are viewing is one into which they would invest every last penny which they themselves possess they should not recommend it for the purpose of the franchisee's business. This may sound drastic, but is certainly a sound principle upon which to operate. No franchisor should expect a franchisee to invest his money in something in which the franchisor would not himself invest. The franchisee should appreciate that in approving a site a franchisor is not infallible and that he cannot guarantee that his judgement is correct. For the franchisee blindly to accept the franchisor's opinion without question can be dangerous. The franchisee should closely question the franchisor, particularly if he has doubts about the site himself.

Having selected a site the franchisor should give assistance to the franchisee in obtaining any necessary consents under the Town and County Planning legislation and the local building By-laws.

He should also assist the franchisee in the design and remodelling of the store, assist him with the shopfitting, and in many cases prepare and submit plans for the shopfitters to work from. The franchisor will, in many instances, give the franchisee assistance in deciding which particular shopfitter's estimates to accept. The franchisor may also give the franchisee assistance in the supervision of the shopfitters while they carry out their work. Most franchisors, although they offer such assistance, will not be prepared to accept the responsibility which the franchisee's own surveyor would, for example, accept. Specialised professional advice is the responsibility of the franchisee.

The franchisor will, if standardised equipment is not already part of the package which he has sold to the franchisee, give advice and assistance in the selection of the correct equipment at the most economic prices. He should have all the relevant information readily available.

A further service which many franchisors offer to franchisees is assistance in negotiating a lease of the premises with the landlords or their agents and assisting the franchisee in completing his arrangements with the benefit of expert and experienced help.

Part of the training which the franchisee will have received will have included some guidance on marketing and promotional principles, and the franchisor should supply to the franchisee initial quantities of marketing and promotional material, point of sale advertising, and the like.

The franchisor will provide for the franchisee a statement setting out the amount of the opening stock inventory, which he should hold, and will make arrangements for the franchisee to purchase these stocks from his own purchasing department or from suppliers who are nominated for the purpose. It is important that the franchisor should give to the franchisee a realistic breakdown of his cash requirements. In particular the franchisee must be able to ascertain what proportion of his investment is required to purchase the franchise package and what proportion is being set aside for working capital. Proper provision must be made for working capital in the calculations of the franchisee's cash requirements. If the franchisor's projections do not take this into account, they must be viewed with some degree of care and the franchisor closely questioned about the matter. Any calculations or projections which do not allow for working capital are bound to be unrealistic, and raise a large question mark about the validity of the franchisor's other statements or representations about the franchise scheme.

The franchisor should provide for the franchisee on-the-spot assistance in the final preparatory arrangements for the store opening.

The franchisor will frequently provide opening assistance by having a team of as many as two or three people present to assist the franchisee in getting the business off the ground. Initially they may have to cope with a rush of customers as the public try out the business. The franchisor's opening crew will seek to ensure that the franchisee is properly putting into practice the principles which have been instilled in him during training. The opening crew should stay on the premises until they are satisfied that the franchisee has got into the swing of things and is coping well enough to be left on his own.

It is only when he is left alone after the initial shock that the franchisee will really come into his own and begin to develop his true potential. At this stage it is important to emphasise again that the franchisee must realise that no franchisor can guarantee to him success, least of all success without work. A franchise is not a passage to wealth without effort. Most franchises will require long hours of solid work on the part of the franchisee in order to achieve success. What the franchisor is offering is a ready-made formula for carrying on business which in similar circumstances has proved to be successful. He will give to the franchisee whatever assistance he can in an endeavour to ensure that the franchisee will achieve a similar degree of success. This cannot be guaranteed, and any franchisor who offers firm guarantees of success to franchisees should be viewed with caution.

CHAPTER 9

The Continuing Services and Franchise Relationship

ONCE the franchisee has opened for business the most obvious help which he will require from the franchisor is the regular visit of the franchisor's field operational man, the trouble shooter. Regular visits should take place, and the trouble shooter should be available at short notice if the franchisee feels that he has a problem.

The trouble shooter may find on a regular routine visit to the franchisee's business that all is not well and that certain retraining is necessary. In such a case he would stay with the business and on the premises while he retrains the franchisee and puts him on the right lines. The franchisee must not rely too heavily on the trouble shooter; he must learn to solve his own problems; he should look to the franchisor merely as a shoulder upon which to lean and as a source of assistance to him when things get a bit too much.

The franchisor's trouble shooter should also be available at all times to the franchisee when required. The words "when required" are used advisedly. The franchisor cannot be expected to know by some telepathic process that the franchisee expects help from him at any particular time. Communication is an essential feature of the relationship. The franchisee must keep in touch with the franchisor and must let the franchisor know when he does have difficulties. The franchisee must not delude himself, he must face up to difficulties as they arise and not try to pretend they do not exist.

The franchisee should telephone the trouble shooter from time to time if he has not been visited, and have a chat with him, for out of these discussions much good can come. He must also read very carefully all literature and circulars which reach him from or through the franchisor, for by this means, if the franchisor is performing his functions correctly, the franchisee will be supplied with a lot of valuable operational information. Nothing could be more annoying to the trouble shooter, or indeed to the franchisee, for the franchisee to call in assistance when the answer to his problems is contained in the literature which has been circulated to him and which he has just not bothered to read.

The franchisee must appreciate that the trouble shooter wants to work with him to help him, but that he must help himself. He cannot expect the franchisor to run his business for him. The franchisee must adjust mentally to the fact that he is a businessman in his own right and behave as one.

The franchisor will, through the trouble shooter and through regularly called meetings and seminars, keep in touch with the franchisee and initiate such retraining processes as are necessary. It may well be that some new equipment or some new line will emerge with which the franchisee has to cope. The franchisor will then have to train the franchisee so that he is familiar and able to cope with the innovation.

While on the subject of innovation, of course, the franchisor should have research facilities in relation to the product, the format, and the market image of its business which is projected. He should constantly be seeking to innovate and introduce ideas and methods for improving the business of the franchised chain and the operational systems.

The franchisor will seek to keep the franchisees in touch with each other and with each other's successes and problems. The franchisor will often run a journal for this purpose. The journal will publicise to the franchisees the successes which are being achieved, set targets for them, and provide an interchange of ideas. Successful schemes which franchisees have evolved for their own benefit are in this way also made available for the benefit of all franchisees within the chain. Much can be done through the imaginative use of journals of this nature to introduce a competitive element among the franchisees and a corporate pride in the activities of the whole chain.

The franchisor invariably will run national and local advertising schemes and also ensure that the important field of public relations is looked after. The advertising schemes will be calculated to exploit to the full the national corporate image of a chain providing services in many areas and to capitalise on the strong features of the franchise.

The cost of advertising will be dealt with in one of the ways described in Chapter 7.

The franchisor will seek to exploit the franchise utilising market research as an aid to discover those areas in which the appeal is strongest. Throughout, the franchisor must be very market conscious and must be prepared to exploit the opportunities which arise.

Indeed, the franchisor must seek to create opportunity where none appear to exist. To this end the franchisor should be seeking to exploit new sources of supply of good quality materials, supplies, or products for the franchisees so that their costs are kept to the most economic level possible. As the chain grows, the bulk purchasing power of the whole group will also grow, resulting in a considerable account with a manufacturer or supplier. This should produce valuable savings for each individual franchisee. Benefits and savings can thus be effected for franchises which would not be available to them outside the franchise scheme with only their own resources as individuals to bring into play.

In the background of all this activity there is, of course, the head office organisation of the franchisor. The organisation should contain specialists in each of the fields in which the franchisee is likely to require assistance. There should be specialists in the management and accountancy aspects of the business; there should be specialists in advertising, marketing, public relations; specialists in product quality control, equipment quality and control; specialists in all the various aspects of the business with which the franchised chain is concerned. There is also the franchisor's field force operating directly with the franchisees, including the trouble shooter.

In these circumstances the franchisee is better off than the manager of a local branch within a national chain. In a national chain the accent will be in ensuring that the manager runs his branch in accordance with the policy of the company. While to some extent this would apply to a franchised organisation, there is not the same rigidity. Each franchisee must be treated as an individual. His problems are treated as those of an individual, and the approach of the team at the highest management level cannot be to dictate to the franchisee what he should do and what company policy is, but rather to try and train him and to instil in him the interest which an individual should have in running and managing his own business, albeit within the established framework. The franchisee must be persuaded to see the sense of what is expected of him.

The franchisor's interest is in seeking to achieve for the franchisee the success of which his business is capable and to bring the best out of him as an individual. The franchisor should certainly not resort to dictating to the franchisee unless the franchisee insists on breaking his contract or fails properly to operate the system.

The franchisor may also be a source for the franchisee obtaining a prospective purchaser for his business. Whether things are going well or not for the franchisee it is quite likely that the franchisor will have contact with many people interested in taking over a business of this sort. The franchisee can often obtain valuable assistance from a franchisor when he does decide, for some reason or other, that the time has come to dispose of his business.

The relationship between the franchisor and franchisee is very special and different from most other business relationships.

It is analogous to a parent/child relationship. In its early stages the franchisee, like a child with a parent, is dependent upon the franchisor for his sources of information and the understanding of how to apply the knowledge acquired. As the franchisee gains practical experience he undergoes a change. He becomes less dependent, and in some cases positively independent, to the point that he no longer sees any value in his association with the franchisor. He regards himself as being totally responsible for his success and he resents the payment he is making to the franchisor. He sees no need to continue to be supplied with any services by the franchisor.

This is similar to the developing parent/child relationships—as the child grows older so it becomes less dependent and more fiercely independent. The child has its own ideas and cannot see the need for parental control and rejects parental influence.

So both the franchisor and parent face a similar problem. It is the recognition of, and response to, the changing and evolving nature of the relationship which is an essential element in the skill of both franchisor and parent. Those who deal with this problem best are most successful in practice.

This peculiarity of the relationship should not be ignored or neglected; it is of fundamental importance. Franchising is not the answer for everyone.

The clear lesson is that the important factors for success in this stage are good communications, co-operation between the franchisor and franchisee, and a clear mutual understanding and respect for the relationship which exists between them.

CHAPTER 10

The Franchise Contract

THE franchise contract is a very important document. It is the moment of truth. It is the occasion when the franchisor's promises have to be presented to the franchisee in writing and be subjected to careful scrutiny.

The contract is a legal commitment which is binding on both parties. The franchisee must therefore at this stage take competent legal advice as to the meaning and effect of the contract. In consultation with his solicitor he will check to see whether the contract confirms what he has been told. The franchisee should realise that the extent of the advice he is given is limited to the meaning and effect of the contract. It is the decision of the franchisee, and the franchisee alone, whether or not to proceed with any particular franchise opportunity. Decision making is an essential part of his role as a businessman.

A franchise contract has to take into account a number of different considerations. The essential considerations may be considered under eleven separate headings.

1. Although basically a contractual relationship between the franchisor and the franchisee, the franchise contract involves two other parties who are not joined as parties to the contract. The other parties are, firstly, all other franchisees within the franchise chain and, secondly, members of the public, the consumer, and it is to both of these parties that the franchisor and the franchisee owe considerable responsibilities. It is simple to see how this arises. Each franchisee within the chain will be affected for good or bad by the actions of his fellow franchisees. If a franchisee runs his operation in a manner which is inconsistent with the standards associated with the franchisor's brand and image, it will damage the goodwill associated with them, thereby adversely affecting the business prospects of other franchisees. So each franchisee owes a

heavy responsibility to the other franchisees and should therefore look on the restrictive provisions of the agreement, which are concerned with the maintenance of the standards and the correct operation of the franchised business, as not merely a tiresome chore, but as a duty and responsibility which he owes to himself and his fellow franchisees to ensure that the reputation and integrity of the franchise chain are always maintained.

The consumer features in this, of course, because the consumer is not concerned with whether or not an outlet is franchised. A consumer is merely concerned with the brand image. A consumer will frequent a business which has given satisfaction in the past and will regard franchised businesses as being branches of a larger chain. He will not accept an explanation "but this was operated under franchise and unfortunately we have problems with that franchisee" if the franchisee does not do his job properly. All the consumer is concerned with is that when he goes into the store he receives the same standards of products and service which he has been led to believe he can expect from that particular "branded" business.

Franchisees therefore owe a great responsibility in the maintenance of these standards to ensure that the consumer is not misled and that, whichever outlet within the franchise chain the consumer patronises, he feels that he is being given the sort of product and service he had reason to expect he would receive.

2. It has already been explained that the franchisor in a business format franchise will be contributing his blueprint which embraces a package comprising trade secrets, method of operation, use of trade marks, trade names, and many of the other features previously mentioned. The franchisor will be concerned in his agreement to ensure that provison is made for the franchisee (a) to use these blueprints, methods of operation, trade marks, trade names, etc., and (b) to preserve the element of trade secrecy which is associated with the franchisor's particular methods and blueprints. The agreement, in essence, is a licence permitting the franchisee to run the business *only* according to the blueprint. If the franchisee wants the freedom to do only as he pleases, then franchising is not for him.

3. In order to achieve the goal, it is inherent in discharging the four-way obligations outlined in item 1 above that consideration is given to the manner in which the necessary standards are imposed upon the franchisee and what provision should be made to enforce those standards.

4. The term of the agreement has to be considered. As a basic principle one should expect the franchise relationship to be capable of subsisting in the long term. There may be legal reasons why the initial term should not exceed five years. Even if this is the case, the franchisee should be given an option to renew the agreement. Some franchisors do not like to grant too long a term on the belief that there may be developments in the law to which they would like to have the opportunity to respond sooner rather than later. In any event it is the invariable practice to grant franchisees an option to renew provided the franchisee has performed his obligations under the agreement and the franchisee enters into a new agreement in the form of the franchisors then current agreement.

5. It will also be advisable that over the passage of years the freshness of the image and appeal to the consumer is maintained, and therefore it will be necessary to ensure that provison is made and means are available to require the franchisee to make provision, by setting amounts aside periodically, for investment in the modernisation and the upgrading of the premises and equipment employed therein, so that with the passage of time the appeal of the business and its attractiveness to the consumer does not fade.

6. Another factor is the method by which the franchisor obtains his income and secures payment.

What will be in the mind of many prospective franchisors will be the extent to which he will be able to protect himself against the franchisee not making full disclosure of all his income against which the percentage fee is calculated. Obviously, there will always be those franchisees who see the payment of fees calculated by reference to gross income as a challenge, but in franchising there is an overall structure which puts the cheat at a disadvantage.

The structure contains a number of features which will inevitably be reflected in the contract and the system which is being operated by the franchisor.

(i) The franchisor in establishing the system by his experience in the market place will have laid down the guidelines of financial achievement. He will be illustrating to franchisees, when training them and in setting them up in business, what their gross and net margins should be at given levels of turnover and the percentage which each group of expense items should be of turnover. A concealment of gross income would inevitably distort those margins. The margins could, of course, also be distorted by incompetence, but if that is the case the franchisor should quickly be able to identify it and advise or initiate appropriate remedial action.

(ii) The franchisor, in order that he can be informed about the performance of each franchisee's business, will establish standard form accounting systems and reporting procedures.

(iii) As part of the accounting system and the monitoring of its correct operation, the franchisor will require the right to do spot audits without prior warning being given.

(iv) The accounting system and reporting procedures will enable the franchisor to monitor the franchisee's performance and to detect warning signs that all is not well.

(v) The franchisor's field operational staff who provide back-up to franchisees by regular visits will have the opportunity of discussing performance with franchisees and making spot checks on stocks, books and other records to verify the accuracy of the information. If the information is inaccurate it naturally devalues the assistance which can be given.

(vi) In collecting and collating the information from each franchisee, the franchisor is building up a record of each franchisee's performance and an average for the whole network. Any franchisee whose achievements are markedly below the average will be a candidate for special attention so that the cause may be identified and remedial action taken.

(vii) The franchisee will be required to make a return of gross income to the Customs and Excise in relation to Value Added Tax. Copies of these returns and any assessments to V.A.T. should be obtained by the franchisor and compared with the figures submitted to him.

(viii) The franchisor will have access to the franchisee's supply sources. If he knows what the franchisee is buying, he will have a very good idea of what his gross sales figures should be if the business is operated properly.

(ix) In some cases the franchisor may be able to obtain information from large customers of the network with whom he has made arrangements for the network to supply goods and/or services.

7. Consideration will have to be given to the question of the circumstances in which the franchise arrangements can be terminated. In doing so, the position of the franchisee must be considered responsibly so that the franchise cannot be terminated capriciously. Consequences of termination also have to be clearly thought out in order that the franchisor's property rights are properly protected.

8. It is also a prime consideration, and in practice an area of some difficulty, in making equitable provision in the agreement for the circumstances in which an assignment might take place. Obviously in a franchise which requires the franchisee to be trained, as most do, or which may require a specialised area of knowledge or the application of particular principles, a franchisee can never be permitted freely to assign his franchise when disposing of his business. Safeguards have to be built in to ensure that the new franchisee will accept the responsibilities, will undergo any necessary training, and provide the same standards of service and product as if, in fact, there had been no change of franchisee. Indeed, the new franchisee has to be acceptable to the franchisor as if he had applied direct to the franchisor. It is usual to demand the same qualification and standards for his acceptance as are being applied to direct applicants for a franchise.

9. Another area to which considerable thought has to be given is what is to happen if the franchisee, being an individual, or if the principal shareholder and director of the franchisee, if it is a limited company, dies? Some franchise agreements make no provision at all for these circumstances; others do make certain provisions. Clearly, it is an area of serious concern for both franchisor and franchisee that the right balance is struck so that the dependants of the franchisee are able either to continue the business formerly carried on by the deceased or, alternatively, are able to turn the business to account by selling and receiving the capital value of the business.

10. The agreement must also be considered from the franchisee's point of view. Quite apart from the consideration which is given to the franchisee's point of view in the aspects already dealt with, the franchisee must satisfy himself that the contract offers him exactly what he has been led to believe he would receive. He should not leave anything to trust; he should ask the franchisor to write into the agreement, or perhaps as an amendment to the agreement, confirmation of all the obligations undertaken. Nothing should be

left to implication. Most franchisors will not accept amendments to their standard form, so they will only have their own lack of foresight to blame if they encounter difficulties.

Furthermore, although the tendency exists for a successful franchisee to forget what he owes to the franchisor for his success, the franchisor will invariably always know just that little bit more about the business than any one individual franchisee. In such a case the franchisor must be able to contain the franchisee within the scope of the franchise scheme.

11. There is an increasing tendency for franchisors to become involved in the property aspects of the transaction. This arises from a number of circumstances:

(i) The franchisor may already be a multiple which is converting some of its existing chain to franchising. He is involved as a freeholder or lessee of the premises which are occupied for the purpose of his business. In granting the franchise he will grant a lease or sublease to the franchisee. He may, of course, if he is a lessee, decide to assign the lease to the franchisee.

(ii) The franchisor may decide as a matter of policy that in order to secure the sites as outlets for his network he wishes to be in control of the situation by buying the freehold or becoming lessee and granting a lease or sublease to the franchisee. He may be more selective and only become involved in a property if it comes into the "flagship" or "irreplacable" category. Into this heading will come scarce sites, such as existing light industrial uses close to residential areas, where, if the franchisee leaves the network, the franchisor may find it difficult (if at all possible) to obtain any suitable alternative from which to trade.

(iii) The franchisor may decide (see Wimpy case study: paragraph 1 on pages 160–161) that he will use the value of his covenant to obtain sites for the network which franchisees may not be able to secure at all.

(iv) The franchisor may find that he is forced into giving his covenant in order to secure a site since the landlord or his agent realise that the franchisor's covenant may be worth having while that of the franchisee is not.

Each franchisor will formulate his own policy towards involvement with property; but if he does get involved, the lease and franchise agreement will have to be linked with each other so that termination and/or renewal of one will result in the same treatment of the other. The rights given to tenants of business premises under the Landlord and Tenant Act 1954 (as subsequently amended) have to be considered in the formulation of policy. If the franchisor does become involved in property, the franchisee should be no worse off upon termination than he would be if the franchisor were not his landlord.

It will be appreciated that not all the provisions referred to in this chapter will apply in every case, but some, indeed most, will feature in all franchise transactions.

The legal topics which have to be addressed in a franchise arrangement often involve a number of areas of law which are not usually dealt with by one practitioner. Indeed some of the topics are quite specialised. Although in business terms the contractual obligations can be split into two stages, which are dealt with below, in framing advice to the franchisor or, even where the franchisor considers his own position, the transaction should be broken down into six phases:

(i) *The preparation of the franchise scheme for marketing.* The development of the concept through the pilot operation during which are developed the industrial and intellectual property rights—the trade mark, the trade name, goodwill, trade secrets and know-how. This is the stage at which these rights have to be protected. The development of the system, apart from solving business problems, must not create legal difficulties which may later cause the system to be changed. This is also the time to consider the structure of the transaction; Will one be involved in property? What will be the policy in relation to territories or catchment areas? and, what will be the range of services to be provided to the franchisee?

(ii) *The marketing of the scheme.* The promotion of the scheme; the preparation of the sales literature followed by the actual negotiations and discussions with the franchisees. When one considers the wide range of services to be provided by the franchisor, and the need to demonstrate to a franchisee the capacity of the business for success, the scope for the franchisor to make representations is very wide indeed. The larger the franchisor's organisation, the more people there are involved in the selling effect, the greater the scope and the greater the risk of mistakes being made.

The next four phases, namely:

(iii) Stage One of the contract,
(iv) Stage Two of the contract,
 (v) Termination, and
(vi) Consequences of termination,

are now dealt with in detail.

For the purposes of considering the contractual arrangements, a franchise transaction conveniently splits into two stages:

Stage One would deal with the position leading up to the opening of the business.

Stage Two is the continuing relationship which regulates the transaction after the business is open.

Some franchise companies accordingly have two contracts, one for each stage. In such cases the Stage One contract is frequently called a purchase agreement and the Stage Two contract the franchise or licence agreement. Let us examine each in turn. It is not necessary to have two agreements, although in some cases where there is a comprehensive equipment and initial services package it can be the better method. It is more likely to find one agreement which can deal with both stages of the transaction, although in practice many agreements which the author has seen do not deal properly or adequately with initial obligations of the franchisor.

The purchase agreement may be conveniently divided into three aspects:

1. The franchise package.
2. The price.
3. The services to be provided.

Before examining each of these aspects it should be noted that it is not essential that the premises from which the franchisee is to trade should be finally agreed upon before the contracts are signed. As long as it is possible to pinpoint an area within which the premises are to be located, the agreements may be entered into conditionally upon a mutually acceptable site being found. This may appear at first sight to be potentially dangerous, but a successful franchise will usually attract more prospective franchisees than can be placed at any given time. A waiting list will develop. In such a case a prospective franchisee will wish to join the queue and reserve an area; indeed it is possible in some cases to obtain an option from a franchisor for an area.

If a site is being sought a purchase agreement will specify the area within which the premises are to be located.

1. *Franchise Package*

The extent and subject matter of the franchise package which is being sold will be listed. The list is sometimes called an inventory or equipment or perhaps just an equipment list. It must contain all items which are included; all items which the franchisee has been told to expect. Some franchise companies regard this list as being confidential and stipulate in the contract that it must be so treated by the franchisee. In such a case there will also be a provision requiring the return of the list if the transaction does not proceed.

2. *The Price*

The price will be specified, as will be the manner of payment. This may be cash in full on signature, although this is rare. More often a deposit is required on signature, with payment of the balance to follow on delivery of the equipment or at other stages of the transaction.

There may be allowance for the fact that finance has to be arranged. In this case the contract may be conditional upon satisfactory finance being obtained. What is to be regarded as "satisfactory finance" should be defined carefully.

The price may not include delivery charges, installation charges, shopfitting works and V.A.T. If this is the case it should be made clear, particularly in respect of the shopfitting work. This latter can often cause confusion, as the equipment list will often include equipment and fittings which will be incorporated in the shopfitting.

If a deposit is paid at this, or indeed at any other, stage it should be made clear whether and in what circumstances it is returnable to the franchisee. The franchisor will wish at this stage to retain the right to withdraw from the transaction. It may be that training will show the franchisee to be unsuitable for the particular type of franchise. In a case where the franchisor withdraws from the transaction the deposit should be returnable to the franchisee in full. However, a different situation obtains if the franchisee wishes to withdraw. The franchisor may be prepared to take a risk on his own withdrawal, but if the franchisee can withdraw without cost, after having caused the franchisor a lot of trouble and expense, then the payment of the deposit will not amount to much evidence of good faith. Provision is therefore usually made for the franchisor to be able to retain the whole or part of the deposit to reimburse him for the expenses in which he has been involved. The franchisee should insist, if a deposit is to be paid, that the circumstances in which he gets it back or in which the franchisor may keep some of it, are very clearly and unambiguously set out in writing. Some franchisees have lost money by failing to read or understand what they were given or told. It is essential to take proper professional advice before parting with any money.

3. *The Initial Services to be Provided*

These services to the franchisee will be set out. They have already been discussed in some detail in Chapter 7.

If there are two agreements the first agreement will contain the provisions relating to the initial training of the franchisee. This will mean that the franchisor will impose upon the franchisee a confidentiality undertaking to ensure that if the transaction does not proceed the trained prospective franchisee cannot make use of, or disclose, the know-how acquired in training.

These are the main features to be expected in a purchase agreement. If in a particular transaction there is no purchase agreement, then such of its features as are relevant to the transaction should be found in the franchise or licence agreement.

The franchise or licence agreement can be conveniently divided into seven sections:

Section 1.   The rights granted to the franchisee.
Section 2.   The obligations undertaken by the franchisor.
Section 3.   The obligations imposed upon the franchisee.
Section 4.   The trading restrictions imposed upon the franchisee.
Section 5.   Assignment/death of franchisee.
Section 6.   The termination provisions.
Section 7.   The consequences of termination.

Section 1

The franchisee will be given the right so far as may be relevant in the particular circumstances:

(a) To use the trade marks, trade names and patents of the franchisor.

(b) To use the brand image and the design and decor of the premises developed by the franchisor in projecting that image.

(c) To use the franchisor's secret methods.

(d) To use the franchisor's copyright material.

(e) To use the recipes, formulae, specifications, and processes and methods of manufacture developed by the franchisor.

(f) To conduct the franchised business upon or from the agreed premises strictly in accordance with the franchisor's methods and subject to the franchisor's directions.

It should be noted that many franchise schemes carry with them the promise of exclusive rights. These exclusive rights will vary according to whether the franchised business is physically immobile (e.g. a retail shop) or physically mobile (e.g. an ice-cream van). In the case of a retail shop the exclusivity would be based upon a radius within which the franchisor will not franchise another similar unit. In the case of a mobile franchise an area within which the franchisee may carry on his business will be exclusively granted and the franchisee will be forbidden to step outside such area.

It is difficult to lay down any set radius, for what is reasonable will vary considerably from case to case. It is important to realise that the franchisor cannot hope for a successful growth in his own business if his units are placed so close together that none can effectively operate. The grant of exclusive rights may give rise to difficulties under the Restrictive Trade Practices Act 1976.

The existence of these difficulties prevents many franchisors from agreeing to grant exclusive territorial rights. In practice this does not give rise to marketing difficulties; franchisees recognise that in economic reality the franchisor cannot succeed if his franchisees fail. The placing too close together of franchisees or the close proximity to a franchised outlet of a franchisor's operation will harm both. Failed franchisees and franchisor operations are hardly the best advertisement for the expansion of a franchise scheme.

The commercial considerations also demand that recognition is given to the practical problems which arise in dealing with territories. With the best will in the world it is extremely difficult, particularly in the early stages of development of a franchise, fairly to define a territory. The tendency is to give an area which is too large. Many franchisors who have tried to establish territories have encountered problems which have inevitably led to them having to purchase back territories which were too large and to change their policy. A franchisee given exclusive territorial rights and who is doing well will not see any incentive in expanding and, maybe, opening or providing more outlets. He will be content with his profits and will wish to avoid more responsibility or expense. This is a short-sighted attitude, since the franchise network will be developing and extending its reputation and the demand for its products and/or services. If the franchisee in a territory does not expand to meet the growing demand, he is leaving a gap in the market place for competitors. The advertising and marketing expenditure by the network will be effectively assisting competitors in establishing themselves. The obvious solution which might be suggested is that one should impose performance targets with which the franchisee should comply. The problem with that solution is that it is just as difficult to establish fair targets which raise annually to reflect improved and expanding business as well as inflation, as it is to define a territory.

An additional factor which must be taken into account in approaching the problem of exclusivity of area is the growing legislative (both domestic and European) intervention. This intervention is sought to be politically justified on the basis that the legislation will curb abuse of monopoly power, anti-competitive practices and encourage the free development of markets. Franchising is likely to be affected by any such legislation, although one is inclined to doubt that many of the arguments justifiably apply to franchising.

(g) The right (as well as the obligation) to obtain supplies from the franchisor and/or nominated suppliers at special prices. The franchisor can often obtain quite good reductions for franchisees using the weight of the bulk-purchasing powers of the whole of the franchised chain.

In some cases the franchisor requires the franchisee to purchase his supplies of products or raw materials from the franchisor. This is often the case where a trade mark is involved and is, for example, a feature of the Wimpy franchise. This type of provision is also likely to attract the same sort of legislative attention to which reference has already been made in relation to exclusivity of territory. Indeed, such tied sales have been the subject of an investigation and report by the Monopolies and Mergers Commission. On the whole the Commission, which considered franchising in a separate chapter, concluded in relation to tied sales in franchise transactions that it did not consider that any public interest issue was likely to be involved, and that the Competition Act 1980 was appropriate for any case which might appear to need investigation.

Section 2

The obligations of the franchisor in the continuing relationship which exists after the business has opened are dealt with in Chapter 8.

Section 3

The franchisee may have the obligation imposed upon him:

(a) To carry on the business franchised and no other upon approved and nominated premises and strictly in accordance with the franchisor's methods and standards. This provision will often be detailed enough to prevent the sale of any items not included in the franchise scheme unless the franchisor expressly gives his consent. In some cases even automatic vending machines and juke boxes are expressly prohibited to maintain the standards and appearance of the operation.

(b) To observe certain minimum opening hours. These will usually be the hours which enable the business to be operated most profitably within the scope of the blueprint and without incurring disproportionate overheads. For example, the cost of staff and other overheads in remaining open for, say, a further two hours a day may not be covered by the additional trading which is done.

(c) To pay a franchise fee. The various methods by which a franchisor receives payment of such a fee are dealt with in Chapter 6.

(d) To follow the accounting system laid down by the franchisor. The purpose is twofold. Firstly, the franchisor has a means of checking and for the purpose of calculating any fees to which he may be entitled. Secondly, the system will be prepared in such a way that it will rapidly reveal if the projected gross and net profit margins are not being maintained.

(e) Not to advertise without prior approval of the advertisements by the franchisor. As has been explained, the franchisor will invariably handle all national advertising, but this will not mean that there is no local or other advertising which cannot benefit the business. The franchisor will wish to have control of the contents of advertisements which make use of his name and relate to one of his franchised businesses.

(f) To use and display such point of sale or advertising material as the franchisor stipulates. Also to use bags, boxes, wrappers, and, in a food franchise, even such items as straws, cups, and serviettes bearing the franchisor's name and trade mark. Point of sale and advertising material is often supplied free of charge, but the other items would, of course, have to be paid for.

(g) To maintain the premises in a good, clean, sanitary condition and to redecorate when required to do so by the franchisor. This is a provision which often causes difficulty. The franchisor will always be striving to ensure that the premises have the best possible appearance while the franchisee will be reluctant to spend his money.

(h) To maintain the widest possible business insurance cover. The purpose of this provision is to protect the franchisee from the consequences of fire or public or employees' liability and other claims. It protects his business and his livelihood.

(i) To permit the franchisor's staff to enter the premises to inspect and see whether the franchisor's standards are being maintained and whether the terms of the agreement are being observed.

(j) To purchase goods or products from the franchisor or his nominated suppliers. This provision would apply in a case where the franchisor manufactures some or all of the products which are to be sold in the franchised business.

(k) To train his staff in the franchisor's methods and to ensure that they are neatly and appropriately clothed.

(l) Not to assign the franchise contract without the franchisor's consent. All franchise contracts should be capable of assignment. If the contract is not assignable there is no incentive to the franchisee to invest and to build. The franchisor, however, will have controls over the acceptance of franchisees and will not wish to have the controls avoided. There is rarely difficulty in practice in arranging a transfer of the franchise provided the incoming person matches the franchisor's selection standards and successfully passes through any necessary training. Many contracts provide for a fixed or percentage fee based upon the sale price to be paid to the franchisor to cover his costs of processing the transaction and of training and establishing the new franchisee. Additionally, some franchisors are able to introduce purchasers from their waiting list of franchisees and charge on a percentage fee basis as would a business transfer agent. Quite often there is a provision which grants to the franchisor an option to purchase if the franchisee wishes to sell. Any such option should secure for the franchisee at least as good a deal as he would get if he were to do a *bona fide* arms length deal in the open market.

Section 4

The restrictions imposed upon the franchisee may prohibit him from:

(a) Carrying on a similar business except under franchise from the franchisor. The franchisor will not wish to train the franchisee only to have him open a similar business trading in competition with the other franchisees without regard to territorial restrictions.

(b) Taking staff away from other franchisees. As all franchisees are dependant upon each other it would not be in the interests of the development of the chain for the franchisees to be attempting to take trained staff away from each other.

(c) Carrying on a similar business in close proximity to the other franchised businesses within the chain for a certain period after the termination of the franchise contract. This provision is to protect all the franchisees within the chain.

(d) Continuing after the termination of the franchise contract to use any of the franchisor's trade names, trade secrets, secret processes, copyright material, recipes, specifications, and the like.

Section 5

The question of assignability has been mentioned in the comments in Section 3. The problem of what should be done in the event of the death of the franchisee, or the principal shareholder of the franchisee if it is a company, has not been faced up to by many franchise contracts. The franchisee should ensure that in the event of death:

(a) His personal representative(s) and/or dependant(s) will be able to keep the business going until one of them can qualify as a franchisee and take an assignment of the franchise agreement; or

(b) That arrangements can be made to keep the business going until a suitable assignee can be found at a proper price. In this respect the franchisor may be able to agree to offer to provide management (for a fee) during the critical few weeks following the death. All reputable and ethical franchisors will be sympathetic and helpful whatever the contract provides, but it is best if the contract clearly specifies what will happen.

Section 6

There is an increasing tendency to introduce into franchise agreements a provision for the arbitration of disputes.

Arbitration is a useful procedure and is particularly apt for the franchise transaction, although it is not considered desirable by all franchisors as a method of resolving disputes.

However, there is a very definite role for arbitration as a method of resolving disputes or differences which can arise in a franchise transaction. A franchise agreement is the basis for a long-term arrangement which should be able to survive genuine differences of opinion. The alternative is confrontation, termination and litigation. Not that arbitration is not a form of confrontation, but it gives the opportunity to deal with a difference speedily in confidence and largely at the convenience of the parties. Also it is usually less expensive and arbitrators can be selected from a specialised panel who will realistically understand and cope with the problems.

There are some aspects of the agreement which are particularly appropriate for the arbitration procedure. Examples include:

(a) whether a franchisee has performed his contract sufficiently well to justify any renewal rights which the franchisee may have; and

(b) differences arising in respect of royalty or franchise fee calculations.

However, most franchisees would not wish to arbitrate about whether or not their standards had been observed. Also care must be taken to ensure that when a franchisor needs to be able quickly to enforce his rights, for example on termination, that he can go to court for immediate action in appropriate cases.

The Chartered Institute of Arbitrators has established rules for arbitration. It also provides a forum for conducting arbitration and can appoint as arbitrators those with the requisite specialised experience from among various panels of arbitrators. These rules are set out in Appendix D, together with a model form of arbitration clause which would be appropriate.

The agreement may be determined after the expiration of the fixed period or there may be express provision for the termination upon the service of a notice. Inevitably, the agreement will provide for termination by the franchisor in the event of any default by the franchisee of his obligations under the franchise agreement. Most agreements provide a machinery for the franchisee to be given an opportunity to remedy any defaults which can be remedied within a specific period before the franchisor can exercise the right of termination subject to safeguards against the habitual offender.

Many franchisors treat breaches with varying degrees of seriousness, but many take a very strong view of breaches which raise questions of whether the franchisee can be trusted. Therefore, some regard cheating over disclosure of gross income, and thus the amount of the fee to be paid, as fundamental and will wish to be able to terminate in such a case without giving the franchisee an opportunity to put matters right. Another instance of lack of trust arises where the franchisee has provided misleading or false information in his franchise application. A franchisor is also bound to take a very serious view of a franchisee who is found to be making confidential information available to competitors or potential competitors.

In whatever circumstances the franchise agreement is terminated, the franchisee should be left with as assets a business and the equipment for which he has paid. He will be stripped of his right to carry on business under the trade name, to use the franchisor's system and know-how, and will lose all the other advantages made available to a franchisee, and he may also have to move trading premises or substantially change his business in view of restrictive covenants in the agreement.

In some cases the franchisor will own the freehold or lease of the premises and will grant a lease or an underlease to the franchisee. In such a case the franchisee may find that upon the termination of the franchise agreement he has lost his lease also. In such a case the franchisee should at the time of the signature of the contract see that there are safeguards for the cash investment he is making. In doing so he must appreciate that the basic cause for him subsequently finding himself in such an invidious position will be his own default.

As will be appreciated, the ultimate consequence of termination for the franchisee can be quite drastic. The objective in framing these provisions is to ensure that the franchisor recovers total control over his industrial and intellectual property rights, his system and his goodwill.

—the use of the brand name and goodwill associated with it must be discontinued;

—the use of the system and know-how must be discontinued;
—all outward signs, appearance of premises and vans must be changed to avoid confusion and to prevent the franchisee from cashing in on the franchisor's goodwill;
—customer contact must stop. Their custom is part of the franchisor's goodwill;
—the franchisee must be prevented from competing with the franchisor and the network, from the premises on which he conducted the franchised business.

In view of the close working relationship that exists between a franchisor and a franchisee all requirements must be clearly stated in the contract. This is a transaction in which no small print should exist.

CHAPTER 11

The Choice of Franchise and What to Ask the Franchisor

BEFORE entering into business by the franchise route it is essential to have sufficient knowledge about four aspects.

1. One has to KNOW oneself.
2. One has to KNOW the particular business.
3. One has to KNOW the franchisor.
4. One has to KNOW the franchise proposition.

1. One has to KNOW Oneself

Let us consider a widely used statement in the franchise context:

"Franchising is safer than independently setting up business on one's own account."

This, broadly speaking, is correct, and certainly in the U.S.A. where statistics are available it is borne out by the information which is provided. In the U.K., in the absence of any statistics, it is difficult to be dogmatic, but the information provided in Chapter 2 and the experience of the British Franchise Association membership as a whole, and of other reputable franchise companies, bears out the assertion.

The danger in making or relying on such an assertion is that a franchisee may:

(i) drop his guard when investigating a franchise just because he has heard this statement and trusts in the system regardless of the specifics of the proposition with which he is faced;

(ii) be lulled into the false belief that to make a lot of money easily all one has to do is sign a franchise agreement.

The lessons to be drawn are that each franchise must be considered on its merits in the light preferably, at the very least, of the guidance contained in this book and the certain knowledge that *franchising is not the easy way to quick money*. What suits the person who successfully establishes a business may not suit another.

In life nothing comes easily, and that is true of franchising. Most successful franchisees have *worked very hard* to achieve what they have. What franchising should do is to reduce the risk inherent in opening a new business because one of the features being sold by the franchisors should be the benefit of the experience he has obtained in running his own business or his pilot operation and in detecting and solving the problems with which any new business is faced. It should also provide the franchisee with a business which has a proved record of success upon which he can build. *It should never offer or be considered as a work-free way of making money*. If it is offered in this way be suspicious, and if you regard it in this way *stop being greedy and come to your senses*.

These factors are important in the process through which all prospective self-employed businessmen should go before taking the plunge. Indeed one must not lose sight of the fact that in deciding whether or not to go into a franchise one is also deciding to go into business on one's own account, albeit a particular type of business structured in a particular type of way. It is necessary, regardless of the fact that it is a franchised business which is contemplated, to indulge in the same sort of self-assessment in which one should indulge when deciding to embark on any business venture.

If one has a particular franchise in mind, the self-assessment exercise is less academic, but one should be asking some, if not all, of the following questions.

—Am I qualified physically and temperamentally for self-employment?
—Do I possess sufficient financial resources to enable me to start a business and survive while it is struggling to become established?
—What are my natural aptitudes and skills?
—Do I do my best with mental or physical tasks?
—Do I mix well with people?
—Do I have the ability to work hard?
—Am I prepared to work unsocial hours?

—How will my family be affected by my decision and the calls the business will make on my time?

—Do my family wholeheartedly support my proposed adventure?

—Will any of the family be able and available to help me?

—How do I assess by financial resources?

—Am I prepared to put whatever assets I now possess at risk?

—Am I able to raise sufficient finance?

—Do I have staying power?

—What am I looking for

    (a) Job satisfaction?

    (b) Capital gain?

    (c) To earn lots of money?

    (d) An investment? (absentee owner)

—Will the business be sufficiently challenging for me?

—Am I determined enough to succeed?

—What do I want to achieve in life?

It is vital to subject oneself and one's attitude to the closest possible scrutiny. The prospective franchisee must be sure he knows himself and what he is looking for. He must ensure that when he looks at himself he can relate his strengths and weaknesses to the proposition which he is considering or is intending to consider. He must remember that he will have to prove to himself his ability to make a decision by deciding to take the franchise route.

2. One Has to KNOW the Particular Business

The place of the business in the market is another vital consideration. Not only is the specific business in relation to its own field important, but so is the assessment of the industry of which it forms part.

The business will either be dealing in goods or products or the provision of services.

We should examine each, and the table which follows contains a comparison of the various considerations.

Goods or Products	*Services*
1. Are the products new?	Is the service to be provided a new one?
2. Has the franchised business been thoroughly proved in practice to be successful?	Same.

Goods or Products	Services
3. Is there a one-product distributorship or agency which is dressed up as a business format franchise?	Does this service have a novelty element about it which clearly distinguishes it from other like and competitive businesses?
4. Does it have staying power?	Same.
5. Is it, alternatively, in a business area which is in decline?	Same.
6. Is it in a growth area?	Same.
7. Is that growth a fad or mere fashion and thus transient?	Same.
8. How competitive is the market for the particular products?	How competitive is the market for the provision of these services?
9. How competitive is the price of the products?	How competitive is the price at which the services are to be offered?
10. Can this competitiveness be maintained?	Same.
11. What is the source of supply of the products?	Not applicable.
12. How certain is it that the source will be available for the future?	Not applicable.
13. Are alternative sources of products of comparable quality and price available?	Not applicable.
14. Are the products based upon a trade mark?	Is there a strong distinctive trade name associated with the provision of the services? If a celebrity name is used, remember celebrities come and go and so can the related franchise.
15. Are the products produced by a patented invention?	Not strictly applicable, although it is possible for a patented product to be featured in a service business so one should still consider this as relevant.

Goods or Products	Services
16. Does the franchisor have his lines of supply properly tied up?	Not applicable.
17. Is there an adequate back-up in terms of guarantees and service facilities?	Not applicable.
18. Could the manufacturer or supplier easily bypass the franchisor and you and set up his own competitive franchise?	Not applicable.
19. What is the reputation of the product?	Not applicable.
20. What is the reputation of the supplier?	Not applicable.

Having considered these factors and decided upon an area of interest, one can now begin to look at the suitable opportunities on offer and assess the prospective franchisors.

3. One Has to KNOW the Franchisor

Your first contact with the franchisor will, if you follow the usual pattern, have come about in one of the following three ways:

1. You will be attracted to the business by a friend who has taken up a franchise or by chatting with an existing franchisee.
2. You will respond to editorial comment about a particularly successful franchise in your usual newspaper.
3. You will see an advertisement in *Franchise World* or the business opportunities column of a newspaper.

You will then either write to or telephone the franchise company concerned and they will send you a package. This package will invariably contain:

1. A glossy presentation describing the franchise company and its success story. Often this is presented in a question and answer form. Most reputable franchise companies are very proud of their success and are very pleased to tell all about it.

2. Another presentation explaining briefly what franchising is and setting out in particular what they do for their franchisees in terms of setting them up and continuing to service them thereafter.

The following questions should be put to a franchisor to enable one to assess him, his financial involvement, and the quality of his personnel.

1. How long have you been in franchising?
2. Did you run your own pilot schemes before franchising?
3. If not, why not? If you did run a pilot operation what do you really have to sell?
4. Whether you did or not, what is the extent of your own cash investment in the business?
5. How many franchised businesses do you have at the moment?
6. What are the addresses of these businesses?
7. May I interview any number of these franchisees? May I choose whom I interview? (Do make a choice. Do not let the franchisor feed to you only his best franchisees.) Can I see them on my own?
8. How many outlets do you yourselves run as at the preent time? How successful are they? May I see details of their financial performance?
9. What does your head office organisation staff consist of?
10. Can I meet your senior executive staff? How long have they each been with you and do they have service contracts which will ensure continuity?
11. Can you demonstrate your capacity to provide the necessary follow-up services? Is your organisation developed sufficiently well to cope with an expansion of the size and area of operations which are envisaged?
12. May I take up your bank references?
13. Are there any other referees whom I may approach?
14. How many business failures have been experienced by your franchisees? What steps did you take to try to solve their problems?
15. On what basis do you choose your franchisees—how selective are you?
16. What is the business background of the directors and executives of your company?
17. Have you or any of your directors or executives ever experienced any business failures? If so, please provide details.

18. Have any of your directors or executives ever been bankrupt, entered into an arrangement with his creditors; been convicted of any criminal offence; been involved as a shareholder or executive in any company which while he was a director or executive, or shortly after he ceased to be a director or executive, went into liquidation? If so, please provide details.
19. Have you or any of your directors or executives been involved in any material litigation with franchisees? If so, please provide details.
20. Are you a member of the British Franchise Association? If not, are you on the British Franchise Association Register?
21. Have you applied for membership of the British Franchise Association or to join the Register and been refused?

The British Franchise Association (B.F.A.)

The formation of the British Franchise Association in 1977 introduced a new element. Membership is open to those whose franchise scheme has been operating successfully for a period of time. The franchisor is investigated before admission to membership and must accept and observe a strict code of ethical behaviour. In Chapter 15 there is set out an explanation of the aims, objectives and practices of the Association so that a prospective franchisee can judge the value of the franchisor having membership of the Association.

4. One Has to KNOW the Franchise Proposition

There are various aspects of the franchisor's business propositions which should be investigated in detail. The following questions should be asked:

The Operational Details

1. What is the initial cost of your franchise?
2. What does this price include?
3. What capital costs will be incurred in addition to this price, and what for?
4. Do I have to pay you a deposit? If so, on what terms? Are there any circumstances in which, if I do not proceed, I will lose my deposit or any part of it?

5. How much working capital do I need?
6. How long will I have to spend in training and setting up the business before it actually opens?
7. What are the costs incurred in the business likely to be, broken down into *gross* profit and *net* profit?
8. May I see actual accounts which confirm or fail to confirm your projections? Can they be relied upon or are they merely illustrations?
9. What financing arrangements can you make and what terms for repayment will there be? What rate of interest will be required and will the finance company want security?
10. Do you have a franchisee finance scheme with one of the Banks who are operating such schemes? If not, have you applied to any of the Banks for a finance scheme and been refused?
11. Is the business seasonal?
12. When is the best time to open up? What opening support staff do you provide?
13. How do you make your money?
14. Do you charge franchise fees?
15. Do you make a mark up on product sales to franchisees?
16. If so, how much, and what protection do I have against an unjustified increase?
17. Do you take any commission on supplies of goods or materials to a franchisee?
18. Do you receive any other commissions from any other source? If so, please provide details?
19. Will I be obliged to maintain a minimum fee or a minimum purchase of goods? What happens if I fail to meet this commitment?
20. What advertising and promotional support do you provide? Does this cost the franchisee anything? If so, please provide details?
21. Do I have to contribute to it? If so, how much?
22. What initial services do you offer?
23. Do you train me?
24. Who pays for my training?
25. Where do I go for training? How about training of my staff?
26. Will I be able to obtain and motivate sufficient able staff?
27. What continuing services do you provide after the business has commenced?

Contracts

1. May I have a copy of your franchise contract?
2. Does this contract permit me to sell my business? What restrictions are there affecting my rights to sell the business?
3. For how long is the franchise granted?
4. What do I get at the end of that period? Do I get automatic renewal?
5. What will happen if I do not like the business? Upon what basis can I terminate the contract?
6. What happens to the business if I die?
7. What will be the position if the contract is terminated?

Other Aspects

1. Who will be my link with you after I have opened my business?
2. Can I meet some of your operational staff?
3. How long have they each been with you and do they have service contracts which will ensure continuity?
4. What point of sale and promotional literature do you supply and what do I have to pay for it?
5. What will the opening hours of business be?
6. Will I own the equipment necessary to operate the business when I have cleared the finance company?
7. How soon will I have to spend money on replacing equipment?
8. Will you find me a site or do I have to find it?
9. What systems do you have for keeping franchisees in touch with you and each other?
10. Do you publish a newsletter?
11. Do you hold seminars?
12. Is there a franchisee association?
13. What help will I receive in local advertising and promotion?
14. What is the nature and extent of the rights I shall be granted?
15. How will I cope with my book-keeping?
16. Are there any restrictions on what I can sell?
17. Do you provide instruction and operational manuals?
18. What would happen if you misjudged the site and it did not produce the anticipated figures but resulted in a loss?
19. What would happen if I ran into operational problems I was not able to solve? What help would I get?
20. How can I be sure you will do what you promise?

The advantages and disadvantages to a franchisee listed in Chapter 3, as well as the replies to the questions above, must be weighed up and considered before making the decision on whether or not to enter into a franchised business venture. One must decide whether the advantages with the training and support they provide are worth having in return for the surrender of some independence to the degree of outside control which is inherent in the franchise transaction. The prospective franchisee must decide whether the particular franchisor is the right person with whom to do business; he must also decide whether he is personally and temperamentally suitable for this type of relationship.

Having weighed up all the factors, considered the contract (see Chapter 10) and taken proper professional advice (he may also consider the advice of his bank manager or a businessman whose judgement he respects; he should certainly discuss the matter with his immediate family) the prospective franchisee then has to make his final decision. The decision should not be rushed and the franchisee should not let himself be weighed down by the advice of others. He must put the advice and comments received into perspective—it is his life and money which will be affected by his decision. If after all this the prospective franchisee is not able to take this decision with confidence, he should consider whether he is indeed capable of running his own business.

A prospective franchisee may find the following guidelines of value. These are the factors to which one *must* pay attention:

1. Weigh advantages and disadvantages.
2. Assess oneself.
3. Assess the business.
4. Assess the franchisor.
5. Assess the franchise package.
6. Speak to existing franchisees.
7. Consider and put into perspective advice of others who are qualified to give it.
8. Consider your family.
9. Make up your mind.

There are *danger signals* which either, as in the case of Pyramid Schemes, rule out the proposition or in the other cases warrant a very deep and careful scrutiny of the franchise offer.

So *beware* of:

1. Heavy initial fees.
2. Pyramid type schemes.

3. Franchisors whose ongoing fee income is too low to support the services with which they should provide their franchisees.
4. Contracts which do not match promises.
5. The hard sell.
6. Fad or fashion franchises which may not have staying power.
7. A franchise consultant purporting to offer objective advice but who is in reality offering a franchise for sale.
8. Get-rich-quick offers.
9. Franchisors who have not invested in pilot operations.

CHAPTER 12

Franchisee Advisory Committees

ONE of the most important features of any successful franchise is the quality of communication between the franchisor and franchisee. Communication is a two-way exercise and the machinery for maintaining the necessary channels becomes increasingly cumbersome as the chain grows.

A franchisee who feels cut off or neglected is an embryonic trouble spot, as, of course, is the franchisee who feels that his good ideas are being ignored for no good reason. Many franchisees with their direct field experience can make a valuable contribution to the development of the franchise system.

There are two types of franchisee committee. There are those born out of the frustration and dissatisfaction of the franchisees and which adopt a hostile adversary position with the franchisor. This must be avoided at all costs.

For a committee to be set up in this way must mean that the franchisor has failed in some of the following areas:

(a) adequately to communicate with his franchisees;
(b) to be receptive to his franchisees' ideas;
(c) to be supportive;
(d) to provide the right link man between the franchisee and franchisor;
(e) in his marketing programmes;
(f) in his innovative functions—he has not kept the system and image up-to-date with market trends;
(g) to organise advantageous purchasing arrangements;
(h) to develop the feeling of mutual trust and dependence which is so

vital—he may have become overbearing or, by contrast, appear disinterested;
(i) in other material respects to discharge his obligations to his franchisees.

A franchisee committee which develops in these circumstances is symptomatic of the problems; it will not solve them; it is an indictment of the franchisor. The franchise scheme would come under attack and the franchisor would find himself with either a combined legal action or tremendous pressure which could lead to the dismantling of his franchise system. Alternatively, the franchisees will try to lead the franchisor back along the path of franchise righteousness. In any event all parties will have suffered traumatically in terms of personal relationships, confidence and undoubtedly financially.

The other type of committee is that which is formed either on the sole initiative of the franchisor or jointly by franchisor and franchisees as a means of improving communications and acting as a means of liaison when problems arise or to ensure that problems are avoided.

It is difficult to state when would be the right point in time in the development of any individual franchise to introduce an advisory committee. Obviously in the early stages it will not be necessary or appropriate, but once the franchisor is established with some experienced franchisees in the field the advantage will become apparent.

The committee which is created in a spirit of goodwill with mutual advantage as its objective extends the climate of understanding which should exist into a practical reality, thus providing a strong weapon in cementing the franchisor and franchisees together in a powerful business alliance.

It acts as a positive synthesis of the franchisor's and franchisee's entrepreneurial talents for their mutual benefit.

What then are the areas of activity in which such a committee can operate?

1. Communications. Practical difficulties and problems can be identified and discussed between the committee and the franchisor. Style and content of communications can be discussed and improved. The franchisor can find out at first hand, and with constructive rather than destructive criticism, why his communications fail to achieve their objective. It may be that the committee would feel that the franchisor could introduce (if he does not already have one) or improve a regular newsletter and make suggestions for topics to be included.

2. Franchisee experience in the field can be passed on to the franchisor and methods of coping with problems discussed. There is often a wealth of experience and ability among franchisees which the franchisor is wise to tap. The size of the group participating will make the discussion more valuable than if all franchisees were present.
3. New ideas can be introduced by the franchisor for the committee's considered views and reaction. The franchisor can either discuss the views before market testing in company-owned stores or operations or report the experience in practice after pilot testing has taken place. This would of course include innovations in products and services.
4. Suggestions can be made for the improvement of operating manuals if perhaps the explanations are not adequate. It may be that there could be introduced additional material which had been lacking.
5. Training or retraining procedures and facilities can be discussed by the franchisor with those who are past or present "pupils".
6. Discussion of detailed problems arising from the failure or inadequacy of field operation staff or the franchisor's support services.
7. Difficulties which may arise with regard to accounting and reporting procedures can be investigated and any remedial steps taken. Many franchisors introduce, at some stage, computer systems to cope with the ever-increasing volume of accounting information with which they have to contend. In such cases, with little additional expense, a full accounting and information service can be produced and made available to franchisees. The introduction of such a service, its scope and cost, can be discussed with an advisory committee and a scheme acceptable in its details can be agreed.
8. Proposals by the franchisor for the introduction of contractual changes. The reason for such changes can be discussed. The franchisor may wish to introduce new provisions to fill gaps. One of the most common of such gaps in franchise agreements is what should happen in the event of the death of the franchisee. Some franchisors also either have little or no provision in the agreements for realistic advertising and marketing programmes. The development and introduction of contract changes to enable a viable programme to be introduced is an ideal subject for discussion between a franchisor and a franchisee committee.

9. Marketing plans. This is a wide subject and includes national advertising, local advertising, point of sale material, promotional activities and public relations. Most franchisees contribute in one way or another towards funding the cost of such activities. Invariably they are keenly interested to know how the funds will be spent and how much it might help them individually.

The ensuing year's activities can be discussed with franchisees through the committee. Frequently a franchisee will have a valid contribution to make because he will be looking at the proposals with his narrow self-interest in mind. This sort of grass roots detail can escape the attention of the franchisor and his marketing advisers.

Promotional activities, in the planning of which the franchisees have participated, will be greeted far more enthusiastically and with greater prospect of success than would be the case if they were forced upon the franchisees.

It will also be possible to discuss such details as—how long before the promotion starts does the franchisee receive:

(a) point of sale material;
(b) any special range of stock and so on.

10. As well as marketing plans there will always be continuing market research and surveys. Franchisees through the committee have a contribution to make in providing information for such research and surveys. In the course of discussion about the introduction of the research and surveys franchisees could assist in the compilation of the terms of reference and the scope of the enquiries.

11. By liaison with a committee, selective trials of new equipment or ideas by franchisees willing to participate can be organised.

12. Franchisees should also have the opportunity to raise topics. Care should be taken to ensure that the committee only really deals with matters of concern affecting franchisees as a whole. It should not allow itself to be used as a vehicle for the promotion of one dissatisfied franchisee's complaints. It cannot act as advocate judge and jury in what would inevitably be a two-sided story. The quality of the relationship between the committee and franchisor should not be placed in jeopardy for the sake of individual problems or disputes. Therefore a strong chairman who commands the respect of the franchisees is essential.

How should the committee be organised?

It should be understood at the outset that the committee is an association of franchisees, but since the object will be to improve communications between the franchisor and franchisee and provide a forum for the discussion of mutual problems and improved liaison between the parties to the franchise transaction, the franchisor must also be represented.

It is, of course, possible to establish a formally constituted committee with a limited company or an unincorporated association. If this is required, the franchisor should incur the expense and organise what is required for the franchisees provided the committee is being set up on a mutual basis.

However, most of the franchisee committees which exist in the United Kingdom at this time have an informal constitution, although it is usually defined in writing by agreement between franchisor and franchisee when it is set up.

Any document should set out the position in relation to the following matters:

The Terms of Reference

The terms of reference to the committee can include all or some of the points already discussed above.

Membership

Membership should be open to all current franchisees.

How it Should be Managed

Normally one would expect to see some sort of representative committee which is kept to a manageable size. A large and unwieldy committee would be counter-productive. It is best to organise some form of regional representation so that committee members can consult with other franchisees within their region. Assuming that there is a nationwide network, one might expect to have the following regions:

Scotland
Wales
North England
Midlands
South-east England
South-west England

There may be one representative from the smaller regions in terms of numbers of franchisees and two for the larger. Each region can select its own representatives. It may be sensible to arrange that an alternate can attend if the selected representative is for some reason not able to attend.

Meetings

It should be sufficient to have three meetings each year to be arranged in consultation with the franchisor, so that any matters he wishes to deal with or raise can be built into the schedule. One of the meetings could coincide with any national get together or seminar which the franchisor may organise. The franchisor would be represented at all meetings by senior staff relevant to the topics to be discussed.

Secretariat

It should be possible to arrange with the franchisor to provide any secretarial needs of the committee. The committee should keep in touch with the members on any topics of note.

Finances

Any financial requirements will have to be arranged between franchisor and franchisees, but apart from the expense of attending meetings and regional get togethers there should not really be any significant expense.

It is essential to bear in mind that the objectives of any franchisee advisory committee should be to work for mutual benefit of all who participate in the franchise scheme and to create an harmonious atmosphere in which problems are dealt with quickly and new ideas are encouraged.

CHAPTER 13

Franchising in Action—Eight Case Studies

To DEMONSTRATE the application in practice of the principles that have been explained, the franchise propositions of the eight founder members of the British Franchise Association have been selected.

Budget Rent a Car (U.K.) Ltd. (Now Budget Rent a Car International, Inc.)	Car hire
Dyno-Rod Ltd. (Now Dyno-Rod plc)	Drain cleaning and hygiene
Holiday Inns (U.K.), Inc.	Hotel
Kentucky Fried Chicken (G.B.) Ltd.	Fast food—Fried chicken
Prontaprint Ltd.	Speedy print service
ServiceMaster Ltd.	On-site cleaning and restoration service
Wimpy International Ltd.	Fast food—Hamburgers
Ziebart Mobile Transport Service Ltd. (Now Zeegard Car Care Ltd. trading as Ziebart U.K.)	Car undersealing service

Each of these companies has prepared a presentation of its franchise proposition for this book.

These eight companies, as will be seen, operate in seven different fields, ranging from the down-to-earth Dyno-Rod drain cleaning service to the international hotel chain, Holiday Inns. Whatever the difference between their areas of operation, each of them offers a franchise which embraces the features of the orthodox business format franchise.

In relation to the Dyno-Rod, ServiceMaster, and Wimpy franchises we have the additional benefit of the statistical information prepared by Professor John Stanworth contained in Appendix C, which is referred to in the comments following each of these company's presentations.

It is interesting to note that some of the conclusions which Professor Stanworth felt were indicated by his researches included:

(i) At least some of the franchisees felt that they would never have become self-employed but for the opportunity which franchising gave them.

(ii) Most franchisees felt that the public did not understand franchising and saw franchisees as employees of the company under whose trade name they operated.

(iii) Most franchisees felt that the quality of the training, equipment, supplies, and general back-up service given by the franchisor was good.

(iv) Nearly 90% of the franchisees felt that franchising had enabled them to set up and develop their business more rapidly than would otherwise have been the case.

(v) Seventy per cent of the franchisees felt that a franchised business reduced the risk of failure.

(vi) Eighty per cent of the franchisees felt that their franchisor's trade mark was an important element in their success.

(vii) Eighty per cent of the franchisees did not consider any franchise other than the one they entered under.

(viii) Most franchisees experienced enough independence within the terms of the franchise contracts to feel they really were self-employed.

(ix) Most franchisees said that their business had fulfilled their original ambitions and that they would recommend others to do as they had done.

Professor Stanworth's research covered a wider field than that with which this work is concerned. The statistics extracted from his survey have been selected by the author solely on the basis of their relevance to the topics covered by this work. Originally the whole of Appendix C, including any comments, were either extracted directly from the survey or contributed by Professor Stanworth. However, in 1981 Jensine Hough, a research assistant (now Research Fellow) in Professor Stanworth's Department, in the course of her research leading to a thesis for her doctorate conducted an enquiry into four companies. The companies were Home Tune, Prontaprint, Zeibart and one other company which did not wish to be featured in this work. The questions asked in some cases were similar to those in the Stanworth research, but there were also different questions and aspects covered. The Hough statistics which are relevant to the topics in this work are also included in Parts One and Two of Appendix C, compared with like questions where possible. In Part Three of the Appendix there are set out responses to questions asked by Hough for which no counterpart exists in the Stanworth research. Prontaprint and Zeibart, who were included in the Hough research, feature in these case studies.

Each company's franchise proposition will be considered in turn.

Budget Rent a Car International, Inc.

The Budget Rent a Car System is represented in more than 85 countries throughout the world and is recognised as one of the world's largest vehicle rental companies, with over 120,000 vehicles being rented from 2,300 locations, more than 500 of them being situated within airport terminal buildings.

It is a subsidiary of the Transamerica Corporation of America, which amongst others encompasses Transamerica Airlines, Occidental Life, TransInternational Life Assurance, Transamerica ICL, and Delavel Inc. The U.K. and European head office is located in Hatfield, Hertfordshire.

In the field of vehicle rental the Budget licensee has the following advantages:

(i) Budget will assist him in finding an appropriate site if he does not already possess one.

(ii) Budget will assist with finance. Indeed, it has made special arrangements with a finance house which has resulted in a tailormade Rent a Car financing system.

(iii) He is financially involved in the business and so has a direct interest in optimising the various factors of the business to produce a maximum profit.

(iv) With Budget's advice and guidance he is in a position to own and service vehicles at the minimum cost per month.

(v) His business has the opportunity to grow in size and profit when small businesses are going to the wall and large businesses find it very difficult to obtain profit-orientated management.

Vehicle rental is a very specialised business which can either be highly profitable or disastrous depending upon the degree of attention and expertise applied to the business.

Budget Rent a Car International, Inc. is in the position of being able to provide the vital expertise and know-how of the vehicle rental industry at a nominal cost compared to the cost to a licensee of acquiring and providing the same expertise himself.

Budget Rent a Car provides the following further benefits for its licencees:

1. ADVERTISING AND PROMOTION

Budget Rent a Car prides itself on its dynamic marketing and promotional approach which is directed at both the national business user and the local renter.

New licensees receive considerable financial support for advertising and promotion activities in their local market during their first twelve months of operation.

2. CORP RATE

This is the name given to the programme which is aimed at the national business user. A team of national sales executives supported by research personnel are constantly selling to major accounts on behalf of the system. A complete range of billing systems has been devised which allows the Budget system to compete directly with other national car rental companies in the U.K. Over 4,000 national companies are registered as regular users of Budget's services; amongst these are many of the largest corporations in the U.K.

3. RESERVATIONS

The Computerised Reservations Department based at the Hatfield head office acts as a central point through which private and Corp Rate reservations are passed out to licensees. International reservations for the U.K. are received via a data and telex link with the worldwide Budget Reservations computer centre in Dallas, U.S.A.

4. IMAGE

One of the most important factors of the success of the system has been the correct application of the brand name Budget Rent a Car. Location signing and vehicle livery is available for all licensees, as are smart uniforms for both male and female staff, which in addition to all the other advertising and promotional material make the name and image of Budget instantly recognisable not only in the U.K. but throughout the world.

A new licensee receives specially designed counter units on free loan, an initial supply of uniforms for his staff and financial assistance towards the cost of the facia sign for the premises.

5. OPERATING SYSTEMS

A complete business system for vehicle rental is made available as part of the overall Budget package. It comprises everything from rental agreements, fleet controls, and daily operating control forms, through weekly and monthly management controls to profit and loss statements.

Regular digests of operation and financial statistics are circulated to licensees to enable them to check their progress.

6. TRAINING

Complete training courses covering all aspects of vehicle rental, including customer qualification (those you should rent to and those you should not), are available free of charge to all rental staff, and the courses are RTITB approved.

These one-week courses are held at head office where a full and modern training facility is located. Refresher training and other motivational courses are held in groups locally as well as personal training on location when required.

7. FIELD MANAGEMENT

A strong field management advisory force, consisting of regional managers, regularly visits and communicates with the licensee and his staff. The team's objective is to assist and advise the licensee on utilising both assets and personnel so that he can obtain maximum profit from his Budget franchise.

8. INSURANCE

The Budget Rent a Car System enjoys an insurance programme unequalled within the vehicle rental industry. Placed with Royal Assurance, it is a comprehensive policy with contingency and conversion cover and is arranged such that premiums are paid monthly in arrears on a percentage of revenue basis. It is therefore easy to cope with as a cost factor.

9. RATES

Full research into the setting of rates, including continuous monitoring of costs and competitive activity, is carried out at head office, and recommendations are regularly made to licensees.

10. VEHICLE AVAILABILITY

Licensees enjoy full fleet priority facilities with several major manufacturers including Ford, Vauxhall and B.L. Fleet finance schemes are also available.

11. MARKET RESEARCH

Surveys of the vehicle rental market are carried out both on a regular and an *ad hoc* basis to obtain full information with regard to the changes taking place in the market, so that licensees can be kept informed of any necessary changes in marketing strategy.

Undoubtedly the potential for achieving a good profit exists. The Budget Rent a Car System has stood the test of time with existing licensees who have operated Budget Rent a Car profitably for several years.

A new licensee is immediately "plugged in" to the system and can enjoy the business which the name Budget Rent a Car generates together with the goodwill inherent in the Budget name throughout the world.

The Budget franchise offers the qualified person or business the opportunity to invest in the growing vehicle rental industry whilst retaining the benefits of running his own business.

This combination of the local Budget licensee supported by the expertise of Budget Rent a Car International, Inc., allows the Budget Rent a Car System to offer its customers:
* Newer cars (generally under six months old)
* Comprehensive insurance
* Proper customer service, including free local area collection and delivery and
* Rates which can save him between 10% and 35% when compared to other international car hire networks

whilst allowing the Budget licensee to enjoy profits which can give him after interest returns of 20% or more on his investment.

Upon examination of this presentation it is seen that the Budget Rent a Car franchisee acquires a brand name which is known not merely nationally but also internationally; a name which is supported by national and international advertising. He is given the benefit of experience which would be very costly to acquire. For example, one vital factor in car hire must be to assess the reliability and acceptability of the prospective customer. A Budget Rent a Car franchisee is given the benefit of the company's international experience in this area right from the outset. This is something which it would be impossible for him to acquire even at great expense and experience, for even if he were to open on his own he would never acquire such a wide experience as the franchisor has acquired.

Budget Rent a Car is able to ensure that the franchisee obtains the right vehicles at the right time and at the right price; is able to advise on the optimum vehicle utilisation and on the disposal of vehicles. Guidance is also given in regard to servicing.

The opportunity exists for the franchisees to co-operate with each other in inter-office bookings and, indeed, inter-continental bookings without using third parties to whom large commissions would otherwise have to be paid.

The vital pre-opening training and continuing supervision is provided. Additional benefits are obtained by the franchisees by virtue of the bulk negotiating power which is vested in a franchisor of Budget Rent a Car's size and scope. From the presentation it is seen that these side benefits include the insurance arrangements which are a very important factor in car hire.

Furthermore, there is the advantage for this franchisee in the securing of national, and indeed international, business accounts. Budget Rent a Car is able to make arrangements with large companies of national or international repute that their car hire requirements will be obtained from the franchisees in the chain. Indeed, it has over 4,000 national companies registered as users of Budget's licensees. This is the sort of contract which no individual franchisee would be in a position to obtain let alone service. The customer obtains a better service that would be obtained from individual branches of a non-franchised chain as each individual franchisee is so keenly interested in retaining the benefit of the account for the contribution that it would make to his profitability. In addition, the franchisee becomes part of the Budget World Wide Reservation System which automatically opens up for him a market to which he would not otherwise have access.

A comparison of the information provided by Budget Rent a Car in the previous two editions of this work with that set out above is quite interesting.

	2nd edition 1979	3rd edition 1982	4th edition 1984
Countries in which represented	30	72	85
Fleet of vehicles	60,000	120,000	over 120,000
Number of locations	1,250	1,750	2,300
Locations in airport terminal buildings	230	450	over 500

This growth rate has been achieved and indeed the progress maintained over a five-year period at a time of world slump. Ignoring the adverse conditions, this growth would make impressive reading. One is inclined to question whether without the franchise method it would be possible to generate such a growth rate on an international scale. First there is the immense capital requirement, the adjustment to and learning of individual national requirements and the recruitment of suitably qualified and motivated staff at each location. This is indeed an impressive endorsement of the success which the use of the franchise method can bring.

Dyno-Rod—A Potted History and Profile

"Drain clearing in the U.K. was traditionally the domain of the plumber. Techniques and methods had not changed since the days of Dickens. But working conditions had, and drain clearing was the "unattractive" end of the plumbing business; it received little priority and the customer just had to wait.

Dyno-Rod changed all that. With the introduction of electromechanical machinery, the likes of which had never before been seen in the U.K., capable of snaking its way through the most tortuous of pipework, Dyno-Rod set out in 1963 to provide the public with a 24-hour emergency service, 365 days of the year. Dyno-Rod vans were white with bold, colourful insignia, very different from the local plumber. Each vehicle was equipped with machinery capable of dealing with blockages in pipes 1 to 12 inches in diameter and in runs of up to 200 feet long. Dyno-Rod made itself known through the major newspapers; in London's Underground trains and on television—methods unprecedented in the world of the plumber. The response was tremendous and Dyno-Rod's London Service Centre was inundated with calls. For the next two years Dyno-Rod operated the business direct and established a sound base from which to expand.

Marketing philosophy dictated that the company should expand rapidly—nationally. Circumstances indicated that this objective could be best achieved by franchising.

London was the first "target" for the franchising programme and, because of the advertising which had been taking place, the response to the announcement for "franchisees" soon secured distribution for the Greater London area. Then the national franchise expansion programme began, thus achieving the main objectives:

Overcoming the problem of extensive funding.
Opening the way for rapid but controlled expansion.
Securing dedicated management up and down the country to meet the needs of the public 24 hours a day, 365 days of the year, good weather or bad.

What had these "franchisees" bought?

First, they had bought the right to use the name and operate "the Service" in a protected territory. They bought into the Dyno-Rod business after much of the risk had been taken out. The system was tried, tested, and proven. They bought into a continuing relationship with the licensor. The relationship was, and is, simple and straightforward.

The franchisor (Dyno-Rod plc as it now is) grants the licence, provides the know-how and training, and promotes the business continually throughout the duration of the licence.

The franchisee (the party taking the licence) provides the manpower and equipment and operates "the Service" in accordance with the contract. In return for the continuing promotion and management support, the franchisee pays a continuing royalty.

This, in simplistic terms, is the basic relationship. Behind it is a well-honed, smooth-running business machine through which Dyno-Rod supports its licensees and develops the business by means of:

1. Extensive advertising on television and radio networks throughout the country.
2. National, regional, and local press advertising.
3. Industrial press advertising.
4. Local promotions, e.g. mailing campaigns, door-to-door distributions, etc.
5. Exhibitions on a national and local scale.
6. Sales promotion materials, e.g. brochures, etc.
7. Field sales support personnel.
8. Public relations activities.
9. External seminars, e.g. for municipal officers, public works engineers, etc.
10. Salesmen's training schemes.
11. Technical advice, information, publications, etc.
12. Financial advice, profitability studies, forecasts, advice on budgeting, etc.
13. In-house communications through house magazines, newsletters, bulletins, etc.
14. Meetings and conferences: visits by head office personnel, committees, and policy groups, spanning administration, pricing and technical matters, regional conferences, annual national conference, and social events.

Dyno-rod provides one of the most comprehensive support programmes in franchising

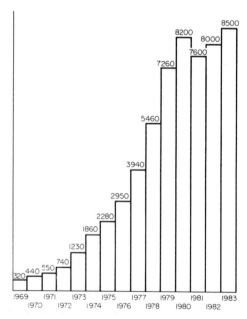

Fig. 13.1. *Dyno-Rod gross organisational turnover (£000s).*

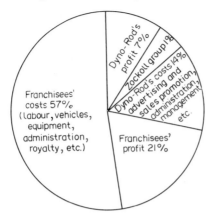

FIG. 13.2. *The revenue "cake".*

and Dyno-Rod personnel are frequently called to lecture on this topic to other businesses, large and small.

Together, Dyno-Rod and its licensees have developed a business which has grown from a gross organisational turnover in 1970 of £443,000 to £8,500,000 in 1983 as shown in Figure 13.1. As can be seen, consistent growth has been maintained with the exception of 1981 where a mixture of the recession and the involvement of Dyno-Rod's parent company (The Zockoll Group plc) in two unsuccessful new ventures caused a hiccup from which Dyno-Rod has now recovered.

In any partnership, both parties must benefit and the benefits must be equitable. The relationship between Dyno-Rod and its licensees has proven to be equitable (Fig. 13.2).

As stated above, Dyno-Rod plc is a subsidiary of The Zockoll Group plc and it is the latter which is the proprietor of the "Dyno Rod" trade marks. The Zockoll Group also set up "Pit Stop", the while-you-wait silencer chain, which proved to be a very successful franchise operation which Zockoll sold off in 1975. In 1979, however, Zockoll set up two further ventures in the field of automobiles but these were unsuccessful. One of these ventures was a franchised chain of car tuning units called Autrac. The one heartening aspect of that episode is that many of the established franchisees are still operating successfully under the Autrac name. The Zockoll Group has now set up a new plumbing franchise trading under the name of "Drips Plumbing". In addition, Zockoll is poised to launch a new franchise in the field of electrical installations and repairs under the trading name of "Dyno-Electrics".

It will be seen that the franchisee earns a profit of approximately 21% of turnover, whilst return on capital employed is in the order of 100%.

(It was estimated that at the end of 1977 the capital employed at service centre level, i.e. the capital employed collectively by all forty-five Dyno-Rod licensees, was in excess of £1,000,000.)

Dyno-Rod management is continually evaluating company performance, anticipating market changes, customer attitudes, technical development and formulating strategies for the future.

Alongside the franchise organisation, Dyno-Rod plc also operates a number of company-owned territories for the purpose of keeping in close touch with the detailed operational aspects of the business and for testing new ideas, equipment, management techniques, etc. (Table 13.3).

Dyno-Rod has now introduced a new job franchise scheme in some of their company-owned territories. This they have christened OMV (One-Man-Van) and the OMV franchisee received a communications link-up with the company's telephone centres, plus central credit control, in addition to the benefits accorded to the territorial franchisees. The royalties are of course higher. The OMV system is designed to put the franchisor and the supplier of the final service in direct contact and ensure that the service is supplied by the person whose return on investment is directly linked to his own personal performance.

The system has limits in terms of market exploitation and the company is building an overlay-branch concept to cater for large jobs, give local technical back-up, and sales input.

The OMV system enables a practical person to get into business on his own for a small outlay and provides extensive operational assistance on an ongoing basis. For the company, standards of service are more easily maintainable and the drive and motivation of the mob franchisee is fully utilised.

Table 13.1. *Typical pro-forma cash flow for a Dyno-Rod franchisee in the £100,000 p.a. turnover range*

	%
Fees	24.00
Payroll	27.70
Rent and rates	1.20
Vehicle running costs	11.33
Equipment	1.86
General administration	0.97
Utilities	2.00
Legal and professional	0.57
Other costs	2.00
Depreciation	2.23
Finance	5.06
Profit	21.00

Dyno-Rod plc is not a capital-intensive business. It relies on having developed a system and a very strong brand name with extraordinary high brand awareness.

A survey carried out in 1978 by Dr. (now Professor) John Stanworth of the Polytechnic of Central London School of Management Studies showed that the public awareness of Dyno-Rod was 79%. Awareness of this high order is normally only achieved in the area of consumer products.

SUMMARY

Some Key Facts

—Eighteen years of consistent growth.
—Pioneer and market leader in the field of drain and pipe cleaning.
—Three out of four people have heard of Dyno-Rod.
—More than just a drain clearing company—pipework of all description located, surveyed and cleared.

—More than just a domestic drain clearing service—industrial and commercial sectors account for 56% of all calls, 75% of the turnover.
—Thirty-six U.K. territorial franchised outlets; forty OMV franchisees; two U.K. company-owned branches; nine overseas franchised outlets; 180 telephone points; 280 mobile units.
—Provides an essential service.
—Experienced management team.
—Founder member of the British Franchise Association.

AREAS OF GROWTH

1. Increased penetration of the drain and pipe cleaning market.
2. Further growth of the preventative maintenance contract.
3. Technical innovation.
4. Extension of service, e.g. TV inspection.
5. Expansion into new market areas, e.g. plumbing, electrics.
6. Licensing of overseas markets, e.g. Singapore, Hong Kong, Bahrain, Kuwait, Gibraltar, Malaysia, Eire.

This presentation is another good example of the way in which franchising has enabled a company comprising a relatively small team of specialists to expand rapidly. Dyno-Rod very thoroughly tested its scheme before proceeding widely to launch it.

It will be seen that Dyno-Rod receives its income by means of the percentage on gross income calculation. The fee is quite considerable, but so are the services provided for the franchisee in return.

The external seminars which are provided is the sort of service one individual would not find available but which can be provided by a franchisor for the benefit of all franchisees.

In view of the fact that the service provided is one which is not frequently required by individuals, the name must be actively promoted. When someone's drains become blocked they should think of Dyno-Rod and contact them. To this end the company spends as much as one-half of its income from franchisees on advertising and promotion and on a corporate scale which makes far more impact than could be made by an individual. Indeed, as is pointed out, Professor Stanworth's field study as long ago as 1978 has demonstrated just how effective this promotional effort has been. In 1982, in order to update and freshen its image, Dyno-Rod relaunched its services with a new corporate style of red vans and red overalls; a corporate theme of "Dyno-Rod 1st—in more ways than one" and a national TV campaign. The theme of the TV campaign was "The Lone Drainer and Pronto". This theme has been extensively employed. It is also interesting to note that the company, as a matter of policy, owns and operates its own territories so as to ensure an ongoing practical experience and providing scope for experimentation and innovation.

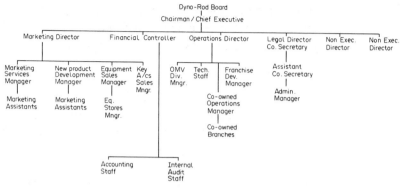

FIG. 13.3. *Organisational structure, Zockroll Group Supervisory.*

Figure 13.3 effectively shows the head office organisation which has developed to service the needs of the company and its franchisees. Each of the seven branches are directly concerned with service to the franchisee either directly or indirectly and it can be seen how wide is the range of skills to which the franchisee has access for advice. It is also apparent that Dyno-Rod is geared to think about the ways of developing its business in a manner which could not be available to the franchisee if he were on his own.

The "hiccup" which affected the group emphasises the point made elsewhere in this work, that it is rare for franchise companies to succeed with more than one franchise. No doubt in deciding to launch "Drips Plumbing" and "Dyno-Electrics", the group has concluded that from its past experience it now knows how to cope with these problems.

In studying the tables in Appendix C the following interesting factors can be noted:

Part One

Table 2. In a franchise which may be considered a "manual job", only three out of the thirty-one franchisees were previously manual workers.

Table 3. Twenty-seven out of the thirty-one franchisees recognised the value of the franchisors' "umbrella", the lowering of risks inherent in establishing a new business or that this was a sound business venture.

Table 6. Twenty-seven out of thirty-one franchisees felt they were given full financial information before signing their contracts.

Table 14. Only one franchisee thought that the public understood the relationship with the franchisor, although (Table 15) six thought that the public saw them as independent contractors.

Table 16. It is somewhat puzzling to find that five franchisees thought they were not provided with training, while nineteen thought that the training was reasonable to excellent.

Table 17. On the other hand, twenty-nine out of thirty-one thought the quality of the equipment supplied was reasonable to excellent.

Table 19. Twenty-three out of thirty-one considered the operating manual reasonable to excellent.

Table 20. Rather surprisingly for a company about whose services there is an exceptionally high level of public awareness, ten out of the thirty-one franchisees thought the national advertising either non-existent or poor.

Tables 22 –24. In the areas of technical support and availability and quality of continuing advisory services, two-thirds of the franchisees thought Dyno-Rod's efforts reasonable to excellent.

Tables 27 and 28. The franchisees are quite positive in recognising the value of the brand name to their business.

Table 29. An impressive twenty-five out of thirty-one (80.7%) felt that their businesses were more successful because they were franchised (see also question 21 in Part 2 of the Appendix).

Table 32. Two-thirds of the franchisees were satisfied with their franchise.

Table 33. Almost unanimously, the franchisees consider the contract weighed in favour of the franchisor.

Table 37. Twenty-two out of the twenty-nine franchisees who replied state that their present intention is to renew the contract, while only four do not intend to do so.

Table 38. Only four were dissatisfied with the profitability of their business, although one cannot judge the position without more facts.

Part Two

Question 8. Fifteen out of the sixteen Dyno-Rod franchisees who were interviewed "would advise anyone else to do what they have done". This is impressive support for the franchise system, although (question 12) the number drops to thirteen when the question is "Would the franchisees still go into franchising if they were starting today?"

Questions 14 Show a generally high level of satisfaction by franchisees
and 15. with the relationship between the franchisor and franchisee.

Holiday Inn (U.K.), Inc.

THE HOLIDAY INN STORY

In 1951 a Memphis home builder, Kemmons Wilson, took his wife, five children, and his mother on a vacation. The inconvenience and high price of family accommodations they experienced made him realise that the lodging business was, he said, "the greatest untouched industry in the world".

In 1952 Wilson built the first Holiday Inn in Memphis, Tennessee. It was so successful that, within the next year, he built three more inns in the city. And the Holiday Inn story began.

Wilson discussed his Holiday Inn idea with another Memphis home builder, Wallace E. Johnson. Together they visualised a nationwide network of Holiday Inns offering the travelling public suitable accommodations at reasonable rates.

In 1953 they formed a partnership that became Holiday Inns Inc. and was later listed on the New York Stock Exchange. In addition to continuing their building programme, they encouraged other independent business and professional men to develop Holiday Inns through a programme of franchise licensing. Over 75% of the Holiday Inn System, of more than 1717 properties in fifty-four countries, has been developed through franchising.

What is a Holiday Inn?

It is a modern hotel facility that offers standardised, quality accommodations and services throughout the world. It embodies a unique concept of hotel marketing and management, especially in that all Holiday Inns are part of an organisation—The International Association of Holiday Inns—known as "The System".

What is the System and how does it work?

The System is the co-operative organisation through which more than 1000 independent businessmen pool their time, talents, and funds in a common endeavour to enable each Holiday Inn to receive marketing power, creative thrust, and management guidance that no individual hotel or group of hotels could achieve on its own. Throughout the year, committees made up of franchisees and representatives of Holiday Inns Inc. meet frequently to resolve pressing issues and participate in the formulation of overall strategies. The efforts of these committees along with the fees contributed by each Holiday Inn in the System have brought about such benefits as the largest marketing and advertising fund in the industry (over £17 million in 1978), the first computerised, instant hotel reservation system—Holidex, and the £2.5 million Hotel Inn University.

What is a Holiday Inn franchise licence?

It is the binding agreement between Holiday Inns Inc. and the franchisee which, while maintaining proprietorship of his own business, bestows upon the franchisee all the benefits of being part of the Holiday Inn System. The licence is granted for a specific site and not for general areas, cities, or countries.

A Holiday Inn franchise represents:

—A brand name with instant recognition, customer acceptance, and goodwill.
—The proven planning, construction, and operating guidelines that have led to the development and operation of more than 1,717 Holiday Inns in fifty-four countries and territories.
—System sales representation throughout the world.
—Referrals to and from more than 1,717 Holiday Inns and sales offices through Holidex—the instant worldwide reservation network.
—System advertising exposure on a worldwide basis.
—Exposure to, and a voice in, the affairs of the System through the International Association of Holiday Inns.
—Management counselling and extensive training programmes through the Holiday Inn University.

What is the size of the investment?

The cost of the project depends on the size of the proposed Holiday Inn, the amount of land and its value, the type of building design, the cost of financing, and local conditions. It could be anticipated that a small (100 room) two- or four-storey Holiday Inn away from metropolitan areas will cost about £8,000 per room or £800,000 for the entire project. A large (600 room), complex, high-rise structure, in an expensive centre city location with large commercial facilities (restaurants, bars, meeting and exposition rooms), could cost about £14,000 per room, or £8,400,000 for the entire project. In general, your equity investment should be about 25% to 40% of total project cost depending on local conditions. Land costs normally represent 10% to 20% of the total project cost. The site may be owned or leased. Lending institutions normally require leased land to be subordinated to the first mortgage.

Can an existing hotel become a Holiday Inn?

Existing hotels, which meet Holiday Inn standards, are eligible for consideration.

How much land is necessary?

Some of the multi-storey, centre city locations are built on as little as 20,000 square feet. Holiday Inns in outlying areas may require 3–5 acres, and resort properties often require even larger areas.

What assistance can be expected in the development phase?

Site selection: Holiday Inn development specialists will help evaluate sites in the area of interest.

Architecture and construction: a representative of the Holiday Inn Projects Development staff will work with the franchisee and his architect to ensure the most feasible and economic approach to design and structure while preserving local architecture and traditions. The choice of architect and building contractor is the franchisee's subject to approval by Holiday Inns Inc.

Furnishings and equipment: all furnishings, fixtures, equipment, and supplies must meet Holiday Inn standards. Items that meet these standards are available from several sources. Holiday Inn's own supply companies can furnish individual items or a furnishings and equipment package.

Project co-ordination: a project co-ordinator will be assigned to the project during the development phase. His attention will ensure that the project meets Holiday Inn requirements.

Development phase inspections: the project will be inspected at least twice during construction, the last inspection serving to verify adherence to standards and to authorise the property to open as a Holiday Inn.

Pre-opening training: Holiday Inn University will train the innkeeper and other key personnel. There is no tuition fee for these courses at the university, but the franchisee will be responsible for transportation, room, board, and other personal expenses. In addition, the university is available on a fee basis to train the entire Holiday Inn staff prior to opening upon request.

What support can be expected when the Holiday Inn is open and operating?

Advertising: the benefits of a worldwide advertising programme, utilising local, national and international media, aimed at selling the travelling public the name and image of Holiday Inns. This is in addition to the franchisee's local advertising effort and gives brand name coverage to all Holiday Inns.

Marketing: marketing specialists carry on continuous research, and design numerous programmes and promotions utilized on a systemwide basis. They are available to consult with franchisees concerning specific marketing needs.

Holidex reservation system: Holidex, capable of using undersea cables and communication in satellites, enables Holiday Inn customers to make free, instantaneous reservations. The Holidex network is also interfaced with some airline reservation computers, enabling travellers to obtain airline and hotel reservations simultaneously. Holidex terminals are being installed in many large corporate offices for direct reservation service.

Sales and reservation offices: a worldwide network of sales and reservation offices gives all Holiday Inns in the System direct sales representation in many of the world's major cities, thus adding to each Holiday Inn's individual sales effort. Major sources of business, especially travel agents, tour wholesalers, and operators, are aggressively solicited by sales representatives from each office.

Public relations: the Public Relations Department works constantly to place stories and articles about Holiday Inns in the media, and to provide the System and individual Holiday Inns with meaningful promotional programmes.

Training aids: in addition to the innkeeper training during the development phase, the Holiday Inn University supplies the franchisee with constantly updated training films in several languages. The university can also retrain personnel on a fee basis at the franchisee's Holiday Inn. Annual conferences are held each year for the innkeeper and food and beverage director at the university and in some overseas locations.

IAHI world conferences and committees: ten committees (marketing/advertising, reservations, rules of operation, construction, education and research, finance, conference, world affairs, legal-legislative, and food and beverage) meet periodically throughout the year to consider and act upon problems and opportunities facing the System. The members of each committee serve voluntarily and are chosen from the IAHI membership by the individual committee chairmen on the basis of the individual expertise and the desire of the franchise owners. The world conference is held by the International Association each year for the exchange of ideas and the presentation and implementation of new System programmes.

What fees are currently required of a franchisee?

—A minimum initial franchise fee of $30,000 plus $300 for each room over 100 rooms.

—Franchise royalty of 3% of gross rooms revenue.

—Holidex reservation terminal lease fee depending upon local costs.

—System advertising fee of 1% of gross rooms revenue.

—System Reservations and Sales Office fee of 1% of gross rooms revenue.
—Holiday Inn University fee of 1 cent per room per night.

For the majority of Holiday Inns, the above fees normally amount to less than 6% of gross rooms revenue. No fees are charged on revenues derived from food, beverage or other sources.

What is the process in obtaining a Holiday Inn franchise?

If a prospective franchisee has sufficient funds and a site which he thinks is feasible and wants to pursue a Holiday Inn franchise commitment, he should contact the nearest Holiday Inn franchise office. The franchise representative will want to discuss the following items with him:

—The location of his property.
—The surrounding area—its industries, airport, highway systems, population, labour force, educational facilities, and general economic strength.
—The number of hotels and rooms already operating in the area and their quality.
—The type of group wishing to make application: individual, partnership, limited partnership, corporation.
—Laws regarding franchise licences which might apply to his area.

After discussing this information in detail, the franchise representative will request materials to assist further in evaluating the proposed site. These materials might include city or highway maps, a plot plan of the specific site, the name of the owner or lessee of the property, certified financial statements and personal and business references from each member of the group, and any other materials which could be pertinent.

If after analysing this information it appears that the prospective franchisee has a potential Holiday Inn location, the franchise representative will encourage him to prepare a formal application. The formal application consists of the submission of all necessary forms and the payment of the application fee. Once these have been received an on-site study of the project will be made by a representative of the franchise department. At that time he will make recommendations regarding the feasibility study which must be completed prior to the presentation of the application to the Franchise Committee. Independent feasibility studies are required for all new applications. It is not recommended that a study be commissioned until a representative of Holiday Inns Inc. has had an opportunity to review the location personally.

If the application is approved by Holiday Inns Inc. the prospective franchisee will receive a commitment agreement to issue a licence agreement. This document is an interim agreement and provides for the timely development of the project. Once all terms of the commitment agreement to issue a licence agreement have been met, construction of the project is complete, and the property receives authorisation to open as a Holiday Inn, a Holiday Inn licence agreement is issued. Both the commitment agreement to issue a licence agreement and the licence agreement itself carry the date of the original approval of the application.

Is the franchisee obliged personally to operate his Holiday Inn?

No. Many franchisees choose to hire management firms for the operation of their Holiday Inns or to lease it to operators. Holiday Inns Inc. must approve all management agreements and leases. Holiday Inns Inc. offers management services through management contracts. Holiday Inn's experienced professionals can provide technical assistance through the development phase of the property and manage it for a franchisee after opening.

The Holiday Inn franchise presentation reveals a franchise which is based on orthodox business format franchise lines. All the elements are present comprising a wide range of services prior to the opening of the business and an extensive continuing relationship thereafter.

Holiday Inns operate in a capital intensive business, and one is left to doubt or to speculate upon the prospects of an individual achieving the exposure of 1,717 outlets in fifty-four different countries within a period of thirty years were it not for the franchise system.

Within that period over 1,000 individuals have become involved in establishing hotel businesses throughout the world to a common format and with many common benefits. It is interesting to note that there has been established a co-operative system between franchisees so that their information is pooled and individual experiences can become part of the common fund of information available from each.

The franchisee on taking up a Holiday Inn franchise is immediately put on the map as part of the Holidex instant hotel reservation system which is operated on a worldwide basis and the Holiday Inn literature which is disseminated widely throughout the world makes known its existence and its location. This is something which an individual would otherwise be incapable of achieving. The presentation which is extremely detailed is an effective and impressive demonstration of the application in practice of the principles as explained in this work relating to the establishment and operation of a business format franchise.

Kentucky Fried Chicken

HOW IT ALL BEGAN

Kentucky Fried Chicken is the original creation of the world renowned Colonel Sanders. He started out selling meals to travellers from his petrol station in Kentucky, U.S.A., and became so well known that the demand for his cooking swiftly persuaded him to set up a resterurent.

This operation was so successful that he developed his now famous and unique Kentucky Fried Chicken using a secret recipe of eleven herbs and spices. Today the recipe remains unchanged and Colonel Sanders was active in the promotion of Kentucky Fried Chicken, travelling thousands of miles each year, until his death in 1980.

The worldwide success of the Kentucky Fried Chicken business is now well established, with over 6000 stores in over forty countries. 4500 of these are in the United States of America, the rest being widely spread over the world, with the U.K. being one of the most important market outside the United States.

KENTUCKY FRIED CHICKEN IN THE U.K.

Kentucky Fried Chicken (G.B.) Limited was formed in 1965. The U.K. network has grown rapidly to over 360 stores, of which sixty-one are company-owned and operated. A Kentucky Fried Chicken franchisee is part of a highly successful fast food retailing operation selling a unique high quality product.

KENTUCKY FRIED CHICKEN—A UNIQUE RECIPE

"Finger Lickin' Good": a well-known phrase that sums up the special nature of Kentucky Fried Chicken. The chicken is cooked by a special method using Colonel Sanders' unique recipe of eleven herbs and spices making it succulent and full of flavour. Kentucky Fried Chicken is offered in stores with a comprehensive range of additional products, including chips and jacket potatoes, fresh coleslaw, barbecue beans, soup, and of course, chicken sauce. There is also a choice of desserts and soft drinks.

New products are being added to the menu. Barbeque spare ribs, for example, were introduced in 1976. With their distinct tangy flavour, they are making a significant contribution to sales. Recently, a new high-quality product, the chicken sandwich, has been introduced. It comprises of $3\frac{1}{4}$ to 4 oz. pure chicken breast in warmed sesame seed bun, with crispy iceberg lettuce and salad dressing. Delicious and selling extremely well. Super for a quick filling snack, ideal for children. Regular additions are made to the range of side dishes, sometimes for specific promotional activities, other items for permanent inclusion in the menu.

Presentation is an area in which great pride is taken. The packaging is well designed, visually attractive, and extremely practical in use. All of this not only adds up to the best takeaway product in the country but means that one can provide bulk catering for outside functions. This service is rapidly growing as customers find it easy to use, highly acceptable, and very economical. Unique product, unique packaging, unique service all promote corporate awareness and help make our product even more popular. But to sell a good product it is necessary to have good stores.

KENTUCKY FRIED CHICKEN—STORE DESIGN

Stores are designed to be bright, warm, and cheerful. Store design and decoration are the subjects of an on-going development programme, incorporating improvements and additions within the framework of the Kentucky Fried Chicken image.

Forty per cent of all Kentucky Fried Chicken restaurants offer seating and dine-in facilities in addition to the regular takeaway service. More restaurants are planned for the future.

"Drive In" and "Drive Through" stores are the latest concept. The company's first "Drive Through" store opened in the Old Kent Road in South London in October 1983. It has its own parking facilities, internal seating area and drive through window—U.S.A. style.

Kentucky Fried Chicken is proud to be setting the highest standards in the fast food industry with its stores and service.

ADVERTISING AND MARKETING

Kentucky Fried Chicken is probably the largest national advertiser in the fast food market. Every franchisee gets all the benefits; he gains from a powerful programme of national TV and radio campaigns, backed up by colourful attention—getting point of sale materials.

There is an Advertising Board with elected franchisee representatives responsible for the advertising strategy and expenditure.

The Marketing Department provides expert support for the franchisee in the field of advertising, promotional activity (at national and local levels), public relations, and operates a continuous programme of market/customer research and new product testing. It also offers help and advice on sales, image-building, customer relations, merchandising, local "events", and over-the-counter selling.

The Marketing Department and Advertising Board is backed up by a front rank national Advertising Agency. Public Relation activity ensures a steady stream of accurate news and feature articles in the top papers, radio, and TV of this country, for example, *The Times, Financial Times, Sunday Times, Guardian, Daily Telegraph, Daily Mail, The Sun*, B.B.C., L.B.C. and the lead item in the very first edition of I.T.V.'s Business Programme have all had very good things to say about the benefits of the Kentucky Fried Chicken franchise.

PUBLIC RELATIONS AND COMMUNICATIONS

Kentucky Fried Chicken (G.B.) Limited have a very active communications strategy retaining a national P.R. agency, political advisers, two firms of specialist solicitors, town planning consultants, and surveyors. All of these organisations are available to offer expert advice over the whole range of business problems that may be encountered by a Kentucky Fried Chicken franchisee.

Kentucky Fried Chicken (G.B.) Limited were founder members of two trade bodies to help raise standards and the public's perception—the British Franchise Association and the Take Away Food Federation. Kentucky Fried Chicken (G.B.) Limited involves itself in litter projects with the Keep Britain Tidy Group and has successfully petitioned Parliament on behalf of its franchisees.

There are standing committees composed of franchisees and company executives on purchasing and wages which exist to inform all Kentucky Fried Chicken operators and improve their business. These committees and the Advertising Board meet regularly. In addition, a National Franchise Conference is held twice a year with a convention (held abroad) once a year to which all franchisees are invited. These meetings help the interchange of ideas and improve the business of each member of the Kentucky Fried Chicken family.

TRAINING AND CONSULTANCY SERVICES

The company holds a series of intensive courses training all personnel in the technical, administrative, and management expertise necessary for the business to run smoothly and profitably. There is a general management course to teach franchisees and their staff the details of the business, and there is a sales course to train and motivate sales staff.

The department also conducts field training courses anywhere in the U.K. and offers advice to franchisees on training methods and systems. Up-to-date training films, slides, charts, and handouts are also made available to franchisees by the department. Road shows for shop staff are now a regular feature on the training calendar.

The company also provides advice and assistance in the following areas:

Site finding, location, surveying, and assessment of stores.
Provision of architects' drawings for local council planning permission.
Shopfitting, equipment, and suppliers.
Weekly financial monitoring operation.
Quality, hygiene, and standards control.
Food purchasing and preparation advice.

When a franchisee's store is opened, marketing and advertising will play an essential part in its success.

A STEADY RETURN ON THE FRANCHISEE'S INVESTMENT

Although all Kentucky Fried Chicken stores are set up within certain strict standards, there is no such thing as an absolute average store. However, the approximate costs as at June 1983 for a standard takeaway store are:

The costs:	£
Operational and training fee	4,000
Shopfitting and equipment	90,000
Solicitor's and architect's fees	4,000
Essential merchandising	2,500
	100,500

N.B. These costs do not include property acquisition.

The return:

As a general guide we have taken a store doing £5,000 a week, which is the average for a new store.

At this level of turnover the store profit would be approximately £850 per week and the capital investment would be returned in under two and half years. Because some of the costs are fixed, profitability, hence return on capital, improves dramatically with increased turnovers.

Sales turnover:		100%
Food and packaging	45%	
Wages	19%	
Royalty	4%	
Advertising	3%	
Rent and rates	4%	
Overheads and utilities	8%	83%
Profit before tax		17%

With the rapidly improving store design and ever-increasing national advertising, the turnover of Kentucky Fried Chicken stores is currently rising faster than at any time in the company's history.

The company has engaged in a drastic review of its position in the market place. In March 1982 54% of business was done between 7 p.m. and midnight and 58% of the business was accounted for by the standard portion of two or three pieces of chicken and chips. During the daytime stores were serving no more than seven or eight customers each hour. The taste of the chicken had a high 86% approval in "blind tests", but complaints were made that portions were too small. It was decided to tackle the problems which had become evident. The following steps were taken:

—larger portions were offered;
—family "bargain buckets" offering meals for four at about £1 per head;
—introduction of party packs;
—lunchtime snacks
—new chicken sandwich;
—new shop livery;
—new staff uniforms;
—new menu cards;
—new equipment to reduce serving time to 1 minute per order;
—better packaging to make the food easier to carry and more convenient to eat;

backed by a big advertising campaign to inform the public of the changes. The package of improvements also had to be "sold" to franchisees. The improvements were introduced in the South West and East Anglia TV areas in September 1982 and in 10 months sales in the South West grew by 43% and in East Anglia by 45%. In Northern Ireland, where the programme was more recently introduced, sales grew by 52% in only three months. The daytime sales had risen from 46% to 54% without harming the volume of sales after 7 p.m. Family "Bargain Buckets" now account for 25% of turnover and sandwiches for 10%. The franchisees have invested £8m in new equipment and £2m in extra advertising (the advertising payment under this programme has been increased from 3% to 5%).

How the Franchisee Benefits

There are many strong and distinct advantages to be gained by becoming a Kentucky Fried Chicken franchisee.

1. He is part of a big, international family, gaining all the security and backing that goes with it.
2. He is offering a top class product—a market leader.
3. He gets the benefit of professional marketing and advertising expertise at all times.
4. Kentucky Fried Chicken is advertised at national and local levels, giving maximum coverage.
5. All the national advertising is backed up by excellent point of sales programmes, plus public relations coverage.
6. Kentucky Fried Chicken offer a wide range of consultancy services, including help with site selection and development, shopfitting advice, a monitoring service, and service to advise the franchisee on preparation, cooking, and storage equipment.
7. The franchisee and his staff can be expertly trained in all aspects of the business.
8. Kentucky Fried Chicken will help the franchisee build sales, with the benefit of well tried and proven methods.
9. If the franchisee puts in the work and the enthusiasm, the profits will show.

Again we have the presentation of an orthodox business format franchise. The worldwide rate of growth is quite startling having taken place in less than the time which has been taken to establish the Holiday Inn chain. The growth rate since the last edition of his work is a powerful compliment to the vigorous development of this franchise opportunity. Worldwide stores up from 5,000 to 6,000; U.S.A. stores up from 4,000 to 4,500; U.K. stores up from 300 to 360; and all in the space of two years! On the other hand, the establishment of each of the stores does not involve the same level of capital as the Holiday Inn operation and the availability of suitable franchisees is undoubtedly much greater.

The operation is simple, the menu range limited and effort is made to ensure that the limited tasks involved are performed well.

Kentucky Fried Chicken (K.F.C.) is a classic example of the effectiveness of updating the decor, design and eye-catching appeal of the stores. In the last edition of this work it was noted that the complete modernisation of each of its many company stores during 1978/9 resulted in a 40% increase in product and cash sales over the previous year. One of the areas in a franchise transaction in which franchisors find great difficulty is in persuading franchisees to update and modernise their stores so as to retain the freshness of the appeal to the customers. K.F.C. vividly demonstrated the commercial sense of taking these steps by introducing them into its own stores with remarkable financial success. With this lead the franchisee had every incentive to embark upon the modernisation of his store in order to obtain the financial returns achieved in practice by K.F.C. Indeed, in the year 1979/80 franchisees followed this example and achieved in a harsh economic climate of 35% increase in product and cash sales over the previous year. How much more effective a form of leadership is this rather than having the situation where one has to rely on strict legal rights and the methods of enforcing them that are available. Nothing could be more damaging to what is effectively to be a continuing "partnership" relationship. We now know that yet again K.F.C. has reorganised its operation and achieved even greater advances for itself and its franchisees. This constant striving for improvement carrying the franchisees with it is a powerful public demonstration of the benefits for franchisees when involved with an effective and concerned franchisor.

Great emphasis is placed upon advertising, marketing, public relations and communications and the benefits in these areas for franchisees are self-evident. K.F.C.'s training method is soundly based, and now firmly formalised in a new training centre in New Malden, Surrey, which was opened in May 1982. The centre is well equipped with lecture rooms with audiovisual aids and even a mock up of a K.F.C. store in which to train staff. The centre can accommodate as many as thirty-six students and has a complete range of relevant topics within its curriculum on which courses are run on a continuous basis throughout the year.

It is interesting to note again, as in so many other cases, that franchisees are regularly called together in order to interchange ideas for the mutual benefit of all the members of the franchise chain.

Prontaprint Limited

Prontaprint operates Britain's largest chain of high-speed printing and copying shops offering a range of simple, small-offset litho printing, photocopying, duplicating, and often a plan copying service. Anything too big for the office copier or too small for the commercial printer, where speed is essential, the Prontaprint Service will fill the gap. By keeping within certain limits and including a full design facility, this need for a service offering speed and quality in relatively small quantities is met.

The first shop was opened in Newcastle-upon-Tyne in February 1971 and was followed by four more company-owned and operated shops in a short space of time. The first franchise was sold in the second year of trading, and there are now (January 1984) over 250 Prontaprint shops in the U.K. stretching from Aberdeen to Plymouth. New units are continuing to open at a steady rate and there are thirty in the pipeline.

Companies large and small and individuals from all sectors of the community find the Prontaprint Service useful—some more than once a week, others even on a daily basis. Cash flow is excellent and potential returns are available for prospective investors.

Being a "business service" with a prestigious image and sociable trading hours, the Prontaprint franchise generally appeals to the "business executive type" of person, male or female, who, for a variety of reasons, are seeking a business of their own, one which will give security and satisfaction not always available when employed even in large international companies. Applicants who were previously printers are no longer accepted as licensees; Prontaprint licensees come from a variety of commercial, managerial, and professional backgrounds. Those with a will to succeed and the ability and willingness to absorb the training provided are ideal potential Prontaprinters.

A typical franchise applicant will probably travel the following route when joining the Prontaprint team:

1. An initial inquiry by telephone or letter which will result in Prontaprint sending a standard brochure.
2. The prospective licensee will contact Prontaprint after having read the literature. An interview at a mutually convenient time will be arranged with the Franchise Sales Manager at the London Regional Office where all details of the Prontaprint package will be thoroughly discussed. After this interview, the prospective licensee will receive authority to visit any number of existing Prontaprint outlets to speak to the licensees and glean from them their feelings about Prontaprint, their service and support and also whether or not they have regretted becoming Prontaprint licensees. Thus, by selecting any Prontaprint shop anywhere in the country, a prospective "Prontaprinter" can assess, by the reactions of each licensee he visits, any areas of doubt in the methods or claims that are made by Prontaprint Ltd.
3. If the prospective licensee wishes to continue with his application he will be invited to Prontaprint's Head Office to meet the Franchise Director and the Franchise Accountant in order to "tailor" the Prontaprint concept to the individual licensee especially in terms of finance. The two interviews will take several hours and should clear up all the uncertainties which are in the mind of the applicant as well as giving both parties a chance to assess each other, for, after all, the relationship can last up to ten years or more.
4. Once the applicant is approved and he accepts Prontaprint, Prontaprint swings into action.
5. The town of interest will be investigated by the prospective licensee along with a member of the Prontaprint team who will help assess the potential of the area within the guidelines established by Prontaprint based upon its previous experience and demographic survey commissioned three years ago, and commence a full search for suitable premises.
6. Once a lease has been finalised, architect's plans are drawn up so that quotations can be obtained for shopfitting work, etc., to the standard Prontaprint design and specification.
7. As soon as the licensee is available, he commences a four-week training course which covers all aspects of running a Prontaprint shop from basic product knowledge to artwork, simple offset printing techniques, customer relations, recruiting staff, basic accounts, sales promotion, use of all ancillary equipment,

and many other aspects which are relevant to the running of a successful business.

8. Each new licensee is supplied with a training manual which underlines the substance and features of the course in detail and contains instructions on the systems, etc. This manual and many other procedure manuals are retained for future reference.

9. During the training course he receives an artwork package which provides standard artwork for such things as quotation forms, letterheads, business cards, promotional leaflets, press advertisements, and so on.

10. The licensee spends at least two weeks of the course at an existing shop where he learns to deal with customers, operate equipment, and experiences the different types of work that he is likely to encounter. This prepares him for confident exposure in his own shop once it opens.

11. During training, equipment is ordered, often at preferential discount terms and timed to arrive at the shop on completion of shopfitting.

12. At the end of the course the licensee acquires a corporate package of items which includes till rolls, point of sale material, invoice sets, standard accounting kit, promotional artwork, and many other useful items.

13. Once the shop is fitted out and the machinery is run in, a launch promotion is organised by the Regional Controller of Prontaprint.

14. On a continuing basis, Prontaprint is regularly in touch with all licensees by telephone, visits and correspondence, feeding out new ideas, innovations and techniques, and assisting in the solution of relevant problems.

15. Regular meetings are arranged for local regions as well as the annual National Conferences.

16. The licensee has full use of the trade marks associated with the Prontaprint service.

17. Prontaprint regularly monitor the cost of basic raw materials and implement new price structures when the retail margins become eroded by increases in costs. This is organised at Head Office and information is sent to every shop to ensure that every licensee maintains gross margins.

The above is only a part of the wide range of services and activities which are available to every licensee. Without successful licensees there can be no Prontaprint Ltd., consequently there is a mutual interest to increase sales and the relationship is a continuing one. Prontaprint continuously encourages sales growth, and to support this guarantees to spend the entire Marketing Services Fund (a levy of 5% on turnover) on promoting and developing the Prontaprint Service. This activity manifests itself for example, by way of advertising for every shop, for example on national TV, Yellow Pages, etc., all paid for from the fund. In addition, various items are available from time to time including point of sale material, direct mail shots, give-away items, standard press, radio jingles, and television advertising—these items are either provided free of charge from the Marketing Services Fund or subsidised.

One advantage of a Prontaprint franchise, as opposed to an independent business, is that as Prontaprint grows and becomes more and more established and a familiar part of the High Street scene, Prontaprint's marketing and sales promotion activities generate an increasing national awareness to every licensee's advantage.

Other long-term advantages of the Prontaprint franchise are:

1. Special group rates on paper, ink, and other consumables.
2. Group discounts on equipment and leasing facilities.
3. Exchange of news and views at regular local and national meetings.
4. Technology advancement—a sharp watch is kept worldwide on relevant developments and information circulated.

5. Re-negotiation of property leases—comparable figures and negotiating skills available.
6. Introduction to sources of finance through schemes specially arranged by major Banks.
7. When the need arises, a Prontaprint shop usually sells quicker and for a higher price than a "Joe Bloggs instant Print Shop" (based on past experience).
8. In the event of unforeseen troubles, help is always available, through the regional staff.
9. The strength of the central Marketing Services Fund is behind each licensee (unit) in the event of unforeseen circumstances making an extraordinary promotional effort necessary.
10. Weaknesses in trading are easily identified and corrected when such an extensive cross-section of the same business and branch activities is available to be used as a guide and assist in forecasting.

Prontaprint has innovated not merely a new field in U.K. franchising, but a new concept in business, by having noticed a gap in the market, providing services in the field of printing and copying, and by stepping in to fill it. It is interesting that five pilot schemes were run before any franchises were sold, and it is interesting to note the source from which the company is obtaining its franchisees. As with some of the other case studies, it is revealing to compare the growth figures for Prontaprint which have appeared in the second and third editions of this work.

In the 2nd edition (1979)—50 stores.
In the 3rd edition (1982)—130 stores.
In this edition (1984)—over 250 stores.

In addition, Prontaprint has expanded its operations overseas and has established a presence in Ireland, France, Germany, South Africa and Kuwait. Overall there are thirty-three stores in operation overseas.

Again this franchise follows the lines of the orthodox business format franchise with which the reader should at this stage be thoroughly familiar. A full range of initial services are supplied, including site selection, training which covers all aspects of running the Prontaprint business, and the provision of a training manual. The inclusion in training of at least two weeks' work in an existing shop, providing real practical experience is invaluable as is the opening sales promotion which is organised by the Company.

Once the business is opened, there are the continuing services, regular meetings of franchisees on a regional basis, as well as the annual National Conference every year. The common marketing fund into which payments are made is utilised to promote the franchised chain and achieves for all franchisees a degree of exposure which their own contribution would scarcely achieve for them if they were sole traders without the benefit of the umbrella of the franchise arrangement and the value of the contribution from the other franchisees.

Prontaprint are also proud of the fact that the benefits of the franchise arrangement achieve for its franchisees much more beneficial margins of profitability than could be obtained by a sole trader without their know-how.

Since the last edition of this work the "Hough" statistics have become available and are set out in Appendix C. The following points are worthy of note.

Part One

Table 2. Just over a third (35.7%) of Prontaprint franchisees were previously manual workers.

Table 3. Obviously some of the franchisees gave more than one reply, but 42.2% were attracted by the support of the franchisor, 64.1% the lower risk and 12.5% the known name and ready-made business. Even allowing for the overlap, these responses constitute a considerable vote of confidence in the franchise concept.

Table 7. As many as 45.3% felt that the franchisor's prediction of profits were over-estimated, 31.3% felt the estimate was accurate. This suggests that franchisees do not understand the purpose and nature of the financial projections which should be better explained. Most financial projections are presented as examples of levels of profitability at stated hypothetical levels of turnover. It is rare indeed for a franchisee to be given a firm estimate of likely turnover for a specific location. There is evidence that newer franchisees felt that profit predictions were more accurate than did the longer-term franchisees. This indicates that with a build-up of experience franchisors are able to give more accurate estimates. This is, of course, what one might expect, although memories do fade with passage of time.

Table 16. In terms of the quality of formal training Prontaprint stands head and shoulders above the rest. Their rating of 73.4% in the good to excellent range is almost twice as high as the next.

Table 19. The manual also is rated quite high with 78.9%, classing it as good to excellent and 21.1% as reasonable. This is matched by a high score (Table 22) for the quality of technical support.

Table 33. Almost half (48.4%) of the franchisees consider the contract to be equally in favour of both parties. The other half quite solidly believe the contract to be weighted in favour of the franchisor.

Table 37. Only 62.5% of the franchisees intended to renew their contracts with 32.8% classed as "don't knows". The high percentage of "don't knows" is undoubtedly attributable to recent franchisees who still have a number of years left under their contract which is for a ten-year term. Unless this is the explanation, the figures are puzzling when contrasted with the 86.7% who say they are satisfied with the franchise.

Table 38. Again bearing in mind the high percentage who are satisfied with the franchise, it is surprising to find 21.9% who are dissatisfied with the profitability of the business.

Part Two

There is only one comparable question in this part and (Table 4) it demonstrates that as many as one-third of Prontaprint franchisees had looked elsewhere before choosing that franchise. Only the Dyno-Rod franchise matches that. Prontaprint clearly stands good comparison with other franchise opportunities—the speedy print franchise segment of the market has at least six major companies perhaps the Prontaprint franchisees carefully compared them before making the final choice.

ServiceMaster Limited

ServiceMaster has developed the world's largest network of independent franchised businesses engaged in professional cleaning services for homes and offices. Today there are more than 2,750 ServiceMaster businesses operating worldwide, with over 159 in the U.K. Two business format franchises are offered in the U.K.: (1) on-location carpet and upholstery cleaning and (2) contract services—daily office cleaning.

ServiceMaster on-location licensees offer a wide range of *in situ* cleaning and restoration services, including carpet cleaning, furniture cleaning, curtain cleaning, wall cleaning, floor cleaning, smoke odour removal and other similar services related to providing and maintaining the appearance and useful life of home and office furnishings and surfaces. Contract service licensees provide daily cleaning services to commercial contractors on a contractual basis.

ServiceMaster has been involved in franchising in the U.K. since the early 1960s. The parent company, ServiceMaster Industries Incorporated, a U.S. corporation, entered into a licence arrangement in the U.K. in 1959. Franchising operations worked under that arrangement until 1976, when ServiceMaster Industries Incorporated re-acquired U.K. franchising rights.

ServiceMaster offers a different franchised business opportunity in that the licensee is not required to purchase and maintain shop premises. ServiceMaster businesses can be operated out of the licensee's home, although many will move to a commercial site as the business grows.

For a total initial investment of £8,500 the new licensee receives all the professional equipment, chemicals, supplies, promotional materials, training manuals, and individualised instruction needed to launch his business. ServiceMaster has arrangements with two leading clearing Banks which will finance up to 50% of the initial cost to approved applicants.

The initial licence agreement is for five years, and is automatically renewed thereafter. All licensees pay a monthly fee of £10 per cent of gross sales, which covers the cost of on-going technical development, training seminars and field counselling, advertising and promotion, etc.

ServiceMaster provides each licensee with a proven marketing plan. Licensees are taught to obtain business from the home market directly and through agencies. They serve the office market on a direct basis. In addition, licensees acquire business through their ability to clean and restore all types of buildings following fires, floods, or other similar occurrences. Licensee individual sales efforts are supported by ServiceMaster staff personnel who liaise with carpet mills, retailers, fibre manufacturers, multi-location businesses and insurance firms.

First year licensee turnover in the on-location business has ranged from £6,000 to £24,000 depending on the degree of salesmanship and effort the individual licensee puts into the building of his business. The average net profit of a licensee operating out of his home, after depreciation but before an allowance for his own salary, is 53%. Once a business is established, turnover can increase to £100,000, with a profit margin of 25% or more. Contract services are still in their infancy but the pilot operation is now achieving annual sales of £113,000 and one licensee in excess of £130,000.

ServiceMaster licensees require no previous experience in on-site cleaning. As a matter of fact, the company has found that the most successful licensees come from backgrounds far afield from cleaning services.

The key to the success of ServiceMaster over the years has been its training programmes. The company provides the most comprehensive initial and on-going training in the industry. In addition to teaching the technical skills required to perform the variety of services, the company also provides systems to teach salesmanship, book-keeping, management, advertising and promotion.

ServiceMaster Industries Incorporated has been committed to the concept of helping individuals build strong independent businesses since 1948, when the first U.S. franchise was established. The company believes that customers seeking services for their homes and offices have the most confidence in the independent, local business owner who is backed by the experience and technical knowledge of a large national firm. The ServiceMaster franchise opportunity couples those two concepts to provide maximum customer benefit.

ServiceMaster is a company with a unique business philosophy. From an economic standpoint, ServiceMaster is in business to grow profitably. But profit is not an end in itself. It is the means by which it expands opportunity for people. ServiceMaster is committed to the idea that profitable growth should be used to help people develop, to help them reach their full potential in their personal as well as their business lives.

ServiceMaster has translated this unique attitude into four corporate objectives. For ServiceMaster licensees and employees alike, these objectives are a way of life:

To Honour God in All We Do
To Help People Develop
To Pursue Excellence
To Grow Profitably

ServiceMaster is yet again another example of the orthodox business format franchise which has the advantage in the early stages of being capable of being operated from the franchisee's home so that he is not involved at a critical early stage in the expenses arising out of the establishment of commercial business premises.

The initial investment is not great and there is a valuable back-up provided by the franchisor. ServiceMaster has been in the franchise business for as long as anyone, the first franchise having been established in 1948, which is the very beginning of the modern business format franchise explosion.

The ServiceMaster growth rate over the last two editions of this work has also been impressive.

	2nd edition 1979	3rd edition 1982	4th edition 1984
Franchisees world wide	1,850	2,300	2,750
Franchisees in U.K.	75	100	159

Since the last edition ServiceMaster have introduced a new franchise which is being pilot tested. It should be noted that even a company with ServiceMaster's experience recognise that they need to pilot test new ideas and cannot assume the previous experience will enable them to eliminate the delays caused by establishing and proving the concept in a pilot operation.

It would appear that one of the keys to the operation of the system lies in the technical aspects in which the franchisee is trained, having been advised on the correct equipment and chemicals to utilise in the conduct of the business. It is interesting to note that ServiceMaster are trying to instil in their franchisees a feeling of business philosophy that should underline all they do in not only their business but also their personal life.

In studying the tables in Appendix B the following interesting factors can be noted:

Part One

Table 2.   By contrast with Dyno-Rod, six out of the thirty-one ServiceMaster franchisees interviewed had previously been manual workers.

Table 3. Twenty-six out of the thirty-one franchisees recognised the value of the franchisor's "umbrella" and the lowering of the risks inherent in establishing a new business and that this was a sound business venture.

Table 6. Twenty-three out of thirty-one franchisees felt they were given full financial information before signing their contracts. This means that eight did not take this view. On the other hand (see Part Two, question 11), all fifteen interviewed in depth felt that their original decision to go into franchising was the right one.

Table 17. Twenty-nine out of thirty-one franchisees thought that the quality of equipment supplied was reasonable to excellent. All thirty-one thought the quality of supplies and the quality of the operating manual was reasonable to excellent. In view of the high emphasis on this aspect of the franchise the franchisees are clearly well served in these respects.

Tables 22 In the areas of technical support and availability and quality
–27. of continuing advisory services, two-thirds of the franchisees through ServiceMaster's efforts reasonable to excellent.

Tables 27 The franchisees are quite solid in recognising the value of
and 28. the brand name to their business.

Table 29. Exactly the same result as for Dyno-Rod in that twenty-five out of thirty-one (80.7%) felt their businesses were more successful because they were franchised (see also question 21 in Part Two of the Appendix).

Table 32. Two-thirds of the franchisees were satisfied with their franchise.

Table 33. As in all cases considered, the franchisees are almost unanimous in considering the contract weighed in favour of the franchisor.

Table 37. Twenty-four out of the twenty-nine franchisees who replied state that their present intention is to renew the contract, while only one does not intend to do so.

Table 38. As many as seven out of the thirty-one franchisees were dissatisfied with the profitability of their business, which is a remarkable result considering the replies set out in Table 37 and in reply to question 11 in Part Two of the Appendix.

Part Two

Question 8. Eleven out of the fifteen ServiceMaster franchisees who were interviewed "would advise anyone also to do what they have done" and the number only drops to ten when the question (question 12) is, "Would the franchisees still go into franchising if they were starting today?" Remarkably, in the light of some of the other replies and data availability, as high a percentage as 60% have some reservations about their relationship with the franchisor. This is difficult to reconcile with the information revealed in Tables 17 to 19.

Questions 14 and 15.

Wimpy International Limited

WHAT IS WIMPY?

Wimpy is the brand name of the most successful and one of the longest standing franchises in the U.K.

Wimpy offers to customers of all types an enjoyable meal, based on hamburgers, served quickly in pleasant surroundings. Only pure beef with seasoning and spices, made to our secret recipe, are used in our manufacturing process. Strict quality control ensures that it is always of the same high standards—delicious every time.

The growth of Wimpy hamburger sales has been dramatic since their introduction in 1955. There are now over 570 outlets trading in the U.K. with a further 400 in thirty-eight countries round the world. In that quarter of a century, thousands of businessmen and entrepreneurs have shared in success and prosperity with Wimpy. That success was built on table service restaurants which were right for the market place of the 1960s and 70s. However, in response to changes in the retail scene and consumer expectations, Wimpy International have developed counter service based systems which are right for the 1980s and '90s.

Rapidly rising rents, rates, wages and energy costs mean that table service outlets will have increasing difficulty in competing in prime trading locations. For this reason Wimpy are not building any new table service stores, although new franchisees may wish to purchase one of the existing Wimpy outlets, which should continue to be viable for some years to come.

Wimpy have built a nucleus of company-owned, counter service outlets to back up the growing number of franchised outlets already open or being developed.

HOW DOES THE WIMPY FRANCHISE WORK?

Essentially it is a partnership in profit where both sides contribute skill and resources to ensure that their mutual benefit is maximised. The franchisee contributes his capital, his management skills and local knowledge. Wimpy International contribute an effective package which has proved successful in a range of operating situations and which no individual operator could hope to match.

The Wimpy package consists of the following key areas:

1. The company will assist in the finding of potential locations, advise on their suitability and will only accept those sites which, in their experience, are likely to be viable. Wimpy International reserve the right to accept or reject a site after an assessment of its trading potential and the overheads involved. It is not their policy to license new Wimpy outlets if, in their opinion, they would materially affect the business of an existing unit, but they do not accept any restriction on

their discretion to license Wimpy outlets in any locations. Wimpy will use the covenant of United Biscuits Ltd., their parent company, to secure the head lease for prime sites which would often be unobtainable by companies of lesser standing.

2. On acceptance of a site the franchisee would make an advance payment of part of the franchise fee to enable Wimpy International to produce detailed plans and specifications, and to assist in obtaining appropriate planning permissions.

3. The franchisee is responsible for acquiring, shopfitting, equipping and converting the site, to the approved specifications of Wimpy International to ensure a durable, attractive outlet.

4. The balance of the franchise fee, £10,000 in total for a counter service outlet and £1,000 "change of hands" fee for an existing table service outlet, is payable prior to the outlet opening at the signing of the agreement setting out the rights and responsibilities of each partner. The agreement is for a ten year period, renewable thereafter with the agreement of both parties.

5. Wimpy International will provide training and practical experience for a franchisee and his management. A comprehensive operations manual is provided covering every aspect of running and operating a Wimpy. Assistance is also given with the training of staff prior to and during the critical opening period.

6. Specific promotional support is given at the opening and thereafter the outlet will benefit from a regular programme of advertising, promotions and merchandising.

7. Advice on the development of the business and problem solving is provided by regular calls from an experienced team of operation supervisors.

8. Wimpy International deliver deep frozen Wimpy products and fresh Wimpy buns, all produced to stringent quality specifications, supervised by their quality control managers.

9. Wimpy International will continue to ensure that their franchisees are able to take advantage of new developments in the market place, systems or equipment, once they have developed and tested them in company-owned outlets.

How Much Profit Will the Franchisee Make?

Individual site circumstances and operating conditions mean that each situation will need to be judged on its own merit. Indeed, the profit profiles of table service and counter service outlets are entirely different. The table service system imposes a relatively low level of turnover on an outlet, so this is compensated for by higher prices and a higher net profit margin (17–20% of net turnover). The counter service system is capable of attracting and handling much higher turnovers, so a higher throughput, low profit margin (14–15% of net turnover) philosophy is adopted. The return on capital employed is competitive with other business ventures and retains the security of using a proven name and system.

Naturally a major factor in the success of a Wimpy is the franchisee's hard work and management control. We are looking for businessmen with the same attitudes as us towards high standards of quality, service and value. A franchisee will need to have, or have access to, at least £120,000, and the return from prime trading locations will normally require and justify greater investment. He need have no knowledge or previous experience of catering or fast food, but he will probably have proved his ability in other successful activities.

The market in which Wimpy operates, fast food, certainly seems to be one of the few that all the pundits agree to be set for real growth throughout the 80s. It is one where the levels of sophistication and competition are also growing, making it almost impossible for an entrepreneur to "do his own thing". Wimpy offers the best opportunity for any businessman to share in the growth of that exciting market.

The Wimpy proposition has changed radically since the second edition of this work. Whereas previously Wimpy were concentrating exclusively on the small simple Wimpy bar (average size 1,400 square feet), they have now added a larger alternative which is to run alongside the existing units. There is obviously room for both. The existing units would be viable in locations which would not justify the new larger unit and they will no doubt benefit from the marketing and promotional activities relating to the new units.

The Wimpy franchise has been successful for many years and many of its franchisees have earned a good income while operating the business as well as making a substantial capital profit on the disposal of the business in due course.

Having traded by means of the franchise system since 1955, the company has acquired a considerable amount of know-how and experience in their field.

Recent invasions of the U.K. by American competitors have found Wimpy ready to use its vast experience to adapt to the changing challenge which a fast developing market has presented. The quality of its system and its existing franchisees are meeting the challenge in a manner which none of the individual franchisees could without the franchise umbrella. The Wimpy franchisee profile for the new style Wimpy restaurant has changed. The capital requirement has quadrupled and Wimpy will have to adjust to dealing with a more sophisticated and independent minded franchisee. It is clear that they recognise the changes and are ready to meet them.

In classical franchising style Wimpy have thoroughly market tested the new units in pilot operations. This has enabled them to make adjustments and variations on their original concept to meet actual operating problems and experience.

Since the new style unit was introduced for pilot testing in 1978 Wimpy have granted thirty-two franchises for these units.

It is significant that Wimpy operated thirteen of its own new style units before granting any franchises and that it presently operates eighteen of these new style units.

Wimpy is now opening new style units at a rate of approximately twenty each year.

The tables relating to Wimpy in Appendix B relate to the existing style unit, the survey having been carried out before the new units were market tested. The following interesting factors can be noted:

Part One

Table 2. The Wimpy franchise attracts almost 50% of previously self-employed and a relatively low number of former manual workers.

Table 3. Twenty-eight out of the fifty franchisees recognise the value of the franchisor's "umbrella", the lowering of risks inherent in establishing a new business or that this was a sound business venture; fifteen (i.e. 28.5%) did not reply.

Table 6. Forty-one out of the fifty-two franchisees felt they were given full financial information before signing the contract; eight did not take this view; on the other hand (see Part Two, question 11), nineteen out of twenty interviewed in depth felt that their original decision to go into franchising was the right one.

Table 16. Again as with Dyno-Rod, there is the puzzling reply that seven franchisees did not think they were provided with training while thirty (out of forty-two replies) thought that the training was reasonable to excellent.

Table 17. Thirty-five (out of forty-three replies) thought the quality of the equipment supplied was reasonable to excellent.

Table 18. Only one of the franchisees who replied thought the quality of supplies was not very good. The others thought it was reasonable to excellent. In a product based franchise this is a good outcome.

Table 19. Thirty-six out of forty-seven considered the operating manual reasonable to excellent.

Table 32. Thirty-seven out of fifty were satisfied with their franchise.

Table 33. Forty-one out of the forty-five franchisees who replied were of the opinion that the contract was weighed in favour of the franchisor.

Table 37. Thirty-two out of forty who replied stated that their present intention is to renew the contract, while only five said they did not intend to do so.

Table 38. Fifteen out of fifty who replied expressed dissatisfaction with the profitability of the business. This, as with Service-Master, is difficult to reconcile with the replies set out in Table 37, and in reply to questions 8 and 11 in Part Two of Appendix B.

Part Two

Questions 8 and 11	Nineteen out of twenty franchisees interviewed stated that they would advise anyone to do what they have done and felt that their original decision to go into franchising was the right one.
Questions 14 and 15.	Clearly there is room for improvement in franchisor/franchisee relations or perhaps there is a communication problem. On the other hand, the problems cannot be too fundamental (see Table 37 in Part One).

Zeegard Car Care Ltd. (trading as Zeibart U.K.)

It has not been the practice in any of the case study sections of previous editions of this work to preface with any remarks a case study submitted by the company concerned. The approach has always been to let the company speak for itself and then to offer comments, which is the approach which has continued to be adopted in all the other case studies in this edition. However, the collapse of Ziebart (G.B.) Limited (Z.G.B.) in 1982 involving a leading company in the U.K. franchise community is so significant that it calls for special treatment.

In reading the company's presentation one should be examining and considering various factors:

A. Why did the franchise fail?
B. What could have been done to avoid that failure and to what extent was it tried?
C. What damage was caused to the franchisees and how was that alleviated?
D. To what extent did franchisees contribute to their own difficulties?
E. What harm has been caused to the customers of the network and how has that been dealt with?
F. To what extent have the problems been overcome for the future?
G. Does the franchise have a future?

Another feature of this franchise is that the ultimate problem rested with the franchisor which is a U.S. company, the Ziebart International Corporation (Z.I.C.). Z.G.B. held a Master franchise from Z.I.C. granting to it the right to operate the Ziebert franchise system in the U.K. This means that in this case there were in effect two franchisors.

Z.I.C. granting rights to Z.G.B., which in turn granted rights to the operational franchisees in the U.K. It is therefore also of interest to see to what extent Z.I.C. was able to influence events and bring their expertise to bear upon the problems and their solution.

THE ZIEBART STORY

In 1979 Ziebart International Corporation, an American company based in Detroit, Michigan, negotiated with a Sussex based company called Mobile Transport Services Ltd., for the grant of the franchise, in the United Kingdom, to the Ziebart process of rustproofing vehicles. The franchise was acquired in July 1970 and operated by Ziebart (G.B.) Ltd, a subsidiary of Mobile Transport Services Ltd. The first operation was opened in London in October 1970 and within a few years a franchise system of some sixty locations had been established.

Through effective public relations activities and good advertising, the network continued to grow in the 1970s during which period up to 50,000 vehicles were processed annually.

In the late 1970s Mobile Transport Services Ltd. changed its name to Envirogarde Group Ltd., and expanded in a multitude of directions. Additional automotive service franchises were offered for windscreen repair, car care services, sun roofs, car polishing, and, at a later stage, the manufacture and distribution of a children's garden game. The additional "Envirogarde" franchises were offered to existing Ziebart franchisees, as an addition to their Ziebart franchise which had to be paid for, as well as to other independent operators.

In addition the group embarked upon a ten-year rustproofing guarantee programme which was not adequately underwritten either by insurance or by financial arrangements with franchisees or from the group's resources.

Ziebart International Corporation, as Envirogarde's franchisor, cautioned the group against such diversification in any event, and advised it to concentrate its efforts on the Ziebart operation. The group was also advised against entering into such a heavy guarantee commitment. None of this advice was accepted.

The group first ran into financial difficulties during the first energy crisis, and Ziebart International provided considerable assistance by agreeing to accept shares in settlement of part of the debts outstanding to it and by converting the balance of short-term debt into a long-term debt supported by a debenture. Subsequently, the U.K. shareholders purchased the shares from Ziebart International and the debt secured by the debenture was repaid.

Ziebart International continued to impress upon the group the folly in diversification, which was resulting in the group (which lacked adequate financial resources) spreading those resources as well as its management resources far too thinly over its total operations. Apart from the guarantee liabilities, undertaken against advice, the Ziebart rustproofing business remained profitable.

When the recession in the early 1980s arrived the group's thin spread of its resources left it with no financial cushion to enable it to weather the storm. The group tried to cut back on its expenditure, but operating losses were too high and in November 1982 the Board of the Envirogarde Group asked its Bankers to appoint a receiver. The group was then put into liquidation. These actions resulted in the termination of the franchise granted to Ziebart (G.B.) Ltd., and also of the sub-franchisees which then numbered eighty-five. The operating losses had been aggravated by excessive costs incurred under the guarantee programme. Ziebart International Corporation had tried to alleviate the financial problems of Ziebart G.B. Ltd., by the introduction of some £100,000 cash and by not enforcing some £50,000 of debts owed to it. Ultimately, it decided that it could not realistically be expected to try to finance the cost of actions taken against its advice. It would be better to invest in a fresh start.

The customers, who are the vehicle owners, have been hurt by the fact that the number of Ziebart rustproofing locations has been drastically reduced. This makes it difficult for them to have the necessary inspections performed in order to keep their rustproofing warranty valid. In addition, they sometimes find that the original processing station, which issued the warranty, is no longer in business and they have no party against whom to make a claim in the event that a "rust-through" occurs. In areas where a Ziebart dealer continues to operate, vehicle owners continue to get the good service which these franchisees have provided for many years. The cost of servicing these guarantees has not been excessive to these franchisees who had always maintained the correct quality standards.

Rustproofing is a service where the workmanship is critical to the success of the process. It is therefore imperative that the processing station guarantees its own work. There is no way that the national sub-franchisor can do more than spot check quality standards to see that proper materials and procedures are used. Ziebart (G.B.) Ltd. at one time purchased annual insurance to back its franchisees, but this proved unsatisfactory. The new national sub-franchisor, Zeegard Car Care Ltd., has negotiated and introduced a new insured warranty for its dealers; however, the insurance naturally will have the normal provisions and limitations, such as excess or deductibles, which would continue to be the responsibility of the franchisee.

Ziebart International Corporation sold the Ziebart rustproofing franchise to Ziebart (G.B.) Ltd., and while the rustproofing business proved profitable until the guarantee programme failed in 1982 it had very little influence over the corporate management of the holding company, Envirogarde Group Ltd., of which Ziebart (G.B.) Ltd. was a wholly owned subsidiary. The objective of Ziebart International was to strengthen the rustproofing franchise, while the objective of the controlling stockholders of Envirogarde Group Ltd. was to diversify and achieve independence from Ziebart in spite of the fact that it was its main moneymaking entity. After the original Managing Director, Keith Tarry, left in May of 1981, Ziebart International assumed a more active role and advanced funds for current operating needs; however, past operating mistakes were too serious to salvage the operation.

Following the collapse of Ziebart G.B. Ltd. Ziebart International Corporation immediately established a wholly owned subsidiary in the U.K. now called Zeegard Car Care Ltd., and offered the sub-franchisees the opportunity to sign a new franchise agreement. Due to the recession in the automotive market and severe competitive conditions, a number of franchisees chose to abandon rustproofing or to switch to competitive processes and only thirty-five franchisees elected to sign an agreement with the new franchisor. Sufficient franchisees elected to remain in rustproofing to demonstrate the underlying quality of the rustproofing business.

Ziebart International Corporation has chosen to make a major investment in funds and management to try to recapture its position in the U.K. market. Additional automotive appearance and protection services were offered under the Ziebart brand name to supplement the existing new car rustproofing business. Such services include pain protection, interior protection and a used care rustproofing service utilising a new product, rust eliminator.

During the spring of 1983, these new services were introduced to existing dealers through a national conference and a series of regional meetings. By the autumn of 1983, the new company, trading as Ziebart U.K., was ready again to offer new franchises. In this new format, Ziebart U.K. had direct access to the American company's research and development and manufacturing know-how, as well as proven marketing programmes. A comprehensive technical manual, which is continually updated as new models are put on the market, is made available to the franchisees.

Both technical training and sales training, as well as continuous quality control, are also part of the business format franchise.

In acquiring a Ziebart franchise the buyer goes through several stages following his initial inquiry, since the buyer and, equally important, the company want the right fit.

1. In response to the inquiry, comprehensive information describing the franchise, the process, the service and the cost are supplied.
2. Contact is made to determine that the information has been received and to carry out an initial assessment of the person or firm concerning their background, business experience, access to premises and financial status.
3. If interest remains high, a discussion/presentation is conducted and all the buyer's questions and queries are answered at this point.
4. The buyer is supplied with a Ziebart franchise agreement with the advice to have the document scrutinized by his solicitors on his behalf.
5. The buyer is invited to visit other Ziebart Centres by himself and have unhindered discussion with other license-holders.
6. The buyer is invited to visit Ziebart headquarters and meet its management and inspect the back-up service departments within the company.

If the buyer chooses to purchase a Ziebart franchise, he will then sign the franchise agreement, pay his franchise fee, and start his training and development activity with the help of the Ziebart staff.

To be acceptable, the buyer is expected to have available a minimum of £15,000 which is allocated as follows:

1. An initial franchise fee of £3,000 to cover two weeks of technical and sales training, technical manuals, marketing manuals, start-up assistance, launch advertising and initial field sales assistance.
2. About £2,100 to cover the specific tools and equipment needed to perform the Ziebart process.
3. About £1,100 to cover the necessary products for rustproofing, paint protection, rust eliminator and interior protection (i.e. consumables).
4. About £350 for promotional materials such as brochures, posters and point of purchase materials.
5. About £950 for normal signage repainting of interior and exterior of the premises.
6. £3,500 will be needed for additional equipment such as vehicle hoist, a compressor and power wash machine.
7. The balance of at least £3,000 will be required as working capital.

In addition to the initial franchise fee, each Ziebart franchise holder pays a weekly royalty of 9% of sales, plus a 3% contribution to an advertising trust fund to support national advertising, public relations, local advertising support, etc.

Benefits to the Ziebart franchisee:

1. Exclusive use of the Ziebart name and trade marks as described in the license agreement to identify the Ziebart process for rust protection, paint protection and interior protection.
2. Consumer awareness associating the Ziebert name with rust protection in excess of 50%.
3. Exclusive use of Ziebart sealants, tooling and manuals.
4. On-site technical services during his opening period, complemented by continuous quality control programmes and technical updating.
5. Field sales activity at all levels, including commercial fleet contacts, assistance with sales presentations, and access to dealing service representatives.
6. Participation in marketing programmes, national as well as regional.
7. Sales literature in the form of brochures, posters, and point of purchase materials to assist in sales presentations.

The original Ziebart rustproofing process was developed in Detroit in the mid-1950s and has been franchised in the U.S.A. since 1963. Ziebart International Corporation, which is the international franchisor for the Ziebart process, operates through a wholly owned subsidiary in the U.S.A. which has over 800 service outlets. In addition, there are some 300 processing centres in over thirty countries outside the U.S.A.

Ziebart International Corporation has been in the forefront in supporting ethical franchising. Both its present and past chairmen have been directors of the International Franchise Association in the U.S.A. Ziebart also supports both the British Franchise Association and the Japan Franchise Association, where it is active through a wholly owned subsidiary operating over ninety franchised stations. In 1982, when the Canadian master licensee put his business on the market, Ziebart International Corporation purchased it. That network has over sixty franchised stations.

The questions posed in the introductory comments have been dealt with in the text. It is undoubtedly plain that mistakes were made and that franchisees and customers have suffered. The effect of the difficulties which were experienced was no doubt accelerated by the general business slump. It would appear that the difficulties were caused by a number of factors.

1. It could be argued that the U.S. franchisor did not retain sufficient control over the business activities of the master franchisee. This led to the master franchisee extending his business activities and diverting his financial and management resources away from the profitable rustproofing business. In addition the master franchisee, against advice, was able to introduce a guarantee commitment, not backed by insurance, which franchisees would find it difficult (and in the event impossible) to fulfil.

   It is not uncommon in an operational franchise agreement to find a provision which would restrict the right of the franchisee to engage in other business activities; furthermore, under such an agreement certainly the franchisee would not be permitted to offer a guarantee out of line with overall company practice. Should a master franchisee not be similarly restricted?

   On the other hand, there are many who would say that in a master franchisee situation the rules change to some extent from those which apply in the case of a direct franchise of an operational unit. After all, the master franchisee will be exploiting the whole of the territory. The business practices and procedures in that territory may require variations in approach and the social and cultural attitudes will differ. The master franchisee is to be the franchisor in the territory, controlling the network making use of the name and know-how of the master franchisor; he should therefore be given greater freedom to develop the business than would be given to the operational franchisee. In view of the distance between master franchisor and master franchisee the latter must be given greater responsibility and, if not regarded as being capable of coping with expanding business responsibilities, should not have been appointed master franchisee in the first place. Ziebart International Corporation can point to the other master franchisee arrangements based upon similar contractual provisions which have proved eminently successful. It may be able to say that it cannot ultimately bear responsibility for a master franchisee who will not accept advice any more than a franchisor will not accept responsibility for its franchisees who ignore advice and end up bankrupt. It is all too easy with the benefit of hindsight to criticise. One should avoid the temptation to be clever after the event, particularly in view of the substantial financial support given by the master franchisor when difficulties emerged.

2. The master franchisee appears to have made a number of mistakes, although one should bear in mind that the presentation does not have the benefit of the views of the then management of that company. These mistakes in summary are:

   (i) It expanded its operations not only against advice but also without adequate capital and manpower resources.

  (ii) It failed adequately to supervise franchisees' operating standards so that substandard work was being performed.

 (iii) The guarantee period was extended for a long term, which made it inevitable that claims would be made in more than the very small number of cases which would be the "norm".

 (iv) The guarantee was not backed by insurance or any other form of adequate financial arrangement. The master franchisee, in order to reduce customer complaints, felt obliged to meet claims where franchisees had gone out of business.

  (v) The number of guarantee claims was unacceptably high owing to the poor operating standards, particularly of franchisees who subsequently went out of business.

The total effect was that as the claims piled up, coupled with the shortage of working capital, inevitably the master franchisee would fail.

There is no doubt that many customers of Ziebart failed to have remedial work carried out or payment made in accordance with the terms of the guarantees which were issued. There is also no doubt that the name Ziebart has suffered much adverse publicity and that the goodwill associated with the name has been damaged.

The recession has affected vehicle rustproofing as has the increased rustproofing protection now given to motor vehicles by manufacturers. These factors affected business in the U.S.A., as much as anywhere, and Ziebart International Corporation developed a marketing strategy during 1981 which was implemented in 1982–3. Basically they have created a far more comprehensive motor vehicle service than the original rustproofing. They set themselves three objectives:

—to diversify the Ziebart business through the addition of new products;
—to diversify distribution of Ziebart services into the fleet and care dealer channels;
—to change the Ziebart pricing system to the "royalty-type" format.

In fulfilling these objectives Ziebart in the U.S.A. have enabled their franchisees to develop and extend their business turnover and profitability when the slump would otherwise have an adverse effect.

So far as the U.K. is concerned, Ziebart International Corporation, the original franchisor, has restructured the programme and is now relaunching in an endeavour to make up for the lost time and to restore its reputation. It is indeed notable that thirty-five franchisees out of eighty-five franchisees of the former Master franchisee have decided to continue with the restructured business. The direct involvement of Ziebart International Corporation should eliminate the problems which affected the U.K. operation in the past.

The "Hough" statistics contained in Appendix C were being gathered in 1980 and 1981, the years immediately before the collapse, when signs of strain and stress should have already been emerging.

The plus factors for Ziebart as appear from responses in Part One were (and presumably will continue to be):

—the quality of formal training: 41.7% good to excellent and 25% reasonable (Table 16);
—the quality of operating manuals: 91.3% good to excellent (Table 19);
—the quality of technical support: 52% good to excellent and 44% adequate (Table 22);
—the rating of the trade name and image: 77.1% (Table 27).

Bearing in mind the admitted failure of the master franchisee to police standards, the low level of threats to terminate, 8.3% (Table 36), is not surprising, although that is the highest level of all the companies in the survey.

The signs of problems are indicated by the following figures.

Table 32. Only 36% satisfied with the existing business. However, of those who were dissatisfied it was not necessarily dissatisfaction with rustproofing; 24% would have liked to continue but outside the franchise, while 24% would have liked to be self-employed but not in rustproofing. That is nearly half of the franchisees said they wanted to leave. These responses are difficult to reconcile with the replies in Table 37, which shows that only 4.2% intended not to renew the contract.

Table 38. Only 8.3% were very satisfied with the profitability of their business, 45.8% were satisfied, while a high 31.3% were dissatisfied.

Part Three

Table 20. Twenty-four per cent of the Ziebart franchisees considered the franchisor slow to respond to requests for assistance as against 2.3% and 4.4% in the case of the other companies.

On the whole the figures seem to bear out the Ziebart contention that the rustproofing business was sound (60% wanted to remain in rustproofing—see Table 32 above) and the franchise had potential if run properly.

We must now wait to see whether the restructured franchise will recover so that the Ziebart name and goodwill will be restored.

CHAPTER 14

Current Developments
in Franchising

THERE have been developments and issues emerging in franchising, some of which are of sufficient significance to warrant discussion.

In this chapter there are five developments or issues which will be looked at:

1. The role of the Banks,
2. The role of franchise consultants,
3. The effect of bankruptcy or failure of a franchisor,
4. The failure of a franchisee, and
5. Applications to which the franchise marketing method have been put.

1. The Role of the Banks

There are two Banks which have taken franchise financing very seriously, namely, National Westminster Bank plc and Barclays Banks plc. Lloyds Bank plc have become involved to a more limited extent and Midland Bank plc* have not formalised any arrangements with regard to franchising. In addition, among the finance houses, First National Securities Ltd. has had a special interest in financing franchising since late 1981.

National Westminster Bank were the first of the Banks to establish a formal approach to franchising by appointing Tim Knowles as franchise manager in July 1981, and he and his team now work within the framework of the Nat West Small Business Section. The franchise team has now grown and comprises a franchise manager, an assistant manager and three other members, apart from secretarial support.

* Midland Bank have now appointed a Franchise Manager.

Barclays Bank followed Nat West quite quickly with the appointment of Patrick Salaun as their franchise manager. Their franchise team now comprises another franchise manager and manager's assistant, as well as secretarial support.

Lloyds Bank were the third of the large Banks to formalise the appointment of a franchise manager, but Midland Bank have not made such an appointment.

The only finance house which has made any serious attempt to tackle the financing of franchises is First National Securities Ltd. and David Owen, the general manager responsible, has been involved since late 1981.

The reason why the Banks have entered the field of franchising is because they have recognised that franchising is a safer way of establishing a new business. Furthermore, with the proven concept and the "umbrella" of the franchisor's organisation, the ability of the business to generate sufficient profit to enable the franchisee to repay his obligation and to live comfortably is more readily recognisable. This enables the Banks to consider lending a greater proportion of the franchisee's ingoing costs than would normally be considered appropriate.

Each of the Bankers which has entered the field has adopted the same approach; the appointment of a franchise manager at the centre and around whom the department can develop. The alternative would be to educate the whole branch network in franchising and in how to evaluate a proposition. This would result in an inconsistency of approach which would be damaging and confusing and ensure that the corporate know-how was spread so thinly as to be incapable of being put to good use.

The specialist manager at the centre, with a developing team around him, enables the Bank to acquire the know-how and pass it on to those who join the department. There is a skilled application of the knowledge acquired which enables rapid evaluation of propositions and the establishment of a consistent attitude towards each franchise. The local manager faced with the prospective franchisee borrower can be provided not only with a brief about franchising in general, but also about the specific proposition which he is being asked to consider.

The Banker's decision about whether or not to be formally involved in any franchise is thus taken by specialists with the requisite knowledge and experience. The Banker's decision on whether to lend to a particular individual is taken by the local manager, who will interview and evaluate him, supported by all the relevant information about the franchise scheme and the franchisor which is supplied by the franchise managers' department.

Although these Banks may well be identified with a particular franchise by the franchisee promoting the availability of a finance scheme, the Banks do not warrant the viability of the franchise or its suitability for any person. The Banks do point out that a prospective franchisee should make a detailed evaluation of the franchise before making his decision.

It is clear that both Nat West and Barclays have committed many millions of pounds to the financing of franchisees and that they are giving a lead to financial institutions in recognising the advantages to lenders of being involved in franchise finance.

The approach adopted by First National Securities Ltd. (FNS) is very similar except, of course, that with no branch network the central control covers all aspects of evaluation. FNS has introduced a three months' "holiday" on capital and interest payments at the start of the loans it makes.

2. The Role of Franchise Consultants

There have been references to franchise consultants in this work. These references have been limited to their possible involvement in the marketing of a franchise. Franchise consultants as a whole do offer a wide range of services, which include:

(i) the evaluation of a business and its suitability for franchising,
(ii) preparing the franchise package,
(iii) assisting with the preparation of, or even writing the franchisor's operational manual,
(iv) marketing the packages and selling franchises,
(v) ongoing development advice, and
(vi) advising franchisees about franchise opportunities.

The mere fact that someone calls himself a franchise consultant does not mean that he is qualified to offer that service. There are no formal qualifications as a franchise consultant; the best that such a person can offer is past practical experience in franchising. Other than this there is the Institute of Management Consultants which establishes qualification criteria and requires members to abide by a strict code of ethical professional conduct. Even so, if one is dealing with a member of that institute his credentials to offer specialised advice on franchising will have to be examined.

Assuming that one wishes to employ the services of a franchise consultant, what are the criteria by which they should be judged and what safeguards are there? There are four general headings:

(i) ethical standards,
(ii) experience in franchising,
(iii) verification of reputation,
(iv) terms and scope of employment (including charges).

(i) Ethical Standards

Any person who is offering consultancy services must be able to approach the client in an objective way. He must place the client's interest first and should be able to advise a client not to proceed with what he proposes, even when it means that the consultant will thereby lose business. He must avoid obvious conflicts of interest between clients and between his own duties. In the author's view it is unethical for a franchise consultant who is assisting franchisors in setting up their business to hold himself out as being able objectively to advise franchisees who wish to have assistance in evaluating a franchise. The strong temptation exists to direct such a person from his area of interest to a client of the consultant, especially if the consultant is part of his client's sale force.

The question also arises as to how far the consultant should properly become involved in the selling of franchises for a client. There are a number of considerations to be taken into account, and those which apply to an employee which are dealt with in Chapter 6 (see pages 73–74) should be reviewed since they apply equally to the use of an outside consultant. While a consultant may be able to give the franchisor advice on franchise marketing and on selection of a franchisee, he should not be employed to sell franchisees; nor should he be paid by reference to the number of franchises sold or upon a sale taking place. He should be paid for the advice given and not because he has persuaded someone to sign up. The decision about the acceptability of a franchisee must rest with the franchisor and no one else, and it must be a decision taken without pressure based solely upon the suitability or otherwise of the applicant.

In advising clients, all ethical consultants should bear in mind the code of ethics of the British Franchise Association. Although not every franchisor will wish to join the British Franchise Association, the code of ethics is a guide to proper conduct by franchisors to which no *bona fide* reputable franchisor could object. Indeed, if a consultant were to set himself as a target the eventual qualification for membership of the British Franchise Association by all his clients, the standards of franchising would undoubtedly benefit.

(ii) Experience in franchising

If a person wishes to offer himself as an adviser on franchising to others, based upon the experience he has in the field, the quality of that experience is important. Ideally he should have been involved in an actual franchise operation and at a sufficiently high level of management to have had responsibility for the operation of the franchise. Someone who is employed in a franchise company at a supervised low level of management is not capable of showing the requisite experience in franchising. After all, if the consultant is holding himself out as competent and able to advise how one should go about setting up, marketing and operating a franchise, it is best if he can demonstrate that he has a level of achievement which justifies his claims. There are a few questions which can be posed under this heading:

(a) What is the consultant's experience in the field of franchising?
(b) Is it general, or is it limited to a specific aspect?
(c) Does he have experience in the particular aspect on which advice is required? (e.g. marketing image; design; retailing; distribution; fast food; practical field experience; manual writing).
(d) Has he actually worked in a franchisor company other than in a consultancy capacity? What was his job? To what extent was he under supervision or direction?
(e) Is he a member of any professional body? What are his qualifications?

(iii) Verification of reputation

It is advisable to verify that the consultant has actually held the positions which he represents to you that he has held. If a consultant or anyone is dishonest, that dishonesty is usually not confined to limited areas, it will be wider. One should therefore check up on the consultant as much as possible. No reputable franchise consultant will object; on the contrary, he will be pleased and proud to demonstrate his "track record". He will also be pleased that you are taking such care, since if everyone did, the business opportunities for the incompetent and less reputable consultant would diminish rapidly.

Additionally, the following questions should be asked:

(a) Can the consultant provide you with references? One should specify the classes of persons from whom one would like to see references (e.g. bankers, accountants or solicitors for his financial position and reputation). Other references could come from persons known and established in franchising who know of his reputation and background by personal contact.

(b) Can, and will, the consultant make arrangements for you to select from his past and present client list and speak to your own selection about their experience with the consultant?

(c) If he offers his services as a salesman of franchises (and you wish to employ him for that purpose despite the views expressed in his work) can arrangements be made for you to speak to franchisees, of your choice, to whom he has sold franchises and also to their franchisors?

(iv) Terms and scope of employment (including charges)

It is the prospective franchisor or franchisor who must decide upon the role which he wishes the consultant to play. The fact that one employs a consultant does not mean that the consultant is able to run the business or advise on every aspect of the business. It is the adaptation of the business to the franchise method of distribution about which the advice is being given. The range of services which are usually offered is set out above and a decision has to be made about the extent of the involvement of the consultant. It would be sensible to have exploratory meetings with the consultant and agree on terms of reference for his role. One should not employ a consultant unless and until those terms are clearly defined in writing. Agreement should also be reached over the method of calculating fees to be charged. A lump sum for a specific task should be avoided. It is far better to be charged an agreed hourly rate when it is easier to control the expenditure and assess the value of the work. It may be sensible initially to set a specific task for the consultant and either develop the relationship further, if the relationship works, or if not, to terminate it.

3. The Effect of Bankruptcy or Failure of a Franchisor

Fortunately, there are not many examples in practice of a franchisor becoming bankrupt or going into liquidation. Nonetheless, the subject is important since there have been failures and there certainly will be more in the future.

The fact that someone sets himself up as a franchisor does not mean that he is thereby invested with an aura of invincibility and cannot fail.

A franchisor may fail for a number of different reasons:

(a) It may have been a deliberate fraud.
(b) It may have been a badly structured franchise.
(c) The franchise may not have been sufficiently well market-tested.
(d) The franchisor may be under capitalised, particularly in the crucial early years.
(e) There may be a good franchise but the franchisor runs his end of the business badly.
(f) The franchisor may make bad policy decisions.
(g) The franchise scheme may fall foul of the law.
(h) Poor selection of franchisees.
(i) Over rapid expansion leading to lack of support for franchisees.
(j) Lack of management ability.

In some of these cases the collapse of the franchisor may cause irretrievable loss, and in this connection one has in mind those losses referred to in (a), (b), (c) and (g), the first three having been avoidable and the last perhaps avoidable or perhaps unforseeable. In such cases the franchisee will probably be left with little except a financial loss and a large headache. He may have some sort of business still left which, with imagination and hard work, he can work up sufficiently to reduce his losses. It may be that what he is left with cannot be worked upon at all and he has to cut his losses and close up as soon as possible. It could also be that the franchisee has so little past experience and training that he is not capable of continuing without a franchisor's support.

It is of little comfort to one who finds himself in that position to be told that he should not have gone into that franchise at all since the weaknesses would have been apparent had proper enquiries been made. In one respect a potential franchisee is not far better placed to judge the good, the bad and the fraudulent than he ever had been in the past. Apart from this work and "How to Evaluate a Franchise", which offer guidance to the would-be franchisee, there are the "Be Your Own Boss" presentations by *Franchise World Magazine*, the Banks involved in franchising and last, but by no means least, the British Franchise Association. The Association runs educational programmes and while not all franchisors qualified for membership are members of the Association there are now some fifty companies who are, and whose credentials and ethical standards have been checked, and are monitored. While membership of the Association is not (and has never been claimed to be) a guarantee of the future business success of the franchisor, it is a strong indication that a successful track record exists and a clear indication that the franchisor is ethical.

In the other cases, where presumably the franchise scheme is basically reasonably sound but the franchisor has failed for the reasons described in (d), (e), (f), (i) and (j) above, the failure is not necessarily fatal for the franchisees.

In the first place the franchisor will be the proprietor of:

—the system under which the franchised business is operated,
—the know-how associated with it,
—trade secrets,
—trade marks and/or a trade name with associated goodwill, and
—copyright material.

None of these will disappear with the franchisor's business failure. They will be assets of the business with which a liquidator or receiver will have to deal, but subject to the rights granted in respect thereof to the franchisees.

The liquidator or receiver will be seeking to obtain whatever is the market price for those assets, but since the rights granted will also be subject to the provision of a franchisor's services, it may not be easy to dispose of them. The value of the assets of which he will be seeking to dispose of will be enhanced by the potential income from the franchise agreements.

There are two potential purchasers of these assets. First, a competitor of the franchisor who may or may not already be a franchisor. If he is a franchisor he may have reservations about whether the former competitor's disgruntled franchisees could fit in. Undoubtedly he would insist on meeting all the franchisees to see whether a working relationship would have any prospect of success. If he is not yet a franchisor the opportunity prescribed to him may have the effect of triggering his entry into the field with a ready-made network. He would, however, have to be very sure of his own franchising ideas and of his ability to develop the right sort of relationships with the franchisees who may resent the intrusion presented by new ideas.

Second, the franchisees themselves. It is unlikely that the franchisor will have become bankrupt or gone into liquidation without some warning signs having been revealed.

The franchisor will usually have contractual obligations:

—to provide management back-up,
—to provide advertising,
—to maintain standards,
—to provide continuing development,
—to supply and/or arrange the supply of products,

and so on, and as his financial resources become stretched his ability to finance the provision of these services will be impaired—his franchisees will notice the deterioration of, or decline, in provision of services and undoubtedly will be complaining. Some franchisees may add to the franchisor's cash flow problems by stopping the payment of franchise fees in retaliation for the failure to provide services.

Additionally, some franchisees may take steps to terminate the franchise agreement for the breach of its provisions by the franchisor and make damages claims. These claims will probably be worth little in view of the franchisor's lack of financial resources. The consequence for a franchisee who terminates will, in all probability, mean that he is prohibited thereafter from using the franchisor's

—system,
—know-how,
—trade secrets,
—trade mark/trade name and goodwill,
—copyright material,

and also limited in his future activities by a restrictive covenant. Termination may not be the best step to take. However, it should also be borne in mind that there may be some bargaining power available to a franchisee, who is in a position to make such a claim, in dealing with a liquidator or receiver.

Depending upon how mature is the franchise system there may be a Franchisee Advisory Committee or there may be some informal liaison between franchisees. In any event it is quite likely, with the franchisor labouring noticeably under the strain of a lack of cash, that the franchisees will get together to discuss their common problem with a common approach to the franchisor. In the author's view therein lies the best course which franchisees can take in these circumstances. Again, there may be different views on what to do and on the degree of involvement which some wish to have. However, the best prospect they have is that the scheme is kept in existence by doing the best job possible.

In most franchise chains there are varying degrees of ability in franchisees and the most able may well have been involved for a sufficiently long time to be capable of providing many of the franchisor's services and of organising the employment or involvement of others with the requisite specialised skills.

The franchisees in this predicament should therefore organise themselves, or such of them as wish to be involved, so that they can negotiate to acquire the assets which can be taken into a joint company which those concerned can own. Some thought will have to be given to the structure in that company and the rights to dispose of shares. The company will then have to be organised to ensure that the requisite services and functions can be provided—it may be that one of the more able and successful franchisees could successfully take over this responsibility.

If it is not possible to negotiate such a purchase of the assets the franchisees may with to go their separate ways using different names. Some may wish to, even if the assets can be acquired. Others may be nervous about breaking free. It may be possible to compromise any claim for damages which franchisees may have against the franchisor by acquiring the right, for a significant period, to continue using the trade marks/trade names, goodwill and system for a nominal charge until the franchisee can reorganise his business or the franchisor's business is restructured and perhaps able successfully to revive its former activities. The franchisees will have a role to play by constructive co-operation with the franchisor.

If the franchisees are able to continue to use the trade marks, trade names and system there will be merit in co-operative effort to ensure the pooling of advertising and promotional resources.

Whatever happens when a franchisor goes into liquidation or becomes bankrupt, it seems best that the franchisees do closely co-operate and co-ordinate their efforts. Therein lies the best prospect they have for emerging from the experience with a continuing successful business.

4. The Failure of a Franchisee

Fortunately, there are few examples of the failure of a franchisee, but cases do exist and it must be accepted as a feature of franchising. There will be failures. It is important to understand why there has been a failure and to investigate to see whether it can be avoided. Much media treatment of franchisee failure is one-sided; it is good for the media to describe the failures but not so good to learn that the failure was more attributable to the deed and misdeeds of the franchisee than those of the franchisor. Perspective is important and there is no doubt that franchisees have failed:

  (i)   because the franchisor had not properly tested the concept before franchising;
 (ii)   because the franchisor was under-capitalised;
(iii)   because the franchisor took bad decisions;
 (iv)   because the franchisor was dishonest;
  (v)   because it was not a franchise but some other fraudulent scheme described wrongly as a franchise; and
 (vi)   because the franchisor failed to provide the continuing services properly or at all.

So clearly the reasons which may lead to the failure of the franchisor may equally well bring down the franchisee. Unless the franchisee has the financial and business resources to seek his own salvation by continuing to trade, he would not have anyone to whom he can turn and will fail.

On the other hand, there have been franchisees who have failed despite their franchisor's support and assistance while other franchisees have succeeded.

Whatever the reason for the failure of the franchisee the symptoms will probably first evidence themselves as a shortage of cash. This shortage (insolvency) does not happen overnight, unless of course the franchisee spends the night at the races and loses his money in one evening.

Basically, insolvency is a developing situation; there will be many signs before the franchisee reaches that point. He will be slow in paying, he will be slow in doing a lot of things which he should be doing to keep his business and his staff on their toes and the franchisor will probably be involved in the developing insolvency a very long time before the point of no return is actually reached.

The reason why the franchisee is sliding into insolvency is important:

—it could be that he will not follow the system; or
—it could be that he will not take advice from the franchisor (and that quite often happens); or
—he may not be suited for the business; or
—he may be under-capitalised; or
—he may not work hard enough.

However hard one may try in selecting a franchisee it is a value judgement and one may or may not be right. Hopefully with experience one is more often right than wrong, but even so, some franchisees will be selected who are not capable of running the business.

Some franchisees who are not familiar with business sometimes assume that every pound which passes into his till is his to spend as he wishes. He does not remember that he has bills and overheads to pay, and consequently his drawings out of his business are much more heavy than they should be. They are not justified by the net profitability of the business. It is very difficult to tell a franchisee how much money he should draw out for himself.

There could well be other reasons which are contributory, but it is important to know why the franchisee is sliding into this situation because without properly identifying the reason it is not possible to prescribe the cure.

It may well be that the circumstances are such that the franchisor will decide long before a bankruptcy situation arises that he will terminate the contract, because however much he tries, he is not able to get the franchisee to comply with the contract or the directions given to him.

If the franchisor decides not to terminate, he may well think, "I made a mistake, this is not the right man for the franchise, he's not capable of running the franchise as well as I thought he was".

The franchisor has a duty to try to help the franchisee, who is running into difficulties, recover as much of his loss as possible. He also has a duty to put someone in to help the franchisee sort out the business and to see if he can sort out the franchisee and put him back on the rails. Ultimately, if the franchisee is unsuitable, the franchisor should assist him in finding a purchaser of the business on a basis which will recover for him as much as possible, at least of his capital investment. Sometimes a franchisee will not respond, but if properly handled experience shows that franchisees (with rare exceptions) usually do respond, and are quite relieved that someone is prepared to assist them and help them out of their difficulties.

One finds in many franchise contracts that the franchisor in the event of termination has the option to purchase the business and ultimately it may be necessary to proceed on this basis.

A reputable franchisor cannot afford to have failed franchisees who have not been given a "fair crack of the whip". On the other hand, no franchisee can expect any franchisor completely to bail him out of his difficulties no matter what are the circumstances.

5. Applications to which the Franchise
Marketing Method has been put

There are six situations in which existing established businesses have become involved in the franchise method of marketing:

(i) The expansion of an established retail chain by:

   (a) adding new franchised stores, thus reducing the need for additional capital and manpower,
   (b) a combination of franchising of existing stores as well as additions to the chain.

(ii) The turning over to franchising of marginally profitable or unprofitable stores in a retail chain. By removing from the profit and loss expense items the cost of employment of staff, including holiday and sickness cover and head office overheads, and replacing them with a franchisee working for himself and paying a franchisee fee, the profit performance of the store can be dramatically transformed.

(iii) By the sale of selected operations coupled with the grant of a franchise to the purchaser a business can raise capital either to enable it to reduce borrowings or to enable it to diversify its business interests.

(iv) A company with underused wholesale storage and distribution facilities can establish a franchise providing additional outlets for the products in which it deals, thus enabling it to make more economic use of its facilities.

(v) In the same way a manufacturer can establish a franchise in order to secure outlets for its products.

(vi) From a prospective franchisee's point of view there are those franchised businesses which can conveniently be added on to an existing business with which it is compatible. A good example of this sort of "marriage" would be the establishment of a car hire business on the forecourt of a motor dealer. This sort of add-on business is often described as a "fractional franchise".

Undoubtedly further applications will be developed. One must avoid approaching franchising as a rigid closely defined business method. It is quite the reverse: it is a flexible marketing method from which may lessons may be learned and applications developed.

CHAPTER 15

The British Franchise Association

THE British Franchise Association Ltd. (B.F.A.), a company limited by Guarantee, was incorporated in 1977. There were eight founder members:

—Budget Rent a Car (U.K.) Ltd.,
—Dyno-Rod plc,
—Holiday Inns (U.K.) Inc.,
—Kentucky Fried Chicken (G.B.) Ltd.,
—Prontaprint Ltd.,
—ServiceMaster Ltd.,
—Wimpy International Ltd.,
—Ziebart Mobile Transport Services Ltd.

Five of these companies, Budget Rent a Car, Holiday Inns, Kentucky Fried Chicken, ServiceMaster, and Ziebart, had clear origins in the U.S.A. Wimpy originated in the U.S.A., although the franchise development was devised and executed in the U.K. Dyno-Rod, the idea of an American, was also developed in the U.K., while Prontaprint of the eight perhaps was the only one devised and developed in the U.K., by an Englishman.

The B.F.A. now has fifty members whose business classifications are set out in Chapter 5 on pages 39 and 40.

In addition there are twenty companies listed in the B.F.A. Register, which is explained below, but basically comprises companies new to franchising.

The origins of the fifty members breaks down in this way:

Fourteen have clear origins in the U.S.A. and operate in the U.K. either directly as subsidiaries or as Master licensees.

Four have clear origins in overseas countries other than the U.S.A. Thirty-two were devised and developed in the U.K.

Applying the same approach to the companies on the Register in the emerging new franchise opportunities, the breakdown reveals:

One has a clear origin in the U.S.A. and operates in the U.K. under Master licence.

Nineteen were devised and developed in the U.K.

The trend towards the development of franchisees in the U.K. is highlighted by these figures. One can expect this trend to continue, although many U.S. franchisors who have set their sights on overseas expansion see the U.K. as a target.

The B.F.A. was originally promoted for two reasons, the first to provide franchising with a collective voice and to perform the normal functions of a "trade association"; the second was to counteract the adverse publicity which franchising had attracted.

The way in which the founder members sought to achieve these are reflected in the B.F.A.'s main objects which are set out in the Association's Memorandum of Association in the following way. It will be noted that these objects incorporate the definition of franchising commented on in Chapter 1.

3. The objects for which the Association is established are the following:

(1) To promote, protect and further the interests of franchisors, that is, those who in the course of their business grant a contractual licence (a franchise) to another party (the franchisee) which:

  (a) permits or requires the franchisee to carry on during the period of the franchise a particular business under or using a specific name belonging to or associated with the franchisor; and

  (b) entitles the franchisor to exercise continuing control during the period of the franchise over the manner in which the franchisee carries on the business which is the subject of the franchise; and

  (c) obliges the franchisor to provide the franchisee with assistance in carrying on the business which is the subject of the franchise (in relation to the organisation of the franchisee's business, the training of staff, merchandising, management or otherwise); and

  (d) requires the franchisee periodically during the period of the franchise to pay to the franchisor sums of money in consideration for the franchise or for goods or services provided by the franchisor to the franchisee; and

  (e) which is not a transaction between a holding company and its subsidiary (as defined in section 154 of the Companies Act 1948) or between subsidiaries of the same holding company or between an individual and a company controlled by him.

(2) Without prejudice to the generality of sub-clause (1):

  (a) to formulate and to establish or to adopt a code or codes of proper business conduct for franchisors and to promote and to secure their compliance with the same and with high standards of business conduct generally.

(b) to consider and to advise and decide upon and generally to deal with all questions and problems connected with or concerning franchises and the carrying on of business by means of the same; and to promote acceptance of and compliance with such advice and decisions.

(c) to promote trust and confidence in the franchises granted by members of the Association.

(d) to inform and to educate in relation to franchises and on all matters concerning the same.

(e) to promote and secure co-operative action on the part of franchisors in advancing their common interests.

(f) to promote business usages and activities likely to increase the efficiency and economy of the carrying on of business by means of franchises.

The Association in a "hand-out" describes its aims, objectives, and activities in the following manner:

The British Franchise Association was formed in 1977 by a number of leading British and international companies engaged in the distribution of goods and services through independent outlets under franchisee and licensee agreements. The aims of the B.F.A. include establishing a clear definition of the ethical franchising standards to assist members of the public, press, potential investors and government bodies in differentiating between sound business opportunities and any suspect investment offers.

The B.F.A. will provide a "forum" for the interchange of information and franchising expertise amongst members and the public, through an advisory information service designed to assist potential franchisees in making a judgement prior to selecting a final investment.

Future objectives include establishing approved education programmes, assisting with arbitration procedures and acting as a common voice in liaison with government bodies where legislation exists or is likely to be formulated.

All B.F.A. members have to conform to a stringent code of business practice, and have to undergo a detailed accreditation procedure prior to acceptance as a full member.

The B.F.A. acts as a "spokesman" for responsible franchising and represents a number of expanding sections of British business including fast food, retailing, specialist cleaning services, car and van hire, automotive protection treatments, hotels and business printing services.

Top executives from member companies bring a broad base of expertise and insight to their roles as officers of the B.F.A. providing an able and qualified leadership.

Member companies operate in diverse areas, sometimes as competitors, but all have a proven track record and successful franchisors combined with a genuine faith in franchising as a system capable of serving the public and industry with economy and responsibility.

ACTIVITIES

The B.F.A. holds regular meetings for the interchange of information and expertise between members. Nominated delegates attend International seminars and report on their findings to all members.

A comprehensive programme of events is being planned which will include seminars and conferences covering topics of interest to the membership and various sectors of the public.

Counsel is retained to act on behalf of the B.F.A. and its members where legislative changes are liable to affect ethical franchising.

An active public relations programme maintains close liaison with the media, trade press, national and provincial newspapers, magazines, radio and television, etc., to ensure they are advised of B.F.A. activities and its views of legislative and administrative proposals.

The B.F.A. also maintains a high level of contact with overseas franchise associations and was provided with valuable assistance during its formation from the U.S. based International Franchise Association.

In accordance with clause 3(2)(a) of the Association's Memorandum of Association it has adopted a code of ethics to which all members are obliged to subscribe and to observe in or about the conduct of their business. The code is as follows:

CODE OF ETHICS

1. The B.F.A.'s Code of Advertising Practice shall be based on that established by the Advertising Standards Association and shall be modified from time to time in accordance with alterations notified by the A.S.A.

   The B.F.A. will subscribe fully to the A.S.A. Code unless, on some specific issue, it is resolved by a full meeting of the Council of the B.F.A. that the A.S.A. is acting against the best interests of the public and of franchising business in general on that specific issue; in this case the B.F.A. will be required to formally notify the A.S.A., setting out the grounds for disagreement.

2. No member shall sell, offer for sale, or distribute any product or render any service, or promote the sale or distribution thereof, under any representation or condition (including the use of the name of a "celebrity") which has the tendency, capacity, or effect of misleading or deceiving purchasers or prospective purchasers.

3. No member shall imitate the trade mark, trade name, corporate identity, slogan or other mark or identification of another franchisor in any manner or form that would have the tendency or capacity to mislead or deceive.

4. Full and accurate written disclosure of all information material to the franchise relationship shall be given to the prospective franchisees within a reasonable time prior to the execution of any binding document.

5. The franchise agreement shall set forth clearly the respective obligations and responsibilities of the parties and all other terms of the relationship, and be free from ambiguity.

6. The franchise agreement and all matters basic and material to the arrangement and relationship thereby created, shall be in writing and executed copies thereof given to the franchisee.

7. A franchisor shall select and accept only those franchisees who, upon reasonable investigation, possess the basic skills, education, personal qualities, and adequate capital to succeed. There shall be no discrimination based on race, colour, religion, national origin or sex.

8. A franchisor shall exercise reasonable surveillance over the activities of his franchisees to the end that the contractual obligations of both parties are observed and the public interest safeguarded.

9. Fairness shall characterise all dealings between a franchisor and its franchisees. A franchisor shall give notice to its franchisee of any contractual breach and grant reasonable time to remedy default.

10. A franchisor shall make every effort to resolve complaints, grievances and disputes with its franchisees with good faith and goodwill through fair and reasonable direct communication and negotiation.

In considering the Association's objectives, the first factor of note is that it is established "to promote, protect and further the interest of franchisors". Quite clearly, while it is an Association of and for franchisors, however, it is of interest to examine the specific ways in which this objective is to be achieved.

Firstly, the Association has established a code of ethics "for the proper business conduct for franchisors and to promote and to secure their (franchisors') compliance with the same and with high standards of business generally". The provisions of the code of ethics are undoubtedly calculated to afford protection to franchisees or would-be franchisees in their dealings with franchisors.

Paragraphs 2 and 3 afford protection against misleading or deceiving franchisees. Paragraph 4 requires full disclosure of all material information before any binding contract is signed.

Paragraphs 5 and 6 regulate the form and procedure to be adopted in relation to the contents of franchise agreements.

Paragraph 7 requires the franchisor to act responsibly in the selection and approval of franchisees.

Paragraph 8 requires the franchisor to provide the "trouble shooting" services to the franchisee in the interests not only of both parties but also in the public interest.

Paragraphs 9 and 10 touch upon similar aspects of the continuing relationship between the franchisor and franchisee and require fairness, good faith, and goodwill to be shown by the franchisor to the franchisee in all their dealings and, in particular, in the case of alleged breaches of contractual obligations and complaints grievances, and disputes.

If members do comply with and observe the express provisions and the spirit of the code of ethics it is obvious that franchisees will obtain the benefit of the code. What, then, will happen if a franchisor fails to line up to the standards required by the code? The Articles of Association of the B.F.A. contain a fairly extensive disciplinary procedure. It is of interest to list the grounds upon which disciplinary action may be initiated which are contained in Article 75.

75. Disciplinary action may be taken against any member who:

(i) commits a breach of any code of proper business conduct adopted by the Association or with which the Association in General Meeting resolves that the members of the Association should comply; or

(ii) is otherwise guilty of illegal business conduct or of business conduct which in the opinion of the Association or of the Council is improper or unfair; or

(iii) commits any act of or involving fraud or fraudulent or negligent misrepresentation; or

(iv) makes any incorrect statement in or in relation to his application for membership of the Association; or

(v) fails to comply with an undertaking required of him by the Council pursuant to Article 84 below; or

(vi) is guilty of conduct which in the opinion of the Association or of the Council is likely to bring the practice of franchising or the Association into disrepute.

The undertaking to be given under the provisions of Article 84 is one which may be required by the Council from a member as a result of a disciplinary proceeding. Presumably this procedure would be used in a case where a franchisor could make recompense in a particular case or would be required to vary a practice or procedure which had been the subject of a valid complaint under the Association's disciplinary procedure.

The Articles establish a detailed procedure providing an opportunity for the member against whom a complaint is made to defend itself. The ultimate decision is made by the Council of the Association in accordance with the requirements of Articles 84, 85 and 86, which are here reproduced.

84. The Council in Disciplinary Meeting, having considered the material and representations put before it, may:

(i) reject the complaint; or

(ii) if they determine that the member who is the subject of the complaint has been guilty of an act or conduct within Article 75 above:

(a) require the member concerned to give such written undertaking to the Association as the Council shall think fit; or

(b) suspend the member concerned for such period (not exceeding eighteen months) as they consider appropriate; or

(c) expel the member concerned from the Association.

85. If a member shall refuse to give a written undertaking required of him pursuant to Article 84 above, the Council may after giving the member concerned an opportunity to make representations to it orally or in writing, suspend him for such period (not exceeding eighteen months) as they consider appropriate or expel him from the Association.

86. Decisions of the Council in Disciplinary Meeting other than a decision to expel a member shall be taken by a simple majority and the Chairman shall in case of an equality of votes have a second or casting vote; a decision to expel a member from the Association shall require a majority of two-thirds of the members of the Council present and voting.

A member against whom an order for expulsion is made has a right to appeal to all the members in General Meeting.

In order to assist new entrants to franchising to participate in B.F.A. activities and to achieve the requisite standard for acceptance as a member the B.F.A. introduced its "Register of Developing Franchises". The B.F.A. introduces the Register to applicants with the following explanation:

1. The B.F.A. receives enquiries from potential franchisees at a rate of 4,000 p.a. and, if telephone enquiries as to the status of various franchising companies are included, this figure is of the order of 8,000 enquiries p.a.

    Further publicity is planned, and the B.F.A. is now established as an authoritative source of information about franchising companies.

    If your company is on the approved Register, it will be brought to the attention of the investing public at every possible opportunity and where enquiries are made about a registered company the B.F.A. will be able to give a qualified and satisfactory response to the enquirer.
2. Companies on the register will have continuing contact with the B.F.A.: registered companies will be invited to attend B.F.A. functions such as workshops (discussion groups), seminars, and working luncheons, so that the executives concerned can benefit directly from contact with experienced members of the franchising community.
3. The B.F.A. executive and elected officers will provide advice to developing companies to help these companies to avoid making mistakes which the established franchisors have identified over the years—mistakes which can inhibit growth and cause unnecessary problems for both the franchisor company and the franchisees.
4. Membership of the B.F.A should follow after a qualifying period on the Register, subject to development proceeding satisfactorily and approval by the Accreditation Committee.

The qualifications for admission to the Register are:

1. That the business offered by the company to the franchisee has been tested in the market-place over a period and is demonstrably sound.
2. That the company is stable and has an effective management and organisation, and appropriate finance or cash flow to match the expected growth.
3. That the terms and conditions offered to the franchisee shall be reasonable and equitable.
4. That franchising knowledge has been acquired or is being developed at a satisfactory rate: in that context pilot schemes (company-owned or franchised), licences from overseas, and a successful track record in the U.K., may all be relevant.

The applicant is also required to enter into undertakings with the B.F.A. to the following effect:

1. The company undertakes to make disclosure of material facts to the potential franchisee and to the B.F.A. by completing and, when necessary, updating the Disclosure Document.
2. The company undertakes to conform to the B.F.A. Code of Ethics, a copy of which is attached to this paper.

The forms of application for membership of the B.F.A. and for inclusion in the Register of Developing Franchisees are set out in Appendix B.

Since its formation, the B.F.A. has become established as a recognised voice of franchising by government and media. It has attracted to its membership most of the leading companies operating in franchising and many companies who are entering the field look to the B.F.A. for guidance. The B.F.A. also receives many enquiries from prospective franchisees who are seeking guidance. The B.F.A. sells basic information packs to both prospective franchisors and prospective franchisees.

The B.F.A. office receives upwards of 10,000 enquiries a year and many of these enquiries are from those seeking advice and assistance.

The B.F.A. also runs an extensive educational programme headed by seminars which have catered for the whole range of interests. Their programme has included:

—Prospective franchisees, and how to evaluate a franchise.
—Is a business franchisable?
—How to set up a franchise.
—International franchising.
—Two-day courses in franchising.
—Franchising seminars in conjunction with the Institute of Marketing.
—Franchising—a brief for the company director, in conjunction with the Institute of Directors.

The B.F.A. is particularly anxious to continue a very full programme of educational activities because ultimately the more understanding there is the greater the likelihood that standards will be raised. The more prospective franchisees understand franchising the less likely they will to be defrauded by those who cloak their activities with an unjustified façade of franchising.

One should not assume that the B.F.A.'s progress has all been achieved without problems. Some member companies have had their difficulties and withdrawn. Some disputes between franchisor members and individual franchisees have emerged, and the B.F.A. has assisted in the resolution of the dispute without the need for costly and lengthy litigation. It would be impossible to achieve the Utopian state in which all problems and difficulties would cease to exist. There will be B.F.A. members who will fail and there will be franchisees of B.F.A.

members who are disgruntled and dissatisfied. The strength of the B.F.A. will be dependent upon:

(a) its skill in investigating applications for membership so as to ensure that no questionable franchisees are admitted;
(b) the observance by its members of the code of ethics, not merely in principle, but also in spirit;
(c) rigorous attention to warning signs about members which emerge from complaints and criticism;
(d) its ability to persuade members to change undesirable practices;
(e) the maintenance of its reputation so that membership is an achievement which enhances the status of the member.

In its brief six years of existence, the B.F.A. has made significant progress under the full-time directorship of Tony Jacobsen, ably assisted by his wife Dr. Christine Jacobsen. Their dedication to the B.F.A. has been a significant factor in its establishment and growth. On 1 January 1984 Tony Dutfield, who was Chairman of the B.F.A. in 1983, in his capacity as representative of Wimpy International Ltd. succeeded Tony Jacobsen as Director of the B.F.A. The B.F.A. is now moving into a new phase of development; one expects that with its present sound foundations it will continue to achieve its objectives.

CHAPTER 16

How to Internationalise
your Franchise

THERE is only one country for which statistics are available which give some indication of the international growth prospects for franchising. The publication *Franchising in the Economy 1981–1983*, published by the U.S. Department of Commerce, provides the following list of the number of U.S. franchisors who have exported their operations and the number of outlets which have been opened.

	Franchisors	Outlets
Canada	209	7068
Carribean	76	541
Europe (excluding U.K.)	75	3393
Japan	63	3999
Asia (excluding Japan)	59	746
U.K.	52	2113
Australia	49	1693
South America	42	318
Mexico	35	403
Middle East	31	184
Africa	29	515
Central America	25	140
New Zealand	13	303

It should be borne in mind that many franchisors involved in international operations are present in more than one of the areas covered. The total number of franchisors involved in overseas franchising is 288 and a further 121 U.S. companies have indicated that they are considering the extension of their operations overseas by the end of 1984.

In reaching the decision to "go international" with a franchise operation, a number of factors will have to be considered. Many of these factors are not peculiar to the franchise system. They are factors which would have to be considered whether or not franchising was involved.

Even if one is not considering the introduction of the franchise into one's domestic operation, the possibility that the business may best be expanded overseas by the franchise method of marketing should be considered. This approach has been adopted by some with advantage.

The first consideration is one which must have attention, even before the actual decision is taken to develop the expansion of the business by the introduction of a franchise. The franchisor is developing and acquiring many industrial and intellectual property rights. The principal visible right will be the trade mark and/or the trade name under which he carries on business. These rights will all need the widest possible protection. With this in mind the possibility of going international must be considered long before the decision to do so is actually taken.

In England, while it is possible to obtain a trade mark in respect of goods, it is not possible to do so in respect of services. While a recent attempt, by a member of Parliament to introduce a private members bill in the U.K. to enable service mark registration to be available was unsuccessful, the Government have now accepted the principle. Legislation should follow in the near future, although when it will be passed and implemented is still a matter of speculation*. There are some countries in which the facility of service mark registration is available. Many franchise operations are developed around names which are associated with the provision of services rather than with the supply or manufacture of goods. In England, therefore, in the case of the supply of services, a franchisor has to rely upon his common law rights which are based on reputation, extent of the knowledge of the name and reputation by the public which might be misled by a third party trying to steal the name.

In those countries where service mark registration is permitted (e.g. the U.S.A.) basically the same protection is afforded to those who register such marks as is available to the holder of a trade mark in respect of goods. It should also be borne in mind that success breeds imitators, and in international terms there are those territories in which it is possible to register a mark in respect of a name which it is not

* The legislation has now been passed by Parliament and Service Mark registration will be available by October 1987.

intended to exploit, except for the purpose of requiring the true owner of the name when he enters that territory to pay a large sum in order to buy the rights to his own name.

It is therefore sensible at the earliest possible moment to review one's international intentions, so that enlightened decisions can be made about whether, and if so where, to register trade marks and/or service marks for future use at the appropriate time.

There is an additional factor to consider, and that is that one will often find that what is a very successful mark in one country is a complete disaster in another. There have been cases in which a successful and inoffensive mark which is employed in one country is an indecent word in the language of a foreign country.

It is important, therefore, to establish as soon as possible after it is appreciated that there is international scope for the development of the franchise, an international registration programme. A balance has to be drawn, and it is desirable to obtain advice from those who practice in the field of international trade marks, be they lawyers or trade mark agents; but in some cases failure to use a mark for a given period of time might lead to a loss of rights in favour of those who are aware of the way in which money can be made out of the exploitation of others' names.

Apart from the trade mark aspects of the industrial and intellectual property rights, there can also be (although this is much more rare in a franchise situation) a patent to be protected. Patent registration requirements are much more stringent than trade mark, in that normally there is a very limited period within which patents can be applied for and registered. Again, if a patent is involved, proper professional advice should be sought immediately. Most lawyers or patent agents who deal in this field will be aware of the need to make application in as many places as might be thought desirable, bearing in mind the future international prospects. The advice given will have to be weighed, of course, against the cost of multiple international registrations.

Apart from the formal methods of registration which are available for trade marks and patents, the other industrial and intellectual property rights such as know-how, ideas and trade secrets are not normally protectable by any form of registration. The protection of these rights depends upon contractual terms entered into between those who own them and those who enter their employment or into licensing arrangements with them.

Furthermore, there is the question of copyright. Very often the franchisor owns the copyright in much of the printed material which is produced for the purpose of the franchise scheme. Methods and effectiveness of copyright protection in the various jurisdictions in which it is intended to expand should be explored. Additionally, appropriate steps should be taken to ensure that the copyright in any translations which have to be prepared into the language of the territory into which one is franchising should be vested in the franchisor and not in those who prepare the translations if translation is to be the responsibility of the franchisee.

These steps then should be taken early on, and before the final decision to go international has been taken.

Having decided to go international, one is then faced with a number of interrelated evaluations, the handling whereof will depend upon the method chosen for going international. It will therefore be sensible to consider the various methods available before dealing with the important area of market research and acceptability.

There are five methods of dealing with the international franchising arrangements.

1. *Master licence*. This would involve the granting of a licence to a company or person in the target territory, granting him the rights for the whole of that territory. He would acquire his know-how and the rights to make use of the package from the franchisor, and he would then either operate his own company and stores under licence or would exploit the territory by means of the franchise system, and by granting sub-licences within the territory to the operational franchisees.

2. *Branch operations*. This would involve the establishment by the franchisor of a branch in the target territory and the exploitation by him of the system in the territory by the granting of franchises.

3. *Subsidiary*. This would involve the establishment by the franchisor of a subsidiary and, in the same way as would be the case with the branch operation, the subsidiary would exploit the territory by the granting of franchises.

4. *Joint venture*. This would involve the franchisor in establishing a joint company with a company or person within the territory, and the exploitation of the territory either by means of operations owned by the joint venture or the franchising route, or a combination of both.

5. *Direct licence*. This would be the grant of a licence (franchise) by the franchisor direct to the operational unit owner, with the franchisor

providing direct back up and support. This can only really work in practice if the franchisor has established some form of presence in the country to provide the on-the-spot assistance, or if the two countries concerned are not that far away from each other, that direct support cannot be given on a frequent basis and without delays. Sometimes a franchisor will grant a direct licence and establish a subsidiary company in the target territory to provide the back-up for the franchisees.

There is not very much evidence in the U.K. of direct franchising of individual units from overseas. Most companies choose one of the other methods. It must be mentioned that the International Franchise Association recently published a survey which did reveal that almost as many of its members who franchise internationally do so by the direct franchising of individual units as by the Master Franchise method. One is inclined to think that the factor which distorts this picture is direct licensing into Canada which, along with Japan and the United Kingdom, is the most popular target for American franchise companies at the moment.

Whichever of the methods is chosen one is vulnerable in the choice of the right local person with whom to work. Frequently in international situations one is confronted with the situation where the selection of the local person, be it Managing Director of a subsidiary, Master Licensee or Joint Venturer, was not very happily made. The person selected did not possess the skills which he professed to have, nor was he able to achieve what both hoped would be capable of achievement.

Even in the case of joint venture arrangements with well-established companies problems have arisen and established arrangements have had to be unwound.

Whichever approach is adopted it is essential to provide operational support for the venture from the franchisor. It is therefore crucial that, before one can commit oneself to the international route, one must be satisfied that one can spare the operational staff.

The greater the speed of growth in one's own country, the greater will be the need to keep the operational staff available for this purpose and the more reluctant the franchisor will be to send them to a foreign country where the returns may be lower and longer in coming. It may seem strange, but there is no doubt whatever that whenever businessmen decide to go international with their franchise schemes, they drop their guard and forget the normal protective measures which they would take in their own territory to ensure that the person with whom they are dealing is what he purports to be. This dropping of the guard only leads to a failure to achieve any forward progress, and it usually turns out to be a costly failure as well. Why it is that businessmen are more trusting of their counterparts in a foreign country than they would be in their own remains to be seen, but it is a phenomenon which exists and which the author has seen over and over. It must be avoided. One should therefore take care to guard against making the mistakes which others have made.

The franchisor going international must be on his guard and must be very careful indeed about the person with whom he chooses to do business. In the same way as one would take great care in the selection of franchisees in one's own country, one must exercise even greater care over the selection of master licensee, joint venture partner, or the local mangement of the subsidiary company.

The most common mistakes which are made in international franchising are:

(i) poor choice of local partner, licensee or staff;
(ii) a failure to recognise the need for and to commit sufficient financial and manpower resources to the venture whatever method is chosen;
(iii) a failure to recognise differences in social and cultural attitudes and in life style; and
(iv) an underestimate of the time which it takes to become established in the target territory.

Bearing these problems in mind one must initially make a decision about the method which it is proposed to adopt. There are then four categories of persons with whom one might deal:

1. one's own staff,
2. locally employed staff,
3. the licensee who may take up the rights for the territory, and
4. a possible joint venture partner.

Once one goes past this stage there may be the assessment and selection of franchisees. Whichever method of exploitation is chosen one will have to decide which of one's own staff are available and free to go to the territory and spend whatever time is needed there initially in order to get things off the ground.

Local staff will have to be selected, taken on and trained and if there is to be a licensee and/or joint venture partner he must be selected very carefully.

In relation to each of these categories the franchisor must give considerable thought to his approach. Criteria must be established for the selection, not only of his own staff whom he may consider suitable, but very much so of local staff, licensees, joint venture partners and ultimately, franchisees. The criteria may well differ in some material respects from those which have already been established in connection with the franchise in the original concept. One cannot emphasise too much how much care and thought must be taken or given to the problem at this stage.

In order that there should be no misunderstanding, the requirement for capital with which to finance the development of the scheme must clearly be identified and quantified. Each of the parties to the arrangement must know who is to provide what and when. Any local financing requirement must be arranged, usually by the licensee or other person present within the territory, although in the case of joint ventures the financing requirements should clearly be specified in the joint venture agreement.

If a prospective licensee or joint venture partner says he has the connections and will be able to raise whatever sums are necessary, do not rest content with such assurances. Check out the capabilities of the licensee to do just what he is asserting. There are many who speak airily of their "magnificent" contacts and their ability to produce finance, whose ability to do just that vanishes into thin air when the task is actually required. Do not take such statements on trust. Check them out. Check them out early so that problems can be identified early enough for the right remedial action to be taken.

One then moves on to the market research. In the same way as one is exhorted to establish a pilot operation before nationally marketing a franchise, it is almost as important if not perhaps even more so (if that is possible) when going international to establish a pilot scheme. There are many factors which will have to be considered in establishing the pilot scheme, quite apart from the availability of the equipment which is necessary and technical differences in specification and capabilities of that equipment.

Equipment manufactured in one country may not be compatible with equipment manufactured in the target country or in the range of utility supplies available. Electricity is one of the supplies which can cause these problems and conversion can be more costly than making use of alternative local supplies.

It is unlikely that a totally unamended scheme or concept will work as effectively in one country as it did in another. Markets are different;

people are different; habits are different; customs are different. All these have to be explored and taken into account; and in a pilot operation fine tuning can take place to ensure that the transition, from what is acceptable in one territory to what is acceptable in another, is made effectively.

An example of the sort of differences with which one is confronted, is the difference between rental values of properties in the U.S.A. and in the U.K. Anyone from the U.S.A. looking at rental values of a property in the U.K. will conclude, on the turnover and margins which he achieves in the U.S.A., that it is not possible profitably to trade in the U.K. using his scheme. However, rental values are invariably related to turnover capabilities and, when one takes into account the differences in currency values and local spending power, very often it is found that the increased rental is more than amply compensated for by the increased turnover and that at the end of the day the rental as a percentage of gross turnover is not that markedly different.

That, as well as other factors which go to make up the overall cost of running a business, will have to be discovered by trial and error; and that is what pilot operations are all about.

It should be mentioned that if one is approaching an international franchise as a prospective master licensee (franchisee) or joint venture partner it is essential—although it may be expensive—to visit the country in which the scheme originates and see how it works in that country. If it has gone international into other territories before the one in which you are interested, then it would be a good thing to visit the operation and see it in action in that territory and to have discussions with the licensees in that country to see how satisfied they are and how well the transition went.

Having decided on the course which is to be adopted, and that the market exists, the franchisor's training programme has to be adapted so that training can be given and for the transference of know-how and trade secrets, bearing in mind that pilot operation lessons can be transferred to the operational personnel in the jurisdiction.

In the initial stages it is not uncommon for this training to take place at the franchisor's existing training establishments in his own country. International expansion can proceed in some cases to the point where training facilities can be established in various parts of the world and training take place on a regional basis; but in the same way as training and transference of know-how have to take place where the franchise is only on a national basis, similar arrangements have to be made on an international basis.

Later on there is discussion of the legal issues which have to be faced but coupled with the training, and embodied in the contract which is entered into, will of course be the grant of the necessary licence which will permit the use of the industrial and intellectual property rights of the franchisor.

Again, whichever course is adopted, the franchisor will have to make arrangements for some presence to exist within the jurisdiction. If there is a joint venture or a master licence arrangement then obviously the presence will be more infrequent and at fewer intervals than would be the case if there were direct licensing branch operations or subsidiaries when some form of local management structure may have to be established; and again, if one is dealing through a number of countries which are clustered together within an area it may be possible to have a regional office out of which the management support, and other services which are to be provided, can be made available to all those within the region.

In addition to this, a marketing strategy will have to be devised and arrangements made for the expenditure of the marketing and advertising funds on a local, national and sometimes international regional basis, as the franchise develops in its international strength.

As we have seen with the development of a franchise on a national basis in the chapters earlier in this book there are many methods for dealing with marketing and promotion and for consultation with franchisees in these respects, and these approaches have equal validity in terms of international operations. This brings us naturally to the crucial area of communications.

Clearly responsibilities will have to be established between the two parties to the arrangement or, if direct licensing takes place, between all the parties to the arrangement, to ensure that each knows his role in the communications network which is established, and that each complies with the requirements. If communications are fundamental to the establishment and development of a national chain, how much more so are they vital in international terms where differences of language and emphasis can cause misunderstandings which are not warranted by the circumstances. Information flows in both directions must be established and maintained. Parties must be available to each other, and the franchisor's responsibilities to provide field support and back up are no less great in the international arrangements than they are in the national; although one must point out that in international terms the back up can often be far less significant a factor than in national terms, unless of course there are branch or direct licensing arrangements.

In terms of master licence and joint venture, back up is normally given to the master licensee or the joint venture partner, whose responsibility it is then nationally to provide the support to the individual operational franchisees. The background of support, visits and back up from the franchisor in his own country to the master licensee or joint venture partner is on a much lower scale than the responsibility which they would each have to the operational local franchises.

These factors are usually spelled out in some detail in the contract.

The fact that one is dealing in terms of an international arrangement; rather than national, will not detract from the franchisor's product and/or services innovation responsibilities. No business can stand still, and the fact that it is organised on an international basis does not detract from the franchisor's responsibility to ensure that in international and national terms his franchise remains just that one step ahead of the opposition. Product and/or services innovation is still a crucial factor which cannot be overlooked.

As has already been mentioned, many of the responsibilities and duties will have been dealt with in the contract, but there are some cautionary notes.

Basically, if one is a potential franchisee on a master licence or a joint venture partner basis, beware of the common approach by successful overseas franchise operations who advertise exclusive rights in your territory for the operation, for a fairly substantial front end fee. The drawback, of course, is that the offeror has never even taken the trouble to see whether the operation is viable in the target territory, or whether they have anything in that territory which can be sold. Often one is offered, under the umbrella of a franchise, exclusive distribution rights for a product, again for payment of a substantial front end fee, not related to the supply of stock and without the market ever having been researched to see whether viable returns could ever be achieved.

Another problem which frequently arises in relation to contracts is an insistence by franchisors from one territory on utilising their own lawyers who lack familiarity with the laws of the target territory, but nonetheless accept the burden of advice as if there were no difference. This can cause a number of problems and indeed, in practice, it does.

For example, as between the U.S.A. and the U.K. there are differences in terminology and expressions which mean one thing in the U.S.A. and something different in the U.K., or indeed may mean nothing at all, and vice versa.

Next we have the problem in that those lawyers will always opt, if they think they can get away with it, for the laws of their own territory to be applied to a contract, and there are many arguments on this issue. The author takes the view that the correct law to apply to any contract is the law of the place where it will have to be enforced, because ultimately—whatever court decisions are obtained elsewhere—enforcement must take place in the area in which the franchisee is to be found.

The next problem which arises from these forms of contractual approach is that the contract is often unacceptable because it is not understood in the target territory. There can be provisions which are valid and binding under the stipulated law which could be void and unenforceable, in some material respects, in the target territory, notwithstanding the applicability of the foreign law specified in the contract.

Furthermore, in master licence arrangements, contracts are sometimes produced which bear no relation whatever to the nature of the transaction but which are merely a botched attempt, by inserting one or two additional provisions, to make applicable as a master franchise contract the provisions of the normal franchise agreement which is used for individual operational units in the franchisor's territory.

If it is the intention of franchisors to save expense by adopting this approach, many who have followed this course have now found that they did not save money. On the contrary, they lost both time and a considerable amount of money in disentangling themselves from the mess into which they had got—a quite avoidable mess, one might add, with a little bit of sensible foresight.

There are a number of legal aspects which should be considered in conducting what one would call a "legal audit" when going into a new territory.

Fortunately, with the growth of international franchising so the sources of information are developing. The Franchising Committee of the Anti-Trust Section of the American Bar Association, under the then Chairmanship of Philip F. Zeidman, has published a *Survey of Foreign Laws and Regulations affecting Franchising* which contains common form information as a reference guide to laws and regulations in some twenty-two countries. In each country a lawyer with experience of franchising was identified and prepared the information. Further, the Section on Business Law of the International Bar Association has established an International Franchising Committee which has members from many countries. The proceedings of that committee's first meeting has been published in 1984 under the title *International Franchising—An Overview*. As international experience and interest grows, the sources of information will expand and be more widely available.

The following areas should be the subject of the "legal audit":

1. Legal Status of Parties and Nature of Legal Relationships

Quite apart from an investigation and assessment of the capacity in which parties can contract, particularly if one of the parties is an overseas company, consideration must be given to whether or not there are special local laws which might result in the franchisee being regarded as an agent or employee of the franchisor. In most franchise arrangements the parties go to great lengths to ensure the establishment of the franchisee as an independent contractor, and to ensure that the franchisee has no power to bind the franchisor and that the franchisee is not the agent or partner or employee of the franchisor. There can be special laws which might affect the contractual arrangement between the parties and impose upon the franchisor obligations both to third parties and of a financial character in the forms of social security taxes which are not part of the normal calculations made or considerations taken into account when establishing a franchise scheme.

2. Government Attitudes

It is important to see whether the Government has an attitude towards franchising and to the import of know-how and trade secrets (see below under No. 16). By investigating government attitudes and existing policies, it may be possible to take advantage of the special incentive schemes and grants which can be available for certain types of business or industry which would make the franchise venture more certain of success and more profitable from the point of view of franchisor and franchisee.

3. Competition Laws

These must always be considered. In the U.S.A. they are such an important factor as almost to overwhelm franchise arrangements.

Many countries are now adopting competition laws, the stated objective whereof is to make anti-competitive practices unlawful with a view to stimulating competition. These laws are not directed at franchise transactions but often affect franchising because of the generality of their application. While one would not advocate that franchising should be free from legal control, certainly it would be better if some of the more rigid systems of anti-trust regulation which exist were capable of taking into account the very many plus factors inherent in franchising which their rigidity does not permit to be taken into consideration. Many of the practices inherent in the franchise transaction—tied sales, price fixing and other controls—are capable of being affected by anti-trust legislation; and the effect must therefore be very carefully considered.

4. Industrial and Intellectual Property Laws

This has already been discussed earlier in the chapter in relation to the protection which should be obtained for the existing package. Having secured the protection for the rights which the franchisor has, the laws to be considered so that the right method for exploitation and protection can be utilised.

5. Taxation

The taxation effects on the franchise scheme have to be considered. There may be local sales taxes to be taken into account and certainly, in operating the pilot scheme, care has to be taken to ensure that the effect of local tax laws on the scheme is fully taken into account. Variations in accounting and reporting systems and procedures which may be necessary also have to be devised properly and incorporated into the locally developed concept.

From the point of view of international tax considerations, one should commence by investigating whether double taxation agreements exist between the franchisor's own country and the target territory, to see what is the effect. If there are no direct double taxation agreements or if the terms are not thought sufficiently beneficial, then investigation should be made of the best route for the income of the franchisor to enable the effects of multiple taxation to be minimised. Very often careful selection of the route through which the monies flow, by taking advantage of double taxation agreements, can achieve a great deal in ensuring that the maximum amount of money reaches its ultimate intended destination. There are, of course, cash flow considerations and if withhold taxes are imposed to any substantial extent it can have a considerable adverse effect on the cash flow of the franchisor and on his ability to finance the operation in the initial stages and from the income generated.

6. Corporate Laws

In deciding whether to set up a branch or operational subsidiary, apart from the taxation implications of operating in this way, the local corporate laws have to be considered to see whether some form of incorporation is necessary or desirable or whether there are, as is in the case of the United Kingdom, requirements for registration of foreign companies which establish a place of business. Some territories have prohibitions against foreign nationals owning the majority of shares in companies which are incorporated. Corporate laws also need to be studied to the extent that franchisees may choose to incorporate the business which is to be licensed. The franchisor will have to evolve some method for ensuring that shareholders and directors cannot acquire the know-how and trade secrets and subsequently use them in competition with the franchisor. A clear understanding of the corporate laws and the roles, duties and responsibilities of shareholders and directors, and the means by which their compliance with any contracts limiting the scope of the use to which they can put the franchisor's know-how and trade secrets, must be undertaken and the appropriate steps taken.

7. Special Franchise Laws

The U.S.A., with its Federal and State system, abounds in a multiplicity of franchise laws. There are disclosure requirements, registration requirements, some statutes affecting franchisors' rights to terminate or to refuse renewal to franchisees. So far as the U.S.A. is concerned, one can almost be offending against some legal requirement even in discussing the grant of a franchise. Legal advice at the earliest point, even before negotiations, is advisable. There are no franchise laws as such throughout the E.E.C. territories but—for example, The Fair Trading Act 1973 in the United Kingdom—there are laws prohibiting the establishment of pyramid schemes. There are some franchise laws in Canada and South America (Andean Pact Countries), while in Australia the sale of a franchise is treated as a sale of a security and Japan has issued guidelines on the application of Antitrust Laws to franchising. At the moment—apart from those countries and the effect which competition laws have on franchising—there are few countries throughout the world which have special laws which directly affect franchising.

8. Special Industry Laws

The franchisor should investigate to see whether the target territory has any laws which concern or affect the type of operation in which he is engaged. For example, in the fast food or restaurant business in the United Kingdom there is legislation which regulates standards of cleanliness in the interests of public health, also By-laws, and similar provisions apply in other countries. These requirements must carefully be checked out by the franchisor because it is only on recognising the existence and extent of these laws that the franchisor can properly adapt his concepts to the target territory's requirements.

9. Property Laws

Laws affecting real estate and leasehold property vary from territory to territory and what may be permissible in one country may not be in another. In some cases there may be protection for business tenants and in others there may not be. Careful evaluation has to be made of property laws to see whether the manner in which the franchisor's scheme is structured in his home territory is capable of being repeated in the target territory. If it is not, adjustments may have to be made to take into account the differences and some fundamental rethinking may have to be engaged in. This is particularly the case where franchisors wish to retain ownership or control of premises.

10. Exchange controls

Some countries have restrictions on the import and export of currency. It is necessary to ascertain whether such restrictions exist and, if so, what they are. There may be a requirement that consent is obtained to inward investment, that it is given only on certain conditions. These considerations may affect the right of the investor to remit profits in whole or in part. Careful evaluation will have to be made to see how these laws affect the franchisor's investment. There is little point in selling know-how and granting rights to others to exercise the opportunity to carry on business under franchise if it is a profitless exercise for the franchisor, in the sense that he is unable to turn is entitlement to income into cash in his hand except in the target territory where he may have little use for it.

11. Limitations on Royalties

In some territories, usually coupled with the exchange control requirements, there can be limitations imposed on the rate of royalties and whether or not royalties can be paid at all. Certain countries take the view that low-grade know-how and trade secrets should not entitle the owner to any royalty income. Some take the view that the royalty income should be limited for a period of time, after which no further charge can be made. One is not speaking of franchising in any denigratory sense when referring to it as "low-grade know-how", but compared wih the high-technology manufacturing industry the know-how which a franchisor has applied to the operation of a service business is usually on a much lower grade. Whether or not the franchisor is prepared to accept that his know-how is low grade it is the attitude of the target jurisdiction which is relevant, and there are some which have very rough-and-ready guides which do not necessarily make sense when approached objectively.

12. Contract Laws

The law of contract will, of course differ from country to country. Our different legal systems—the common law system, the civil law system—and even where the same systems apply different legislative approaches, lead to differences in the legal requirements which have to be considered and taken into account. One cannot assume that contracts can necessarily be entered into on the same basis from one country to another. Great care must be taken before entering into any commitments to ensure that the correct form and procedure is followed.

13. Zoning/Planning Laws

Careful investigation has to be made to discover the extent to which any restrictions on the use to which premises can be put—any building requirements or building regulations—affect the proposed schemes. Again, we have the classic example of roadside locations, particularly for fast food operations in the U.S.A., for which planning permission would just not be obtained in the U.K. This difference can have a marked effect on the operation, the layout of facilities and the rate at which the franchise chain can grow: so much that it is possible when calculations of growth rate are taken into account, coupled with the difficulty in obtaining suitable sites for particular types of business, a completely different financial projection emerges from what the franchisor might originally have anticipated.

The local regulations in relation to building may require a higher standard of construction that is normally built into the capital requirement projections, and unless a thorough investigation is made of these factors, the franchisor is not in a position to give the right guidance to franchisees or indeed to know the extent to which his operation is viable.

14. Employment Laws

There are wide variations in employment laws, and a wide range of add-on costs to the employer, depending upon the degree of social security available in the jurisdiction. There can also be legislation which inhibits the ability of the franchisor or the employer to fire staff without being liable for compensation payments. These laws must be assessed and realistic decisions made about how to cope with the differences which exist between different territories.

15. Excise and Duties

The cost of importing materials and equipment, plant and machinery must take into account—apart from shipping costs—any excise or other duties which may be levied on them in the target country. This, coupled with the need to make technical changes in equipment to which reference has already been made, may require the franchisor to use locally manufactured products or products manufactured in the same trading area to which the excise, taxes and duties may not apply or may not bear such a high rate. It is clearly a crucial factor to know the precise cost of import and excise taxes and duties which are a significant element in cost calculations.

16. Import/Export Controls

Some territories have restrictions on what may or may not be imported or exported, and also certain standards may be set which must be achieved before imports are allowed. There are also, sometimes, quotas limiting how much can be imported from certain countries. The franchisor must be sure that whatever he requires to import into a target territory, it must be possible to do so; and his product requirements in this respect must be capable of meeting the criteria established by the target territory in order to qualify for import or alternative arrangements made.

International franchising can have many rewards, but the rewards will only be commensurate with the thoroughness with which the franchisor prepares to take this giant step. In the same way as one is cautioned against nationally franchising prematurely just because the franchisee is there, one is also to be cautioned against franchising prematurely on an international basis. The pitfalls are just as great and the risk that someone will steal your ideas and know-how, and establish better rights to them in the other territory than you yourself can establish, is much greater.

International franchising approached with enlightened caution, and with care and thoroughness in preparation and researching the territory, the market and the people with whom you will be dealing, can be a very profitable exercise.

Extracts of Franchises from *Franchise Opportunities Handbook* published by U.S. Department of Commerce

THE *Franchise Opportunities Handbook* is published each year by the U.S. Department of Commerce. It is prepared by Andrew Kostecka in the Office of Consumer Goods and Service Industries Bureau of Industrial Economics. The publication, which lists 1,142 franchise opportunities, does not constitute an endorsement or recommendation by the Department of Commerce, nor does it represent a complete list of franchisors in the U.S.A.

One surprising feature is the amount of turnover each year in the franchisees which are listed. In compiling the list which follows it was noted that approximately 40% of the companies which were listed in the 1980 edition did not appear on the list in 1983 and there are therefore many franchises which come and go on a very short-term basis. The remarkable success of franchising is probably sustained by the fact that in the U.S.A. fifty-seven companies with 1,000 or more units each dominate franchising and account for 53% of all sales and 55% of all outlets.

The list well illustrates the diverse nature of franchise opportunities and the many applications of the principles of franchise marketing to many different types of business.

Automotive Products/Service
(22 out of a total listing of 90)

AAMCO Automatic Transmissions Inc.	Repair and reconditioning of automatic car transmissions

ABC Mobile Brake	Mobile brake and silencer repairs
Aid Auto Stores Inc.	Retain sales of car parts and accessories
Automatch, Inc.	Computerised listing of used vehicles
Cap-A Radiator Shops of America, Inc.	Service against radiators, heaters and conditioners
Drive Line Service, Inc.	Complete drive shaft repair service
Econo Lube N'Tune, Inc.	Lubrication and tune-up shop
E.P.I Inc.	"Sparley Washmobile" car wash equipment
The Firestone Tire & Rubber Co.	Tyre sales and service
B.F. Goodrich Company	Tyre sales and service
The Goodyear Tire & Rubber Company	Tyre sales and service
Interstate Automatic Transmission Co., Inc.	Transmission centres
Jiffiwash, Inc.	Mobile industrial vehicle cleaning
MAACO Enterprises, Inc.	Car spraying
Midas International Corp.	Exhaust brake and shock absorber service
Miracle Auto Painting	Car spraying
Mollen's Auto Audio Marketing Corp.	Sale installation and servicing of auto sound equipment and electronics
Parts Plus	Car parts and accessories
Perma-Shine, Inc.	Preservation of automotive paint
Precision Tune, Inc.	Tune-up centres
Tuff-Kote Dinol, Inc.	Rustproofing
Ziebart Rustproofing Co.	Automotive appearance and protection service

Beauty Salons/Supplies
(4 out of a total listing of 19)

Edie Adams Cut & Curl	Beauty salons

The Barbers, Hairstyling for Men and Women, Inc.	Men's and women's hairstyling
Joan M. Cable's La Femma Beauty Salons, Inc.	Unisex haircutting/Beauty salons
Roffler Industries, Inc.	Hair styling and hair care preparations

Business Aids/Services
(24 out of a total listing of 122)

Allied Business Brokers, Inc.	Assist in sale and merger of mid-sized businesses
American Dynamics Corp.	Financial advisors
Audit Controls, Inc.	Collection of overdue accounts
Barter Systems International	Organising the trading of goods and services between businessmen
H & R Block, Inc.	Preparation of income tax returns
Business Consultants of America	Business advisory service
Business Data Services, Inc.	Financial and management service to business
Comprehensive Accounting Corp.	Computerised book-keeping services
Contacts Influential	Business directories
Eastern Onion, Inc.	Singing telegrams
Federal Energy Systems, Inc.	Energy management
The Headquarters Companies	Leases executive offices with full support services
Hicks Pension Services	Pensions and profit-sharing administration and planning
HomeCall, Inc.	Home care services
Mail Boxes Etc. U.S.A.	Postal and business service centres
Marcoin, Inc.	Business advisory services
Muzak	Sound systems
Nationwide Income Tax Service Co.	Income tax returns for individuals
Newcomers Service	Service to introduce newcomers to local businesses and services
Telecheck Services, Inc.	Personal cheque verification systems

TV Facts   Localised television guides
Unified Neighbors of America, Inc. Localised consumer oriented
                                             newletter
Western Appraisers   Loss adjusters
Edwin K. Williams & Co.   Advisory and book-keeping
                                             services to small businesses

Camp Grounds
(2 out of a total listing of 4)

Kampgrounds of America, Inc.   Camping and service facilities,
                                     accommodation for vehicles
Yogi Bear's Jellystone Park   Rental and condominium camp
  Camp-Resorts   research developments

Car/Caravan/Truck/Rentals
(5 out of a total listing of 17)

Avis   Car and truck rentals
Budget Rent A Car Corp.   Rental of new cars
Rent-a-Wreck   Used car rentals
Dollar Rent A Car Systems, Inc. Car and truck rentals, particularly
                                   at airports
Hertz Corp.   Car and truck rentals and vehicle
                                   leasing

Children's Stores/Furniture/Products
(New category)
(1 out of a total listing of 2)

Lewis of London, Inc.   Retail juvenile furniture and
                                   accessories

Clothing/Shoes
(9 out of a total listing of 15)

Athlete's Foot Marketing Associations, Inc.	Top quality footwear and accessories for athletes
Fleet Feet	Footwear with emphasis on sporting lifestyle
Gingiss International, Inc.	Sale and rental of men's formal clothes
Just Pants	Jeans and accessories shops for teenagers
Knapp Shoe Company	Retail shoe shop selling "Knapp Shoes"
Lady Madonna Management Corp.	Women's maternity apparel
Salley Wallace Brides Shop, Inc.	Complete bride shop and bridal service
T-Shirts Plus, Inc.	Personalised T-shirts
Tyler's Country Clothes	Retail family apparel stores

Construction/Remodelling-Materials/Services
(12 out of a total listing of 37)

B-Day System, Inc.	Basement water proofing
Eldorado Stone Corp.	Manufacture and sale of "Eldorado Stone" and brick-building products
Energy Doctor, Inc.	Energy conservation in homes
GNU Services Corporation	Porcelain and fibreglass repair
Independent Home Builders of America	Do-it-yourself custom home construction
New England Log Homes, Inc.	Sale of log homes
Perma-Jack Co.	Foundation stabilising system
Poraflor, Inc.	Sale and installation of seamless flooring
Porcelite International, Inc.	Process to repair bathroom suites
Renaissance Refacers, Inc.	Refacing kitchen cabinets with solid oak
Wick Homes	Wet-core closed panel home manufacturer
Zell-Aire Corporation	Promotion of electric heating

Cosmetics/Toiletries
(2 out of a total listing of 7)

Natural Cosmetics

Syd Simons Cosmetics, Inc.

Cosmetic boutique

Completely equipped makeup and skin care studios

Dental Centres
(New category)
(1 out of a total listing of 6)

United Dental Network, Inc.

Dental marketing and management services

Drug Stores
(1 out of a total listing of 6)

Medicine Shoppes International, Inc.

Retail sale of pharmaceutical products

Educational Products/Services
(9 out of a total listing of 22)

Child Enrichment Centers

Dootson Driving Schools

Gymboree

Kindergartens

Driving tuition

Pre-school movement education programme

Image Improvement, Inc.

Teaching of improvement course for women based on biblical principles

International Travel Training Courses, Inc.

Training prospective travel agents

Leisure Learning Centers, Inc.

Mary Moppets Day Care School, Inc.

Educational products

Day care centre for children

Patricia Stevens International, Inc.

Educational residential schools

Teller Training Distributors, Inc.

Teaching systems

Employment Services
(17 out of a total listing of 52)

Adia Temporary Services, Inc.	Temporary white collar and industrial staff placement
Bailey Employment System, Inc.	National chain agency for placement of professional and office staff
Dr. Personnel, Inc.	Paramedical placement service to the medical profession
Dunhill Personnel System, Inc.	National chain of office and technical staff placement
Engineering Corporation of America	Temporary technical personal service
Gilbert Lane Personnel Service	Executive and office personnel
HRI Services, Inc.	Executive search and placement services
Manpower, Inc.	Complete range of temporary staff
Norrell Temporary Services, Inc.	Temporary office and computer staff
The Olsten Corporation	Temporary office industrial and nursing staff
Parker Page Associates, Inc.	Specialised executive recruitment
Personnel Pool of America, Inc.	Temporary staff
Phone-A-Writer, Inc.	National "computerised" centre placement agency
Ritta Personnel System of North America, Inc.	Complete personnel placement service
Sanford Rose Associates International, Inc.	Job placement service, some specialisation
Snelling & Snelling, Inc.	Employment service in white collar and industrial field
VIP Personnel Systems	Permanent executive placement

Equipment/Rentals
(3 out of a total listing of 9)

Sounds Easy Franchise Corp.	Rental of video, stereo, TV, electronic games

Taylor Rental Corporation

United Rent-All, Inc.

Commercial, industrial, and
    domestic equipment rental
Domestic appliances and
    equipment rental

Foods—Doughnuts
(2 out of a total listing of 14)

Dunkin' Donuts of America, Inc.

Spudnuts, Inc.

Coffee and doughnut shops

Retail doughnut shops

Foods—Grocery/Speciality/Stores
(10 out of a total listing of 48)

Alpen Pantry, Inc.

Convenient Food Mart, Inc.

Cookie Factory of America

International Aromas

Jo Ann's Nut House, Inc.

Mr Dunderbak, Inc.

The Southland Corp.

Swiss Colony Stores, Inc.

Tiffany's Bakeries, Inc.

White Hen Pantry Division,
    Jewel Companies, Inc.

Gourmet food shops

Convenience-type grocery stores

Retail sale of biscuits and bakery
    products

Retail coffee, tea and spice shops

Candy and nuts kiosks

Delicatessens

Convenience grocery stores

Delicatessen and European
    speciality foods

Fresh baked pastries and breads

Delicatessens and bakeries

Foods—Ice Cream/Yoghurt/Candy/Popcorn/Beverages
(6 out of a total listing of 33)

Baskin Robbins, Inc.

Ernie's Wine and Liquor Corp.

Karmelkorn Shoppe, Inc.

Main Street Original Ice Cream
    Parlors

Mister Softee, Inc.

Swenson's Ice Cream Co.

Retail ice cream shops

Off-licences

Popcorn and sweet shops

Old-fashioned ice cream parlour
    and soda fountains

Van sales of ice cream

Retail sale of ice cream from old
    secret recipe

Foods—Pancake/Waffle/Pretzel
(2 out of a total listing of 7)

International House of Pancakes Restaurants	Full service family restaurant with variety of pancake specialties
Perkins Restaurants, Inc.	Pancakes, waffles and omlettes

Foods—Restaurants/Drive-ins/Carry Outs
(44 out of a total listing of 259)

Arbey's, Inc.	Fast food specialising in roast beef sandwiches
Bagel Nosh, Inc.	Manufacture of bagels and sale of Deli products
Big Daddy's Restaurants	Snack bars
Bonanza International, Inc.	Bonanza sirloin pit restaurants
Boy Blue of America, Inc.	Frozen yoghurt and limited menu stores
Burger King Corporation	Limited menu specialising in hamburgers
Charlie Chan Restaurants, Inc.	Quick service Chinese American foods
Chicken Delight	Sit-down and take-away restaurants
Country Kitchen International, Inc.	Sit down service restaurants
Dairy Cheer Stores	Fast foods and sandwiches
Dairy Sweet Corporation	Drive-in and take-away fast food
Der Wienerschnitzel International, Inc.	Fast food, hot dog restaurants
Dosanko Foods, Inc.	Japanese fast food restaurants
Duff's Enterprises, Inc.	Smorgasbord cafeterias
El Polo Coco Franchise Corp.	Mexican style broiled chicken
Frostop Corporation	"Frostop Root Beers" and limited fast food menus
Golden Chicken Franchises	Fast food chicken, pizza, and seafood carry outs
Gulliver's, Inc.	Quick service limited seafood menu
Howard Johnson Company	Full service restaurants
The Hush Puppy Corporation	Fast food limited menu restaurants

Jake's International, Inc.	Pizza
KFC Corporation	"Kentucky Fried Chicken" take aways
LaRosa's, Inc.	Full service Italian style
Long John Silver's, Inc.	Fast food, wide menu restaurants
McDonald's Corporation	Fast food, hamburger restaurants
Michel's Baguette French Bakery Cafe	Retail French bakery and cafe
Mr. Pizza, Inc.	Pizza restaurants
Mr. Steak, Inc.	Steak houses
Orange Julius of America	Fast foods and brand drink "Orange Julius"
Pepe's, Inc.	Pepe's Mexican restaurants
The Pewter Mug	English pubs and restaurants
Philly Mignon	Fast food restaurants
Pizza Time Theatre, Inc.	Family entertainment pizza parlours with simulated characters
The Pizza Inn, Inc.	Pizza restaurants
Ponderosa System, Inc.	Cafeteria-style steak houses
Popeyes Famous Fried Chicken, Inc.	Fast food
The Salad Bar Corporation	Garden like restaurants—light healthy foods
Skippers, Inc.	Limited fish menu
Stuckey's, Inc.	One-stop freeway traveller centre
The Straw Hat Restaurant Corporation	Limited menu family pizza restaurants
Subway	Submarine sandwiches
Taco Bell Corporation Headquarters	Mexican food restaurants
Wendy's Old Fashioned Hamburgers	Hamburger restaurants
Western Sizzlin Steak House	Semi-cafeteria style family steak house

General Merchandising Stores
(2 out of a total listing of 3)

Ben Franklin	General merchanidise stores
Gamble Stores	Houseware stores

Health Aids/Services
(6 out of a total listing of 33)

Diet Centre, Inc.   Five phase weight reduction and
                                           management programme
Fat Fighters, Inc.   Weight reduction centres
MacLevy Products Corporation   Health clinic and salon
MGI Aerobic Fitness Centres   Isokinetic treadmills and exercises
Omni Health International, Inc.   Weight loss, stress and smoking
                                           control through subliminal
                                           hypnosis
Woman's World Health Spas   Women's Health spas

Hearing Aids
(only 1 listed)

RCI, Inc.   Hearing aids in "Montgomery
                                           Ward" and other major retail
                                           stores

Home Furnishings/Furniture—Retail/
Repair—Services
(11 out of a total listing of 38)

Carpeteria, Inc.   Franchising retail carpet outlets
Crossland Furniture Restoration   Furniture restoration services
  Studios
Decorating Den Systems, Inc.   Custom-made draperies, carpeting
                                           and wallpaper
Dip'N Strip, Inc.   Removal of paints from wood and
                                           metal
Duraclean International   On-location cleaning of carpets
                                           and upholstery
Guarantee System Carpet   Carpet and upholstery cleaning
  Cleaning and Dye Company
"Jack The Stripper"   Stripping of paint and varnish
                                           from wood and metal
Scandia Down Corporation   Top range bedding store
Siesta Sleep Shop, Inc.   Retail sale of bedding

Spring Crest Company — Retailing of drapery, drapery hardware and accessories

Steamatic Incorporated — Carpet and upholstery home cleaning service

Insurance
(New category)
(2 out of a total listing of 7)

Insurance Consortium of America, Inc. — Franchise for independent insurance agents

Underwriters Adjusting Company — Adjusters providing services for insurance companies, agents, brokers

Laundries, Dry Cleaning—Services
(5 out of a total listing of 9)

A Cleaner World — Dry cleaning and shirt laundry

Bruck Distributing Co., Inc. — Drapery dry cleaning

Coit Draper & Carpet Cleaners, Inc. — Supply and maintenance of draperies and other window furnishings

Martin Franchises, Inc. — Fast service "Martinising" dry cleaning stores

Speed Queen Coin Operated Laundromat and Dry Cleaner, Inc. — Coin-operated laundromat and dry cleaning

Lawn and Garden Supplies/Services
(2 out of a total listing of 9)

Lawn-A-Mat Chemical and Equipment Corporation — Sale of lawn products and lawn service

Lawn Doctor Incorporated — Automated lawn services

Maintenance/Cleaning/Sanitation-Services—Supplies
(11 out of a total listing of 41)

Chem-Mark International, Inc.	Commercial dish-washing
The Gentleman Plumber	Business system for plumbing industry
Lien Chemical Company	Commercial and industrial sanitation service
The Maids International	Maid's Service
Master-Kleen	High pressure washing systems
Mr. Maintenance	Commercial building maintenance service
Mr. Rooter Corporation	Sewer and drain-cleaning service
Port-O-let Company, Inc.	Temporary restroom facilities for construction sites
ServiceMaster Industries	Cleaning of homes and offices, public buildings and institutions
Sparkle Wash, Inc.	National mobile power cleaning for all buildings
Ultrasonic Predictable Maintenance, Inc.	Detection of gas, water leaks, and electrical faults

Motels/Hotels
(8 out of a total listing of 19)

Days Inns of America, Inc.	Nationwide "budget-luxury" motels and restaurants
Econo-Travel Motor Hotel Corp.	Budget hotels and motels
Family Inns of America, Inc.	Motels
Hilton Inns, Inc.	Hotels
Holiday Inns, Inc.	Hotels and restaurants
Ramada Inns, Inc.	Hotels and motor hotels
Sheraton Inns, Inc.	Hotels
Travelodge International, Inc.	Motels

Optical Products/Services
(New category)
(2 out of a total listing of 5)

Pearle Vision Centres	Full-service optical retail outlets

Texas State Optical (TSO)   High quality retail optical
                                   dispensing office

Paint and Decorating Supplies
(1 out of a listing of 2)

Davis Paint Company   Retail paint and wallpaper stores

Pet Shops
(2 out of a total listing of 4)

Docktor Pet Centres, Inc.   Retail pet shops
PetMaster, Inc.   Mobile pet grooming service

Printing
(5 out of a total listing of 16)

Insty-Prints, Inc.   Instant printing services
Kwik-Kopy Corporation   Production and sale of high-quality
                                   printing
Postal Instant Press (PIP)   While-you-wait printing operation
Quik Print, Inc.   Quick copying of letterheads,
                                   envelopes, price lists, etc.
Sir Speedy, Inc.   Instant print centres

Property (Real Estate)
(3 out of a total listing of 30)

Century 21 Real Estate   Estate agents for established
  Corporation   proven agents
The Deltona Corporation   Real estate for development and
                                   investment
Realty World Corp.   Full service network for estate
                                   agents and brokers

Recreation/Entertainment/Travel—Services/Supplies
(12 out of a total listing of 23)

Balfing Range PRO	Coin-operated baseball pitching machine
Canoe Outpost, Inc.	Canoe ships
Curtis Mathes Soles Co. Inc.	Home entertainment centres
Empress Travel Franchise Corp.	Travel agencies
Fugazy Travel Franchises, Ltd.	Full service travel agency
Fun Services, Inc.	Fun fairs
Go-Kart Track Systems	Go-kart track
Golf Players, Inc.	Sir Goony golf miniature golf courses
Miss American Teen-Ager Pageant	Beauty contest promotions
Putt-Putt Golf Courses of America, Inc.	Miniature golf courses
Putt-R-Golf, Inc.	Miniature golf and baseball batting ranges
2001 Clubs of America, Inc.	Entertainment complexes

Retailing—Not classified Elsewhere
(23 out of a total listing of 87)

Athletic Attic Marketing, Inc.	Retail sports goods
Bathtique International Ltd.	Retail bath, bed and gift speciality shop
Budget Tapes & Records, Inc.	Retail tapes and records
Buning The Florist, Inc.	Florists
Computerland Corporation	Retail computer stores
Consumer Products of America, Inc.	Rack merchandising footwear
FauxPas Incorporated	In-store jewellery fashion centres
Friedman Franchisors	Microwave ovens
The Great Frame Up Systems, Inc.	D-I-Y picture frames
Little Professor Book Centres, Inc.	Book shops and newsagents
Miss Bojangles, Inc.	Fashion jewellery

National Video, Inc.	Rental video cassette and/or video disc
Plywood Ranch	Home centre
Radio Shack	Audio products
The Ringgold Corporation	Retail picture framing and art shops
Software City	Retail sale of packaged computer programmes
Sport Shacks, Inc.	Sports shops
Sketch & Sew, Inc.	Quality fabrics
Team Central Incorporated	Audio and domestic appliances stores
That's My Bag International, Inc.	Specialty bag stores
The Tinder Box International, Inc.	Tobacconists and gift shops
Wedding Bell Bridal Boutiques	Bridal stationery, unusual wedding accessories and supplies
Wicks 'N' Sticks, Inc.	Candle shops

Security Systems
(3 out of a total listing of 5)

Dictograph Security Systems	Sale of security devices
Honor Guard Security Service	Uniformed security guards
Rampart Industries, Inc.	Sale and installation of security alarm systems

Swimming Pools
(1 out of a total listing of 4)

Cascade Industries, Inc.	Sale and installation of Buster Crabbe pools, accessories and supplies

Tools/Hardware
(2 out of a total listing of 4)

Mac Tools, Inc.	Mobile sale of tools to mechanics and light industry
Vulcan Tools	Mobile sales of tools

Vending
(1 out of a total listing of 5)

Ford Gum and Machine Co., Inc.	Chewing gum and sweets from vending machines

Water Conditioning
(2 out of a total listing of 6)

Culligan International Co.	Water-conditioning equipment for all users
Rainsoft Water Conditioning Co.	Sale and leasing of water treatment equipment to homes and businesses

Miscellaneous Wholesale and Service Businesses
(16 out of a total listing of 26)

The Armoloy Company	Metal Coating
Asi Sign Systems, Inc.	Sign business
Badgeman International Ltd.	Production of name badges
Balloon Bouquets, Inc.	Balloon delivery and decorating services
Diversified Arts	Part-time distribution of paintings
Foliage Design Systems Franchise Co., Inc.	Leasing of live plants to businesses
Key Korner Systems, Inc.	Locksmiths
Machinery Wholesalers Corp.	Computerised seller-to-buyer service

Meistergram	Monogram embroidery equipment
Redd Pest Control Company, Inc.	Pest control
Selectra-Date Corporation	Computer dating
Tempaco, Inc.	Heating, air conditioning, refrigeration supplies
Tepco, Inc.	Air-purification systems
United Air Specialists, Inc.	Smokeeter electronic air cleaners
Vacationquest, Inc.	Time share units in resort areas
Wilbert Inc.	Designer and manufacturer of quality burial vaults

The British Franchise Association Ltd.

THE B.F.A.'s current form of application for membership of the Association is:

BRITISH FRANCHISE ASSOCIATION
Application for Membership

PART I

QUALIFICATION

1. Members shall be actively engaged in the franchise system of distribution of goods and services.
2. Members shall have established and be operating an ethical franchise network which shall be based on sound business principles, and providing a genuine and adequate service to both franchisee and consumer.
3. Members will be required to demonstrate to the Accreditation Committee the intention to provide, on a continuing basis, the service offered to the franchisee and, where relevant, to the public. The viability of the operation, both with respect to the franchisee and the franchisor, must also be demonstrated.
4. Members will be required to satisfy the Accreditation Committee that the systems established by the member company are adequate to protect both the public and the franchisee, where money is advanced in anticipation of a service to be provided at a future date.
5. The member company shall give an absolute undertaking that it will subscribe to the Code of Ethics adopted by the British Franchise Association. This Code of Ethics draws heavily on the Code established by the International Franchise Association and on the Code of Advertising Practice established by the British Advertising Standards Authority (A.S.A.). Members shall also have completed the following Declaration:

DECLARATION AND APPLICATION

We, the applicant company .... Ltd., give our undertaking that we are prepared at all times to subscribe to the Code of Ethics adopted by the British Franchise Association. We declare, to the best of our knowledge and belief, that the franchise system we offer is based on sound business principles and provides a viable and ethical business opportunity for the franchisee and a genuine end product or service for the consumer. It is our belief that the systems we operate, satisfactorily protect both the franchisee and the consumer and, accordingly, we hereby apply for membership of the British Franchise Association and, if granted membership, we undertake that we will notify the Association of any changes in the financial status or company structure or of any other material change which is likely to give rise to an adverse effect on our ability to perform our obligation to our franchisees.

Signed ....

For and on behalf of .... Ltd.

Registered Office ....

Position held ....

Date ....

The Form shall be signed by the Chairman or Managing Director of the company making the application.

Application for Membership

PART II—DATA SHEET

SECTION A. COMPANY INFORMATION

Name of Company ....

Name of designated representative ....

Position in Company ....

Address for correspondence ....

Telephone ....

Chairman of Company ....

Managing Director ....

Other Directors ....

Name of Parent or Holding Company ....

Names of Subsidiary Companies ....

Name of Franchise ....

SECTION B. SERVICE INFORMATION

Nature of service provided by the Company thro' franchisees & company-owned outlets:

....

....

Date your Company first offered this service ....

Date of opening the first detached company station ....

Date of opening the first franchised outlet ....

Number of franchised outlets operating ....

Number of company outlets operating ....

SECTION C. REFERENCES

Names, Addresses & Telephone numbers of *three* established franchisees:

1. ....

2. ....

3. ....

Bank ....

Auditor ....

Solicitor ....

Trade (1) ....

(2) ....

SECTION D. CONTRACTS

Please attach copies of current Contracts & Licences: please note any changes under consideration or planned, which you consider to be relevant to future operations. Also kindly enclose with your Application Form any Promotional Literature used in your relationship with:

(a) Potential Licensees.

(b) The Consumer.

Please supply copy of registered Trade Mark/Logo.

The B.F.A.'s current form of application for membership of the B.F.A. Register of Developing Franchises is:

BRITISH FRANCHISE ASSOCIATION
Application Form
for
Registration as a Qualified Non-member
Developing Franchise Company

We, the applicant company .... Ltd., declare, to the best of our knowledge and belief, that the franchise system we offer is based on sound business principles and provides a viable and ethical business opportunity for the franchisee and a genuine end-product or service for the consumer and it is our belief that the systems we operate, satisfactorily protect both the franchisee and the consumer.

We give our Undertaking that we are prepared at all times to subscribe to the Code of Ethics adopted by the British Franchise Association and, accordingly, we hereby make application to the B.F.A. for Registration as a qualified non-member Developing Franchise Company.

It is our intention to present an accurate picture of our franchise at all times as it passes through the various stages of development and we Undertake to disclose all relevant information to potential franchisees during negotiation and to the B.F.A. and to complete and regularly update the standard Form of Disclosure.

Signed ....

For and on behalf of .... Ltd.

Registered Office ....

Position held ....

Date ....

The Form shall be signed by the Chairman or Managing Director of the Company.

Information for B.F.A. Register
PART I. For general disclosure
PART II. Confidential to the B.F.A.

PART I	Current Information	Updated Information

Name of the Company holding
the right to the use of the
name & mark and the total
technology package,
including the know-how.

U.K. Company Registration
Number

Date company established

Address

Chairman

Managing Director

Other Directors:
1.
2.
3.

Banker

Accountant

Solicitor

Executive to contact

Telephone Number

Address

Description of franchised
business activity.

If relevant, Material Supply
arrangements.

State whether territory
franchised or address only.

Date when Business Format
first established to your
satisfaction.

Royalty payable

Initial Franchise Fee
(excluding charges for
initial supply of goods,
training, manual, launch,
equipment, premises &
shopfitting).

Attachments to Part I General Disclosure Document

Please enclose for information:

1. Copy of current Contract. (Please indicate term).
2. Prospectus or equivalent letter and papers, including projections, if any.
3. Current copy of advertisement for franchisees. (If available).
4. If relevant to your business and available, literature describing your product to the consumer.

To complete Part I—Please fill in Pages 3 and 4 covering Pilot-Schemes, Launch & Supporting Services.

Pilot-schemes

	Place	Date	Company Owned or Franchised
Company first offered service			
2nd operation opened			
3rd operation opened			
4th operation opened			
5th operation opened			
6th operation opened			
7th operation opened			
8th operation opened			
9th operation opened			
10th operation opened			

	Current	Updated
Please summarise: Number of operations achieving expected standard		
Number of operations below expected standard		
Current Number of Franchisees		
Current Number of Company Operations		

PART I	Current Information	Updated Information
INITIAL DEVELOPMENT PACKAGE & LAUNCH Training & Manual: estimated cost.		
Initial Marketing Operations, including Launch: estimated cost.		
Goods & Material: cost of initial supply.		
Equipment: total cost.		
Preparation of Premises: estimated cost.		
Other items—please specify		
SUPPORTING SERVICES Brief Summary of Management, Technical, Marketing & Training resources available.		
Proportion of Royalty allocated to Promotion & Advertising.		

Statistical Survey of Selected Franchises

Introduction

The tables which appear in this Appendix have been drawn from two research studies which have been conducted under the auspices of the School of Management Studies of the Polytechnic of Central London. The first study was made by Professor John Stanworth (then Dr. Stanworth) in 1975 based on three leading franchise operations in the UK.: Wimpy, Dyno-Rod and ServiceMaster, and appeared in the second and third editions of this work. The study was broken down into four segments:

(1) Recorded in-depth interviews with key franchisor executives.
(2) Recorded in-depth interviews with a sample of fifty-one franchisees.
(3) A mailed questionnaire to a larger sample of franchisees (total number of respondents = 114).
(4) A questionnaire survey of over 200 respondents currently considering entry into self-employment.

In the tables which follow, the data is drawn largely from stage (3) of the research, but is supplemented with additional tables drawn from data gathered from stage (2).

Some of the tables which have clearly become out of date since the third edition of this work have been omitted.

The second study was carried out by Jensine Hough in 1980 and 1981 in the course of her research into franchising while preparing her thesis for a Doctorate. There were four companies in her study: Home Tune, Prontaprint and Ziebart, whose results are presented here, while the fourth company did not want the statistics which relate to it to be published.

This study was more comprehensive than the exploratory investigation undertaken by John Stanworth and differed in its aims and emphasis, although many similar questions were asked. Although similar research strategies were used, these were modified in the light of experience gained during his research. Jensine Hough's differed in that in-depth interviews with franchisees were conducted before, and not after, the mailed questionnaire was sent to franchisees. However, as with the in-depth interviews, the majority of questions were left open so as to allow those responding the maximum freedom to express their own opinions.

In addition to the surveys of franchisors and franchisees, Jensine Hough examined franchise agreements, along with other documentary material and, where possible, attended national conferences and other franchising events. She did not survey people considering self-employment.

Jensine Hough's tables presented here, mainly in Sections One and Three, have like those from John Stanworth's survey, been selected by the author on the basis of their relevance to this work. While the majority of her tables show the responses given by the 183 Home Tune, Prontaprint and Ziebart franchisees responding to both the in-depth and mailed surveys, in some cases the questions were put only to the seventy franchisees who were interviewed in-depth, or to the further 113 who returned the mailed questionnaire. This can be ascertained from the number of respondents ($N =$) included with each table.

Where the questions are similar the results are set alongside each other for ease of comparison and in the index of tables the letter "H" indicates where this has been done. Hough's questions which are of interest for the purpose of this work, but which do not have a counterpart in John Stanworth's study, are set out in Part Three of this appendix.

The tables represent only a proportion of the questions put to the franchisees only in each study, and should be viewed in that light. The reader should take into account that the franchisees surveyed may have entered their franchise some years prior to being surveyed and so their recall on certain questions may not be perfect. Also, franchisors have changed certain of their practices over time, which may again lead to differing responses depending on when a franchisee joined the franchisee. With regard to this latter aspect, it should also be borne in mind that John Stanworth's survey was undertaken in 1975 and

Jensine Hough's in 1980 and 1981. As such, the studies reflect the attitudes, opinions and recollections of franchisees at the time and so should not be taken as necessarily reflecting current franchisee attitudes or current franchisor practices or policy.

The tables which follow show various aspects of franchisees' transactions with their franchisors, including their first meeting, setting up, operational elements and thoughts about termination. Each of the companies has a different approach and this must be borne in mind when assessing the replies. It will also be helpful to re-read the appropriate Case Studies before tackling this Appendix.

While the responses to all the questions which are set out in Part Three of the Appendix are of interest, there are aspects of the franchise relationship which are dealt with which warrant specific comment.

The first ten tables are concerned with precontractual considerations.

The main information requested by franchisees at their first meeting with the franchisor relates to the financial returns and cost of entry. The franchisors' integrity and the marketability of the product was given a lower priority. Invariably the financial information requested was provided in any event. It is reassuring to note that the vast majority of prospective franchisees consulted existing franchisees prior to taking up a franchise.

Bearing in mind that the survey preceded the final establishment of franchisee departments by some of the Banks, it is interesting to note the then relatively high level of understanding and support from the Banks reported by franchisees.

Many of the tables which follow provide an interesting insight into operational features. Table 11, which provides the franchisee's assessments of the quality of the franchisor's advice, shows the strains which were emerging in the Ziebart franchise.

Invariably the franchisors responded quickly to requests for assistance (Table 20) and on the whole the assistance was adequate or better (Table 24). Where a franchisee had a need for special assistance when experiencing difficulty, the franchisors rose to the occasion with an average 81.5% favorable reaction with an average 7.7% still receiving assistance (Table 29).

Both franchisor and franchisees seem quite relaxed about enforcement of contract provisions. It is not surprising to find that Home Tune and Prontaprint pay most attention to fee payments and maintenance of standards, while Ziebart, who received payment of fees in a product mark-up, were more concerned to ensure that the franchisees did not buy elsewhere (Table 36).

The franchisee grapevine obviously works well (Table 45) and the fact that other franchisees have been terminated presumably for breach is well known.

Franchising reflects the personality and style of both franchisor and franchisee: the varied attitudes and responses illustrate that the uniformity which many associate with franchising is only a uniformity of name and system. The individual and his talents and attitudes are catered for and the range of responses indicates just how flexible franchisors are.

The last two of Jensine Hough's tables (53 and 54) raise the interesting question of whether franchisees should have a place in the B.F.A. and whether they should have a national association of their own. It is interesting to note that just under two-thirds of the franchisees who replied to the mailed questionnaire thought they should have a place in the B.F.A., while only approaching 40% of all the franchisees thought that they should have their own national association.

The B.F.A., as an association of franchisors, has a number of interests in common with franchisees, but also, of course, a potential conflict in some other respects. The difficulty for franchisees in establishing an "across the marketplace" association is that they have little in common with each other. Within a franchise there is a place for a franchisee association (see Chapter 12), but none of these franchises had one.

LIST OF TABLES

Part One

Part Two

Section One—The Decision to Become Self-employed

Question No.	*Question*
1.	Did franchisees really understand what franchising involved when they first contacted ServiceMaster/Dyno-Rod/Wimpy?
2.	Did the availability of capital influence franchisees' decision to take a franchise rather than set up a totally independent business?
3.	What was the approximate time gap between the decision to become self-employed and taking up a franchise?
4.	Was their present franchise the only one that franchisees considered? (H)
5.	Did franchisees consider any alternative forms of self-employment?
6.	If they had not gone into franchising did franchisees feel they would still be working for themselves?
7.	Have their businesses fulfilled their original ambitions?
8.	Would they advise anyone else to do what they have done?
9.	Did franchisees feel, taking into account both the benefits and difficulties associated with being their own boss, that self-employment was worthwhile?
10.	Did franchisees experience sufficient freedom within terms of their franchise agreements to really feel they were working for themselves?

11. Did franchisees still feel their original decisions to go into franchising was the right one?
12. If franchisees were starting in business again today would they still go into franchising?
13. How long did franchisees think they would continue in their present businesses?

Section Two—Relationships with Others

14. Did franchisees encounter any problems in their relationships with their franchisors?
15. Did franchisees feel that their franchisor gave a fair service for the return he got from them?
16. Did franchisees think the public was generally aware that ServiceMaster/Dyno-Rod/Wimpy was franchised?
17. Did franchisees think their franchisors made any attempt to inform the public that ServiceMaster/Dyno-Rod/Wimpy was franchised?
18. Did franchisees' customers generally realise that they worked for themselves?
19. How well did franchisees think their brand name was known to:
    (a) the general public; and
    (b) their potential customers?
20. Was the brand name ServiceMaster/Dyno-Rod/Wimpy important to franchisees' businesses?
21. In franchisees' opinions, were their businesses more successful as a result of being franchised than they would otherwise have been?
22. Did franchisees feel that there was less risk in running a franchised business than in running a totally independent business?
23. Did franchisees have employees working for them?
24. Did franchisees find the task of organising other people satisfying?
25. Did franchisees have problems obtaining staff?
26. Did their employees know they were franchisees?
    If "yes" did this affect their attitude to working for them?
27. Did franchisees experience any problems in their relationship with customers?

Section Three—Advantages and Disadvantages of Franchising

28.   Were there any aspects of franchising that franchisees did not like?

29.   Were there any benefits franchisees' customers got from them as a franchise that they would not have got from an ordinary managed branch of a large company?

30.   Were there any ways in which franchisees could perhaps have given their customers an even better service, but could not because of restrictions in their agreements with their franchisor?

Part Three

Table 1   Main information sought by franchisees at their first meeting with the franchisor

Table 2   Main type of financial information initially provided to franchisees

Table 3   What financial projections were supplied by the franchisor once the franchisee's own territory or site had been agreed upon

Table 4   Were visits made to existing franchisees prior to entry?

Table 5   Did their franchisor advise them to consult an independent third party prior to signing their agreement?

Table 6   Was the independent third party consulted knowledgeable about franchising?

Table 7   Proportion of franchisees' initial funding obtained from a bank

Table 8   Did your bank manager appear to understand the concept of franchising?

Table 9   What do you think was your bank manager's attitude toward franchising?

Table 10   Did you undertake training before starting to operate as a franchisee?

Table 11   Franchisee assessments of the quality of franchisor advice

Table 12   Does your franchisor see your primarily as an independent small businessman or essentially as a manager?

Table 13   How much individual freedom does your franchisor give you in running your franchise?

Table 14   Has there been renegotiation or attempted renegotiation of your territory since you started to operate the franchise?

Table 15   Why did the renegotiation of the territory take place?

The Guide to Franchising

Part One

TABLE 1. *Qualifications gained at the end of secondary education*

Stanworth:		ServiceMaster		Dyno-Rod		Wimpy		Total	
			%		%		%		%
CSE	2		6.5	—	—	1	1.9	3	2.6
School Certificate/ O-level GCE	9		29.0	12	38.7	25	48.1	46	49.4
Higher School Certificate/ A-level GCE	5		16.1	5	16.1	10	19.2	20	17.5
No qualification obtained	20		64.5	17	54.8	24	46.2	61	53.5
Non-response	—		—	2	6.5	2	3.8	4	3.5

Hough:	None	CSE	O-level GCE	A-level GCE	Other	N.R.*	N =
	%	%	%	%	%	%	
Total	33.9	4.4	31.7	24.0	3.3	2.7	183
Home Tune	49.3	4.2	31.0	9.9	5.6	0.0	71
Prontaprint	23.4	1.6	34.4	35.9	1.6	3.1	64
Ziebart	25.0	8.3	29.2	29.2	2.1	6.3	48

* No response.

TABLE 2. *Last occupations of franchisees prior to entry into franchising*

Stanworth:		ServiceMaster		Dyno-Rod		Wimpy		Total
			%		%		%		%
Manual	6	19.4	3	9.7	5	9.6	14	12.3
Lower level white collar	1	3.2	1	3.2	3	5.8	5	4.4
Supervisor to middle management/ semi-professional	16	51.6	13	41.9	13	25.0	42	36.8
Higher managerial/ professional	2	6.5	2	6.5	2	3.8	6	5.3
Self-employed	5	16.1	11	35.5	25	48.1	41	36.0
Other/NR	1	3.2	1	3.3	4	7.7	6	5.3
	$N=31$	100.0	$N=31$	100.0	$N=52$	100.0	$N=114$	100.0

Hough:	Manual	White collar	Self- employed	Other	$N=$
	%	%	%	%	
Total	21.4	45.7	24.3	8.6	70
Home Tune	35.7	25.0	28.6	10.7	28
Prontaprint	35.7	25.0	28.6	10.7	28
Ziebart	8.7	65.2	17.4	8.7	23

TABLE 3. *Reasons for taking up a franchise*

Stanworth:	ServiceMaster		Dyno-Rod		Wimpy		Total	
		%		%		%		%
An opportunity to have own business and still be part of a national organisation	14	45.2	13	41.9	7	13.5	34	29.8
To make money/ sound business venture	4	12.9	6	19.4	8	15.4	18	15.8
Less risky than starting in business on your own because of proven product/ service and technical "know-how" available/ easy to run/ ready-made market	8	25.8	8	25.8	13	25.0	29	25.4
Opportunity to build a business for the future and/or family	1	3.2	—	—	1	1.9	2	1.7
Greater job satisfaction	2	6.5	1	3.2	—	—	3	2.6
Had appropriate experience or related business	2	6.5	1	3.2	4	7.7	7	6.1
Other	—	—	2	6.5	4	7.7	6	5.3
Non-response	—	—	—	—	15	28.6	15	13.2
	$N=31$	100.0	$N=31$	100.0	$N=52$	100.0	$N=114$	100.0

TABLE 3 (*cont.*)

Hough:	Home Tune	Prontaprint	Ziebart	Total
	%	%	%	%
Umbrella/support of the franchisor	62.0	42.2	41.7	49.7
Lacked experience/ less risk	35.2	64.1	25.0	42.6
Known name/ready made business	25.4	12.5	45.8	26.2
Employee of franchisor or franchisee	4.2	3.1	10.4	5.4
Chance	4.2	6.3	14.6	7.6
Other	18.3	18.8	20.8	18.5
$N=$	71	64	48	183

N.B.: Columns total more than 100% due to multiple responses.

TABLE 4. *Would respondents be otherwise self-employed if they had not taken up franchises?*

Stanworth:	ServiceMaster		Dyno-Rod		Wimpy		Total	
		%		%		%		%
Yes	20	64.5	24	77.4	—	—	44	71.0
No	7	22.6	3	9.7	—	—	10	16.1
Don't know	2	6.5	1	3.2	—	—	3	4.8
Non-response	2	6.5	3	9.7	—	—	5	8.1
	$N=31$	100.0	$N=31$	100.0	—	—	$N=62$	100.0

Hough:	Yes	No	Don't know	No response	$N=$
	%	%	%	%	%
Total	71.7	24.8	1.8	1.8	113
Home Tune	60.5	34.9	2.3	2.3	43
Prontaprint	73.3	22.2	2.2	2.2	45
Ziebart	88.0	12.0	0.0	0.0	25

TABLE 5. *How franchisees first approached their franchisors about buying a franchise*

Stanworth:	ServiceMaster		Dyno-Rod		Wimpy		Total	
		%		%		%		%
In response to an advertisement for franchisees	15	48.4	17	54.8	8	15.4	40	35.1
Contacted the franchisor directly or via a franchisee after using an outlet or service	4	12.9	6	19.4	29	55.8	39	34.2
Attended a franchise exhibition	—	—	1	3.2	—	—	1	0.9
Other	12	38.7	7	22.6	13	25.0	32	28.1
Non-response	—	—	—	—	2	3.9	2	1.8
	$N=31$	100.0	$N=31$	100.0	$N=52$	100.0	$N=114$	100.0

TABLE 6. *Did respondents feel they were given full financial information before signing their franchise contracts?*

Stanworth:	ServiceMaster		Dyno-Rod		Wimpy		Total	
		%		%		%		%
Yes	23	74.2	27	87.1	41	78.9	91	79.8
No	8	25.8	3	9.7	9	17.3	20	17.5
Non-response	—	—	1	3.2	2	3.9	3	2.6
	$N=31$	100.0	$N=31$	100.0	$N=52$	100.0	$N=114$	100.0

TABLE 7. *Respondents' feelings, prior to signing a franchise contract, on the franchisors' prediction of likely profits*

Stanworth:	ServiceMaster		Dyno-Rod		Wimpy		Total	
		%		%		%		%
Grossly overestimated likely profits	2	6.5	4	12.9	5	9.6	11	9.7
Overestimated likely profits	8	25.8	13	41.9	12	23.1	33	29.0
Neither overestimated nor underestimated profits	17	54.8	9	29.0	23	44.2	49	43.0
Underestimated likely profits	3	9.7	5	16.1	5	9.6	13	11.4
Grossly underestimated likely profits	—	—	—	—	2	3.9	2	1.8
Non-response	1	3.2	—	—	5	9.6	6	5.3
	$N=31$	100.0	$N=31$	100.0	$N=52$	100.0	$N=114$	100.0

Hough:	Over estimated	Accurately estimated	Under estimated	Not predicted	Don't know/ No response	$N=$
	%	%	%	%	%	
Total	44.8	28.4	11.0	7.7	8.1	183
Home Tune	39.4	32.4	12.6	7.0	8.4	71
Prontaprint	45.3	31.3	15.6	3.1	4.7	64
Ziebart	52.1	18.8	2.1	14.6	12.5	48

TABLE 8. *Did respondents consult a solicitor or other adviser before signing their franchise contracts?*

Stanworth:	ServiceMaster		Dyno-Rod		Wimpy		Total	
		%		%		%		%
Solicitor:								
Yes	11	35.5	25	80.7	31	59.6	67	58.8
No	20	64.5	6	19.4	18	34.6	44	38.6
Non-response	—	—	—	—	3	5.8	3	2.6
	$N=31$	100.0	$N=31$	100.0	$N=52$	100.0	$N=114$	100.0
Other adviser:								
Yes	11	35.5	17	54.8	12	23.1	40	35.1
No	20	64.5	14	45.2	26	50.0	60	52.6
Non-response	—	—	—	—	14	26.9	14	12.3
	$N=31$	100.0	$N=31$	100.0	$N=52$	100.0	$N=114$	100.0

Hough:	Home Tune	Prontaprint	Ziebart	Total
	%	%	%	%
Consulted third party	71.8	87.6	89.6	81.9
Didn't consult	28.2	12.5	8.3	17.5
No response	0.0	0.0	2.1	0.6
	100.0	100.0	100.0	100.0
Description of third party consulted:	%	%	%	%
Solicitor	29.6	71.9	70.8	55.2
Bank manager	45.1	68.8	27.1	48.6
Accountant	19.7	59.4	47.9	41.0
Other	12.7	10.9	6.3	10.4
$N=$	71	64	48	183

TABLE 9. *Party from whom franchisees purchased their franchises*

Stanworth:	ServiceMaster		Dyno-Rod		Wimpy		Total	
		%		%		%		%
Directly from the franchisor	24	77.4	23	74.2	30	57.7	77	67.5
Directly from another franchisee	7	22.6	8	25.8	20	38.5	35	30.7
Non-response	—	—	—	—	2	3.9	2	1.8
	$N=31$	100.0	$N=31$	100.0	$N=52$	100.0	$N=114$	100.0

TABLE 10. *Decision on site or area location made by*

Stanworth:	ServiceMaster		Dyno-Rod		Wimpy		Total	
		%		%		%		%
The franchisor	7	22.6	9	29.0	19	36.5	35	30.7
The franchisee himself	22	71.0	17	54.8	25	48.1	64	56.1
Other	1	3.2	5	16.1	4	7.7	10	8.8
Non-response	1	3.2	—	—	4	7.7	5	4.4
	$N=31$	100.0	$N=31$	100.0	$N=52$	100.0	$N=114$	100.0

Basis of initial territorial allocation

Hough:	Home Tune	Prontaprint	Ziebart	Total
	%	%	%	%
Franchisor's decision	60.7	42.1	60.9	55.7
Renegotiated	28.6	15.8	21.7	22.9
Joint decision	10.7	42.1	17.4	21.4
	100.0	100.0	100.0	100.0
$N=$	28	19	32	70

TABLE 11. *Owner of franchisees' business premises*

Stanworth:	ServiceMaster	%	Dyno-Rod	%	Wimpy	%		Total %
The franchisor	1	3.2	—	—	—	—	1	0.9
The franchisee	20	64.5	15	48.4	4	7.7	39	34.2
Owned by a third party	8	25.8	16	51.6	46	88.5	70	61.4
Non-response	2	6.5	—	—	2	3.9	4	3.5
	$N=31$	100.0	$N=31$	100.0	$N=52$	100.0	$N=114$	100.0

TABLE 12. *Average number of hours per week worked by franchisees*

Stanworth:	ServiceMaster	%	Dyno-Rod	%	Wimpy	%		Total %
Less than 30 hours	—	—	1	3.2	2	3.9	3	2.6
30–40 hours	—	—	2	6.5	3	5.8	5	4.4
40–45 hours	4	12.9	—	—	4	7.7	8	7.0
45–50 hours	9	29.0	6	19.4	4	7.7	19	16.7
50–55 hours	5	16.1	7	22.6	2	3.9	14	12.3
55–60 hours	4	12.9	5	16.1	6	11.5	15	13.2
60–65 hours	6	19.4	3	9.7	8	15.4	17	14.9
65–70 hours	1	3.2	2	6.5	4	7.7	7	6.1
70–75 hours	1	3.2	3	9.7	7	13.5	11	9.7
75–80 hours	—	—	1	3.2	2	3.9	3	2.6
80–85 hours	1	3.2	1	3.2	3	5.8	5	4.4
85–90 hours	—	—	—	—	1	1.9	1	0.9
90 hours or more	—	—	—	—	2	3.9	2	1.8
Non-response	—	—	—	—	4	7.7	4	3.5
	$N=31$	100.0	$N=31$	100.0	$N=52$	100.0	$N=114$	100.0

TABLE 13. *Extent of assistance provided by wife*

Stanworth:	ServiceMaster		Dyno-Rod		Wimpy		Total	
		%		%		%		%
"However and whenever needed	11	35.5	6	19.4	14	26.9	31	27.2
Less than 10 hours	1	3.2	2	6.5	2	3.9	5	4.4
10–20 hours	3	9.7	1	3.2	—	—	4	3.5
20–30 hours	4	12.9	2	6.5	3	5.8	9	7.9
30–40 hours	2	6.5	2	6.5	2	3.9	6	5.3
40–45 hours	1	3.2	—	—	3	5.8	4	3.5
45–50 hours	—	—	—	—	1	1.9	1	0.9
50 hours or more/full time	4	12.9	2	6.5	2	3.9	8	7.0
Other	—	—	1	3.2	1	1.9	2	1.8
None	5	16.1	15	48.4	24	46.2	44	38.6
	$N=31$	100.0	$N=31$	100.0	$N=52$	100.0	$N=114$	100.0

Hough:	Assists	Doesn't assist	No response	Not married	$N=$
	%	%	%	%	
Total	59.6	28.4	2.2	9.8	183
Home Tune	81.7	12.7	0.0	5.6	71
Prontaprint	57.8	29.7	1.6	10.9	64
Ziebart	29.2	50.0	6.3	14.6	48

TABLE 14. *Did franchisees think that the public with whom they have contact understand their relationship with the franchisor?*

Stanworth:	ServiceMaster		Dyno-Rod		Wimpy		Total	
		%		%		%		%
Yes	5	16.1	1	3.2	8	15.4	14	12.3
No	24	77.4	29	93.6	38	73.1	91	79.8
Other/don't know	—	—	1	3.2	2	3.9	3	2.6
Non-response	2	6.5	—	—	4	7.7	6	5.3
	$N=31$	100.0	$N=31$	100.0	$N=52$	100.0	$N=114$	100.0

TABLE 15. *How do the public think of franchisees?*

Stanworth:	ServiceMaster		Dyno-Rod		Wimpy		Total	
		%		%		%		%
As an independent operator	6	19.4	6	19.4	5	9.6	17	14.9
As someone working for a larger organisation	16	51.6	23	74.2	38	73.1	77	67.5
"Some understand, some do not"	6	19.4	2	6.5	1	1.9	9	7.9
As both independent and working for larger organisation	1	3.2	—	—	3	5.8	4	3.5
Other	—	—	—	—	—	—	—	—
Non-response	2	6.5	—	—	5	9.6	7	6.1
	$N=31$	100.0	$N=31$	100.0	$N=52$	100.0	$N=114$	100.0

TABLE 16. *Quality of formal training*

Stanworth:	ServiceMaster		Dyno-Rod		Wimpy		Total	
		%		%		%		%
Excellent	3	9.7	2	6.5	9	17.3	14	12.3
Good	8	25.8	5	16.1	6	11.5	19	16.7
Reasonable	13	41.9	12	38.7	15	28.9	40	35.1
Not very good	4	12.9	1	3.2	3	5.8	8	7.0
Poor	3	9.7	4	12.9	2	3.9	9	7.9
Franchisor does not provide/ not applicable	—	—	5	16.1	7	13.5	12	10.5
Non-response	—	—	2	6.5	10	19.2	12	10.5
	$N=31$	100.0	$N=31$	100.0	$N=52$	100.0	$N=114$	100.0

Hough:	Good to excellent	Reasonable	Poor to very low	Not provided/ Not required	No Response	$N=$
	%	%	%	%	%	
Total	45.8	22.9	15.3	10.4	5.6	173
Home Tune	22.5	28.2	35.2	11.3	2.8	71
Prontaprint	73.4	15.7	6.3	3.1	1.6	64
Ziebart	41.7	25.0	4.2	16.7	12.5	48

TABLE 17. *Quality of equipment supplied by franchisor*

Stanworth:	ServiceMaster		Dyno-Rod		Wimpy		Total	
		%		%		%		%
Excellent	10	32.3	10	32.3	14	26.9	34	29.8
Good	11	35.5	11	35.5	12	23.1	34	29.8
Reasonable	8	25.8	8	25.8	9	17.3	25	21.9
Not very good	1	3.2	—	—	1	1.9	2	1.8
Poor	1	3.2	—	—	2	3.9	3	2.6
Franchisor does not provide/ Not applicable	—	—	—	—	5	9.6	5	4.4
Non-response	—	—	2	6.5	9	17.3	11	9.7
	$N=31$	100.0	$N=31$	100.0	$N=52$	100.0	$N=114$	100.0

TABLE 18. *Quality of supplies sold by franchisor to franchisees*

Stanworth:	ServiceMaster		Dyno-Rod		Wimpy		Total	
		%		%		%		%
Excellent	11	35.5	7	22.6	14	26.9	32	28.1
Good	17	54.8	10	32.3	15	28.9	42	36.8
Reasonable	3	9.7	7	22.6	16	30.8	26	22.8
Not very good	—	—	1	3.2	1	1.9	2	1.8
Poor	—	—	—	—	—	—	—	—
Franchisor does not provide/ Not applicable	—	—	3	9.7	—	—	3	2.6
Non-response	—	—	3	9.7	6	11.5	9	7.9
	$N=31$	100.0	$N=31$	100.0	$N=52$	100.0	$N=114$	100.0

TABLE 19. *Quality of operating manual/s*

Stanworth:	ServiceMaster	%	Dyno-Rod	%	Wimpy	%		Total	%
Excellent	19	61.3	5	16.1	14	26.9	38		33.3
Good	8	25.8	10	32.3	13	25.0	31		27.2
Reasonable	4	12.9	8	25.8	9	17.3	21		18.4
Not very good	—	—	2	6.5	4	7.7	6		5.3
Poor	—	—	3	9.7	2	3.9	5		4.4
Franchisor does not provide/ Not applicable	—	—	1	3.2	5	9.6	6		5.3
None-response	—	—	2	6.5	5	9.6	7		6.1
	$N=31$	100.0	$N=31$	100.0	$N=52$	100.0	$N=114$		100.0

Hough:	Excellent	Good	Reasonable	Not supplied	$N=$
	%	%	%	%	
Total	40.0	20.0	11.4	28.6	70
Home Tune	17.9	3.6	7.1	71.4	28
Prontaprint	36.8	42.1	21.1	0.0	19
Ziebart	69.6	21.7	8.7	0.0	23

TABLE 20. *Quality of national advertising*

Stanworth:	ServiceMaster	%	Dyno-Rod	%	Wimpy	%		Total	%
Excellent	3	9.7	5	16.1	8	15.4	16		14.0
Good	9	29.0	3	9.7	9	17.3	21		18.4
Reasonable	8	25.8	12	38.7	15	28.9	35		30.7
Not very good	3	9.7	4	12.9	4	7.7	11		9.7
Poor	3	9.7	5	16.1	7	13.5	15		13.2
Franchisor does not provide/ Not applicable	5	16.1	1	3.2	3	5.8	9		7.9
Non-response	—	—	1	3.2	6	11.5	7		6.1
	$N=31$	100.0	$N=31$	100.0	$N=52$	100.0	$N=114$		100.0

TABLE 21. *Quality of book-keeping assistance/advice*

Stanworth:	ServiceMaster		Dyno-Rod		Wimpy		Total	
		%		%		%		%
Excellent	2	6.5	1	3.2	2	3.9	5	4.4
Good	7	22.6	4	12.9	3	5.8	14	12.3
Reasonable	12	38.7	7	22.6	6	11.5	25	21.9
Not very good	1	3.2	1	3.2	2	3.9	4	3.5
Poor	1	3.2	6	19.4	4	7.7	11	9.7
Franchisor does not provide/ Not applicable	8	25.8	10	32.3	26	50.0	44	38.6
Non-response	—	—	2	6.5	9	17.3	11	9.7
	$N=31$	100.0	$N=31$	100.0	$N=52$	100.0	$N=114$	100.0

TABLE 22. *Quality of technical support*

Stanworth:	ServiceMaster		Dyno-Rod		Wimpy		Total	
		%		%		%		%
Excellent	4	12.9	4	12.9	—	—	8	12.9
Good	8	25.8	4	12.9	—	—	12	19.4
Reasonable	9	29.0	14	45.2	—	—	23	37.1
Not very good	3	9.7	1	3.2	—	—	4	6.5
Poor	3	9.7	7	22.6	—	—	10	16.1
Franchisor does not provide/ Not applicable	3	9.7	—	—	—	—	3	4.8
Non-response	1	3.2	1	3.2	—	—	2	3.2
	$N=31$	100.0	$N=31$	100.0	—	—	$N=62$	100.0

Hough:	Good to excellent	Adequate	Poor to very poor	No response	
	%	%	%	%	%
Total	55.7	35.4	8.0	0.9	113
Home Tune	41.9	41.9	14.0	2.3	43
Prontaprint	71.1	24.4	4.4	0.0	45
Ziebart	52.0	44.0	4.0	0.0	25

TABLE 23. *Quality of day-to-day business advice*

Stanworth:	ServiceMaster	%	Dyno-Rod	%	Wimpy	%	Total	%
Excellent	3	9.7	1	3.2	7	13.5	11	9.7
Good	7	22.6	9	29.0	7	13.5	23	20.2
Reasonable	10	32.3	8	25.8	8	15.4	26	22.8
Not very good	2	6.5	1	3.2	5	9.6	8	7.0
Poor	2	6.5	5	16.1	10	19.2	17	14.9
Franchisor does not provide/ Not applicable	7	22.6	5	16.1	6	11.5	18	15.8
Non-response	—	—	2	6.5	9	17.3	11	9.7
	$N=31$	100.0	$N=31$	100.0	$N=52$	100.0	$N=114$	100.0

TABLE 24. *Availability of franchisor for advice*

Stanworth:	ServiceMaster	%	Dyno-Rod	%	Wimpy	%	Total	%
Excellent	8	25.8	12	38.7	—	—	20	32.3
Good	12	38.7	8	25.8	—	—	20	32.3
Reasonable	5	16.1	3	9.7	—	—	8	12.9
Not very good	5	16.1	2	6.5	—	—	7	11.3
Poor	—	—	5	16.1	—	—	5	8.1
Franchisor does not provide/ Not applicable	1	3.2	—	—	—	—	1	1.6
Non-response	—	—	1	3.2	—	—	1	1.6
	$N=31$	100.0	$N=31$	100.0	—	—	$N=62$	100.0

TABLE 25. *Franchising enables you to own and develop a business more speedily than starting a business on your own account*

Stanworth:	ServiceMaster		Dyno-Rod		Wimpy			Total
		%		%		%		%
Strongly agree	13	41.9	18	58.1	—	—	31	50.0
Agree	13	41.9	11	35.5	—	—	24	38.7
Neither agree nor disagree	4	12.9	1	3.2	—	—	5	8.1
Disagree	—	—	—	—	—	—	—	—
Strongly disagree	1	3.2	1	3.2	—	—	2	3.2
Non-response	—	—	—	—	—	—	—	—
	$N=31$	100.0	$N=31$	100.0	—	—	$N=62$	100.0

TABLE 26. *Franchising enables you to own and develop a business with less risk than starting a business on your own account*

Stanworth:	ServiceMaster		Dyno-Rod		Wimpy			Total
		%		%		%		%
Strongly agree	8	25.8	11	35.5	—	—	19	30.7
Agree	15	48.4	10	32.3	—	—	25	40.3
Neither agree nor disagree	4	12.9	4	12.9	—	—	8	12.9
Disagree	1	3.2	1	3.2	—	—	2	3.2
Strongly disagree	3	9.7	4	12.9	—	—	7	11.3
Non-response	—	—	1	3.2	—	—	1	1.6
	$N=31$	100.0	$N=31$	100.0	—	—	$N=62$	100.0

TABLE 27. *How well known did franchisees think their franchise company's brand name was?*

Stanworth:	ServiceMaster		Dyno-Rod		Wimpy		Total	
		%		%		%		%
Very well known	6	19.4	17	54.8	—	—	23	37.1
Well known	2	6.5	3	9.7	—	—	5	8.1
Fairly well known	12	38.7	4	12.9	—	—	16	25.8
Not very well known	8	25.8	2	6.5	—	—	10	16.1
Hardly known	1	3.2	—	—	—	—	1	1.6
Not known	—	—	2	6.5	—	—	2	3.2
Don't know	—	—	—	—	—	—	—	—
Non-response	2	6.5	3	9.7	—	—	5	8.1
	$N=31$	100.0	$N=31$	100.0	—	—	$N=62$	100.0

TABLE 28. *How important did franchisees feel their brand name was to the success of their business?*

Stanworth:	ServiceMaster		Dyno-Rod		Wimpy		Total	
		%		%		%		%
Very important	22	71.0	28	90.3	—	—	50	80.7
Important	2	6.5	—	—	—	—	2	3.2
Fairly important	1	3.2	1	3.2	—	—	2	3.2
Makes little difference	—	—	—	—	—	—	—	—
Not very important	3	9.7	—	—	—	—	3	4.8
Not important	1	3.2	—	—	—	—	1	1.6
Don't know	—	—	—	—	—	—	—	—
Non-response	2	6.5	2	6.5	—	—	4	6.5
	$N=31$	100.0	$N=31$	100.0	—	—	$N=62$	100.0

TABLE 29. *Did franchisee believe their businesses were more successful because they were franchised?*

Stanworth:	ServiceMaster		Dyno-Rod		Wimpy		Total	
		%		%	%			%
More successful	25	80.7	25	80.7	—	—	50	80.7
Less successful	2	6.5	4	12.9	—	—	6	9.7
Other/Don't know	3	9.7	—	—	—	—	3	4.8
Non-response	1	3.2	2	6.5	—	—	3	4.8
	N=31	100.0	N=31	100.0	—	—	N=62	100.0

Hough: re: Tables 27 to 29
Proportion of Franchisees Mentioning the
Franchisor's Name and Know-How

	Home Tune	Prontaprint	Ziebart	Total
	%	%	%	%
As a reason *for taking* *their franchise*				
Name	9.9	1.6	33.3	13.1
Know-how	42.3	31.3	25.0	33.8
As a current *advantage of* *their franchise*				
Name	38.0	18.8	77.0	41.5
Know-how	57.8	57.8	31.3	50.8
N =	71	64	48	183

TABLE 30. *What did franchisees feel were the main advantages of franchising to themselves?*

Stanworth:	ServiceMaster		Dyno-Rod		Wimpy		Total	
		%		%		%		%
Independence/ An opportunity to run own business	2	6.5	5	16.1	5	9.6	12	10.5
Benefit of a well-known protected trade name	11	35.5	17	54.8	20	38.5	48	42.1
Less capital risk	1	3.2	2	6.5	3	5.8	6	5.3
Backing of a large organisation/ training, advice, etc.	20	64.5	13	41.9	21	40.4	54	47.4
National advertising	7	22.6	11	35.5	12	23.1	30	26.3
Security	—	—	1	3.2	3	5.8	4	3.5
Standard formula for presentation and quality	—	—	—	—	10	19.2	10	8.8
Other	6	19.4	1	3.2	5	9.6	12	10.5

Hough:	Home Tune	Prontaprint	Ziebart	Total
	%	%	%	%
Backing available from their franchisor	57.8	57.8	31.3	49.3
Trade name and image	38.0	18.8	77.1	42.8
National advertising	4.2	12.5	10.4	9.3
Independence/ Opportunity to run own business	12.6	3.1	2.1	7.4
Reduced risk/ Security	8.5	7.8	2.1	6.1
Ready-made business	2.8	17.2	6.3	8.8
Other	5.6	18.8	12.5	12.0
$N =$	71	64	48	183

TABLE 31. *What did franchisees feel were the main disadvantages of franchising to themselves?*

Stanworth:	ServiceMaster		Dyno-Rod		Wimpy		Total	
		%		%		%		%
Tight control of franchisor via the contract	5	16.1	11	35.5	16	30.8	32	28.1
Royalties	16	51.6	15	48.4	15	28.9	46	40.4
Not truly independent	5	16.1	8	25.8	3	5.8	16	14.0
Remote from franchisor	1	3.2	1	3.2	2	3.9	4	3.5
Lack of direction and leadership by franchisor	2	6.5	—	—	1	1.9	3	2.6
National trade name could be tarnished by bad franchisees	1	3.2	—	—	5	9.6	6	5.3
Other	1	3.2	2	6.5	5	9.6	8	7.0
None	5	16.1	3	9.7	9	17.3	17	14.9

Hough:	Home Tune	Prontaprint	Ziebart	Total
	%	%	%	%
Royalties	18.3	35.9	2.1	20.2
None or few	25.4	18.8	18.8	21.3
Not truly independent	12.7	10.9	18.8	13.5
Tied supplies/ restricted range	2.8	1.6	8.4	3.8
Territorial restrictions	7.0	4.7	4.2	5.5
Trade name could be tarnished by poor franchisees	5.6	3.1	0.0	3.3
High prices	0.0	0.0	22.9	6.0
Other	19.7	9.4	20.8	16.4
No response	8.5	15.6	4.2	9.8
	100.0	100.0	100.0	100.0
$N=$	71	64	48	215

TABLE 32. *How did franchisees feel about their businesses?*

Stanworth:	ServiceMaster		Dyno-Rod		Wimpy		Total	
		%		%		%		%
I am satisfied with my present franchise	20	64.5	21	67.7	37	71.2	78	68.4
I would prefer to be a completely independent operator in a similar business to the one I have now	8	25.8	8	25.8	10	19.2	26	22.8
I would prefer to be a completely independent operator in a different business	2	6.5	1	3.2	1	1.9	4	3.5
I would prefer not to be in business for myself whether franchised or not	1	3.2	—	—	2	3.9	3	2.6
Non-response	—	—	1	3.2	2	3.9	3	2.6
	$N=31$	100.0	$N=31$	100.0	$N=52$	100.0	$N=114$	100.0

Hough:	Satisfied with present franchise	Like to run same business independently	Like to run different business independently	Prefer to be an employee	No response	$N=$
	%	%	%	%	%	
Total	70.8	12.4	11.5	0.9	4.4	113
Home Tune	74.4	14.0	9.3	0.0	2.3	43
Prontaprint	86.7	4.4	6.7	0.0	2.2	45
Ziebart	36.0	24.0	24.0	4.0	12.0	25

TABLE 33. *In franchisees' opinions, which of the following statements most accurately describe their contracts?*

Stanworth:	ServiceMaster		Dyno-Rod		Wimpy		Total	
		%		%		%		%
Weighted very much in favour of franchisor	13	41.9	11	35.5	11	21.2	35	30.7
Weighted moderately in favour of franchisor	11	35.5	9	29.0	17	32.7	37	32.5
Weighted slightly in favour of franchisor	3	9.7	9	29.0	13	25.0	25	21.9
Weighted slightly in favour of franchisee	2	6.5	1	3.2	2	3.9	5	4.4
Weighted moderately in favour of franchisee	—	—	—	—	1	1.9	1	0.9
Weighted very much in favour of franchisees	1	3.2	—	—	1	1.9	2	1.8
Other	1	3.2	1	3.2	—	—	2	1.8
Non-response	—	—	—	—	7	13.5	7	6.1
	$N=31$	100.0	$N=31$	100.0	$N=52$	100.0	$N=114$	100.0

Party Toward Whom the Franchise Agreement is Weighted

Hough:	Weighted towards franchisor	About equal	Weighted towards franchisee	Other	$N=$
	%	%	%	%	
Total	51.9	39.9	6.6	1.6	183
Home Tune	43.7	46.5	7.0	2.8	71
Prontaprint	43.8	48.4	6.3	1.6	64
Ziebart	75.0	18.8	6.3	0.0	48

Including non-respondents.

TABLE 34. *Understanding by franchisees of their right to sell their franchise*

Stanworth:	ServiceMaster		Dyno-Rod		Wimpy		Total	
		%		%		%		%
Franchisee does not have the right to sell his franchise	1	3.2	—	—	4	7.7	6	4.4
Franchisee may sell but only to his franchisor	1	3.2	3	9.7	—	—	3	3.5
Franchisee may sell to an approved person but his franchisor has the right of first refusal	4	12.9	7	22.6	4	7.7	15	13.2
Franchisee may sell to anyone who is approved by his franchisor	23	74.2	19	61.3	34	65.4	76	66.7
Franchisee may sell to anyone without his franchisor's approval	1	3.2	1	3.2	7	13.5	9	7.9
Don't know	1	3.2	—	—	—	—	1	0.8
Non-response	—	—	1	3.2	3	5.8	4	3.5
	$N=31$	100.0	$N=31$	100.0	$N=52$	100.0	$N=114$	100.0

Hough:	Sell through franchisor only	Franchisor has first refusal	Can sell with franchisor approval*	Sale unrestricted	Don't know/ No response	$N=$
	%	%	%	%		
Total	10.4	28.4	59.0	1.6	0.5	183
Home Tune	25.4*	15.5	57.7	0.0	1.4	71
Prontaprint	0.0	28.1*	70.3	1.6	0.0	64
Ziebart	2.1	47.9*	45.8	4.2	0.0	48

* Specified in contract.

TABLE 35. *Had franchisors ever expressed an interest in buying-back?*

Stanworth:	ServiceMaster	%	Dyno-Rod	%	Wimpy	%	Total	%
Yes	1	3.2	3	9.7	—	—	4	3.5
No	30	96.8	27	87.1	44	84.6	101	88.6
Non-response	—	—	1	3.2	8	15.4	9	7.9
	$N=31$	100.0	$N=31$	100.0	$N=52$	100.0	$N=114$	100.0

TABLE 36. *Had franchisors ever threatened to terminate franchisees' contracts?*

Stanworth:	ServiceMaster	%	Dyno-Rod	%	Wimpy	%	Total	%
Yes	3	9.7	5	16.1	2	3.9	10	8.8
No	27	87.1	25	80.7	46	88.5	98	86.0
Non-response	1	3.2	1	3.2	4	7.7	6	5.3
	$N=31$	100.0	$N=31$	100.0	$N=52$	100.0	$N=114$	100.0

Hough:	Yes %	No %	$N=$
Total	4.9	95.1	183
Home Tune	4.2	95.8	71
Prontaprint	3.1	96.9	64
Ziebart	8.3	91.7	48

TABLE 37. *Provided the franchisor is willing, do franchisees plan to renew their contracts when they expire?*

Stanworth:	ServiceMaster	%	Dyno-Rod	%	Wimpy	%	Total	%
Yes	24	77.4	22	71.0	32	61.5	78	68.4
No	1	3.2	4	12.9	5	9.6	10	8.8
Don't know	3	9.7	2	6.5	3	5.8	8	7.0
Non-response	3	9.7	3	9.7	12	23.1	18	15.8
	$N=31$	100.0	$N=31$	100.0	$N=52$	100.0	$N=114$	100.0

Hough:	Yes	No	Perpetual contract	Don't know	$N=$
	%	%	%	%	
Total	68.9	2.7	6.6	21.9	183
Home Tune	84.5	0.0	1.4	14.1	71
Prontaprint	62.5	4.7	0.0	32.8	64
Ziebart	54.2	4.2	22.9	18.8	48

TABLE 38. *Level of satisfaction of franchisees with the profitability of their businesses*

Stanworth:	ServiceMaster	%	Dyno-Rod	%	Wimpy	%	Total	%
Very satisfied	3	9.7	5	16.1	4	7.7	12	10.5
Satisfied	15	48.4	12	38.7	15	28.9	42	36.8
Neither satisfied nor dissatisfied	4	12.9	10	32.3	16	30.8	30	26.3
Dissatisfied	5	16.1	1	3.2	12	23.1	18	15.8
Very dissatisfied	2	6.5	3	9.7	3	5.8	8	7.0
Non-response	2	6.5	—	—	2	3.9	4	3.5
	$N=31$	100.0	$N=31$	100.0	$N=52$	100.0	$N=114$	100.0

Hough:	Very satisfied	Satisfied	Neither	Dissatisfied	Very dissatisfied	Non-response/ don't know	$N=$
	%	%	%	%	%	%	
Total	15.3	42.6	19.1	13.7	6.0	3.2	183
Home Tune	22.5	46.5	16.9	8.5	1.4	4.2	71
Prontaprint	12.5	35.9	25.0	17.2	4.7	4.7	64
Ziebart	8.3	45.8	14.6	16.7	14.6	0.0	48

TABLE 39. *For anyone who is willing to work hard in Britain it is possible to create a successful and profitable business*

Stanworth:	ServiceMaster		Dyno-Rod		Wimpy		Total	
		%		%		%		%
Strongly agree	14	45.2	19	61.3	16	30.8	49	43.0
Agree	11	35.5	8	25.8	18	34.6	37	32.5
Neither agree nor disagree	3	9.7	2	6.5	2	3.9	7	6.1
Disagree	—	—	—	—	3	5.8	3	2.6
Strongly disagree	2	6.5	2	6.5	10	19.2	14	12.3
Non-response	1	3.2	—	—	3	5.8	4	3.5
	$N=31$	100.0	$N=31$	100.0	$N=52$	100.0	$N=114$	100.0

Part Two

Section One: The Decision to Become Self-employed

1. *Did franchisees really understand what franchising involved when they first contacted ServiceMaster/Dyno-Rod/Wimpy?*

	ServiceMaster		Dyno-Rod		Wimpy		Total	
		%		%		%		%
Yes	8	53.3	11	68.8	9	45.0	28	54.9
No	7	46.7	5	31.3	11	55.0	23	45.1
	$N=15$	100.0	$N=16$	100.0	$N=20$	100.0	$N=51$	100.0

2. *Did the availability of capital influence franchisees' decision to take a franchise rather than to set up a totally independent business?*

	ServiceMaster		Dyno-Rod		Wimpy		Total	
		%		%		%		%
Yes	10	66.7	6	37.5	4	20.0	20	39.2
No	5	33.3	10	62.5	16	80.0	31	60.8
	$N=15$	100.0	$N=16$	100.0	$N=20$	100.0	$N=51$	100.0

3. What was the approximate time gap between the decision to become self-employed and taking up a franchise?

	ServiceMaster	%	Dyno-Rod	%	Wimpy	%	Total	%
Up to 1 year	13	86.7	12	75.0	16	80.0	41	80.4
1–2 years	1	6.7	1	6.3	2	10.0	4	7.8
More than 2 years	—	—	2	12.5	1	5.0	3	5.9
Other	1	6.7	1	6.3	1	5.0	3	5.9
	$N=15$	100.0	$N=16$	100.0	$N=20$	100.0	$N=51$	100.0

4. Was their present franchise the only one that franchisees considered?

Stanworth:	ServiceMaster	%	Dyno-Rod	%	Wimpy	%	Total	%
Yes	13	86.7	11	68.8	17	85.0	41	80.4
No	2	13.3	5	31.3	3	15.0	10	19.6
	$N=15$	100.0	$N=16$	100.0	$N=20$	100.0	$N=51$	100.0

Hough:	Yes %	No %	$N=$
Total	76.5	23.5	183
Home Tune	88.7	11.3	71
Prontaprint	62.5	37.5	64
Ziebart	77.1	22.9	48

5. Did franchisees consider any alternative forms of self-employment?

	ServiceMaster	%	Dyno-Rod	%	Wimpy	%	Total	%
Yes	7	46.7	6	37.5	6	30.0	19	37.3
No	8	53.3	9	56.3	12	60.0	29	56.9
Other (already self-employed)	—	—	1	6.3	2	10.0	3	5.9
	$N=15$	100.0	$N=16$	100.0	$N=20$	100.0	$N=51$	100.0

6. *If they had not gone into franchising did franchisees feel they would still be working for themselves?*

	ServiceMaster	%	Dyno-Rod	%	Wimpy	%	Total	%
Yes	9	60.0	9	56.3	16	80.0	34	66.7
No	6	40.0	7	43.8	4	20.0	17	33.3
	N = 15	100.0	N = 16	100.0	N = 20	100.0	N = 51	100.0

7. *Have their businesses fulfilled their original ambitions?*

	ServiceMaster	%	Dyno-Rod	%	Wimpy	%	Total	%
Yes	*12	80.0	13	81.3	13	65.0	38	74.5
No	3	20.0	3	18.8	7	35.0	13	25.5
	N = 15	100.0	N = 16	100.0	N = 20	100.0	N = 51	100.0

* Includes: "partly" and "commencing to".

8. *Would they advise anyone else to do what they have done?*

	ServiceMaster	%	Dyno-Rod	%	Wimpy	%	Total	%
Yes	11	73.3	15	93.8	19	95.0	45	89.2
No	2	13.3	1	6.3	1	5.0	4	7.8
Other	2	13.3	—	—	—	—	2	3.9
	N = 15	100.0	N = 16	100.0	N = 20	100.0	N = 51	100.0

9. *Did franchisees feel, taking into account both the benefits and difficulties associated with being their own boss, that self-employment was worthwhile?*

	ServiceMaster		Dyno-Rod		Wimpy		Total	
		%		%		%		%
Yes	*14	93.3	15	93.8	18	90.0	47	92.2
No	1	6.7	**1	6.3	1	5.0	3	5.9
Other	—	—	—	—	1	5.0	1	2.0
	N = 15	100.0	N = 16	100.0	N = 20	100.0	N = 51	100.0

*   Includes two personally "yes", financially "no".
** Same "no" as question 11.

10. *Did franchisees experience sufficient freedom within terms of their franchise agreement to really feel they were working for themselves?*

	ServiceMaster		Dyno-Rod		Wimpy		Total	
		%		%		%		%
Yes	11	73.3	13	81.3	15	75.0	39	76.5
No	4	26.7	3	19.8	5	25.0	12	23.5
	N = 15	100.0	N = 16	100.0	N = 20	100.0	N = 51	100.0

11. *Did franchisees still feel their original decision to go into franchising was the right one?*

	ServiceMaster		Dyno-Rod		Wimpy		Total	
		%		%		%		%
Yes	15	100.0	16	100.0	19	95.0	50	98.0
No	—	—	—	—	1	5.0	1	2.0
	N = 15	100.0	N = 16	100.0	N = 20	100.0	N = 51	100.0

12. *If franchisees were starting in business again today would they still go into franchising?*

	ServiceMaster		Dyno-Rod		Wimpy		Total	
		%		%		%		%
Yes	10	66.7	13	81.3	14	70.0	37	72.5
No	5	33.3	3	18.8	6	30.0	14	27.5
	$N=15$	100.0	$N=16$	100.0	$N=20$	100.0	$N=51$	100.0

13. *How long did franchisees think they would continue in their present businesses?*

	ServiceMaster		Dyno-Rod		Wimpy		Total	
		%		%		%		%
Indefinitely	8	53.3	14	87.5	12	60.0	34	66.7
Other	7	46.7	2	12.5	8	40.0	17	33.3
	$N=15$	100.0	$N=16$	100.0	$N=20$	100.0	$N=51$	100.0

Section Two: Relationships with Others

14. *Did franchisees encounter any problems in their relationships with their franchisors?*

	ServiceMaster		Dyno-Rod		Wimpy		Total	
		%		%		%		%
Yes	9	60.0	4	25.0	9	45.0	22	43.1
No	6	40.0	12	75.0	11	55.0	29	56.9
	$N=15$	100.0	$N=16$	100.0	$N=20$	100.0	$N=51$	100.0

15. *Did franchisees feel that their franchisor gave a fair service for the return he got from them?*

	ServiceMaster	%	Dyno-Rod	%	Wimpy	%	Total	%
Yes	9	60.0	11	68.8	13	65.0	33	64.7
No	6	40.0	5	31.3	7	35.0	18	35.3
	$N=15$	100.0	$N=16$	100.0	$N=20$	100.0	$N=51$	100.0

16. *Did franchisees think the public was generally aware that ServiceMaster/Dyno-Rod/Wimpy was franchised?*

		%		%		%		%
Yes	—	—	2	12.5	3	15.0	5	9.8
No	15	100.0	14	87.5	17	85.0	45	90.2
	$N=15$	100.0	$N=16$	100.0	$N=20$	100.0	$N=51$	100.0

17. *Did franchisees think their franchisors made any attempt to inform the public that ServiceMaster/Dyno-Rod/Wimpy was franchised?*

	ServiceMaster	%	Dyno-Rod	%	Wimpy	%	Total	%
Yes	4	26.7	2	12.5	1	5.0	7	13.7
No	11	73.3	14	87.5	19	95.0	44	86.3
	$N=15$	100.0	$N=16$	100.0	$N=20$	100.0	$N=51$	100.0

18. *Did franchisees' customers generally realise that they worked for themselves?*

	ServiceMaster	%	Dyno-Rod	%	Wimpy	%	Total	%
Yes	*6	40.0	*3	18.8	8	40.0	17	33.3
No	8	53.3	13	81.3	11	55.0	32	62.7
Other	1	6.7	—	—	1	5.0	2	3.9
	$N=15$	100.0	$N=16$	100.0	$N=20$	100.0	$N=51$	100.0

* Regular customers, i.e. large companies, generally realised they worked for themselves or were told.

19. *How well did franchisees think their brand name was known to:*
(a) *The general public:*

	ServiceMaster	%	Dyno-Rod	%	Wimpy	%	Total	%
Well known	2	13.3	15	93.8	20	100.0	37	72.5
Not well known	13	86.7	1	6.3	—	—	14	27.5
	$N=15$	100.0	$N=16$	100.0	$N=20$	100.0	$N=51$	100.0

(b) *Their potential customers:*

	%		%		%		%
Well known	4	26.7	13	81.3	20	100.0	37	72.5
Not well known	11	73.3	3	18.8	—	—	14	27.5
	$N=15$	100.0	$N=16$	100.0	$N=20$	100.0	$N=51$	100.0

20. *Was the brand name ServiceMaster/Dyno-Rod/Wimpy important to franchisees' businesses?*

	ServiceMaster	%	Dyno-Rod	%	Wimpy	%	Total	%
Yes	10	66.7	15	93.8	17	85.0	42	82.4
No	4	26.7	1	6.3	2	10.0	7	13.7
Other/ Don't know	1	6.7	—	—	1	5.0	2	3.9
	$N=15$	100.0	$N=16$	100.0	$N=20$	100.0	$N=51$	100.0

21. *In franchisees' opinions, were there businesses more successful as a result of being franchised than they would otherwise have been?*

	ServiceMaster		Dyno-Rod		Wimpy		Total	
		%		%		%		%
Yes	12	80.0	14	87.5	14	70.0	40	78.4
No	3	20.0	1	6.3	4	20.0	8	15.7
Other/ Don't know	—	—	1	6.3	2	10.0	3	5.9
	N = 15	100.0	N = 16	100.0	N = 20	100.0	N = 51	100.0

22. *Did franchisees feel that there was less risk in running a franchised business than in running a totally independent business?*

	ServiceMaster		Dyno-Rod		Wimpy		Total	
		%		%		%		%
Yes	10	66.7	15	93.8	13	65.0	38	74.5
No	5	33.3	1	6.3	6	30.0	12	23.5
Other/ Don't know	—	—	—	—	1	5.0	1	2.0
	N = 15	100.0	N = 16	100.0	N = 20	100.0	N = 51	100.0

23. *Did franchisees have employees working for them?*

		%		%		%		%
Yes	10	66.7	16	100.0	20	100.0	46	90.2
No	5	33.3	—	—	—	—	5	9.8
	N = 15	100.0	N = 16	100.0	N = 20	100.0	N = 51	100.0

24. Did franchisees find the task of organising other people satisfying?

		%		%		%		%
Yes	6	40.0	14	87.5	14	70.0	34	66.7
No	2	13.3	2	12.5	5	20.0	9	17.6
Other	—	—	—	—	1	5.0	1	2.0
Non-response/ Not applicable	7	46.7	—	—	—	—	7	13.7
	$N=15$	100.0	$N=16$	100.0	$N=20$	100.0	$N=51$	100.0

25. Did franchisees have problems obtaining staff?

	ServiceMaster		Dyno-Rod		Wimpy		Total	
		%		%		%		%
Yes	5	33.3	3	18.8	5	25.0	13	25.5
No	3	20.0	13	81.3	15	75.0	31	60.8
Non-response/ Not applicable	7	46.7	—	—	—	—	7	13.7
	$N=15$	100.0	$N=16$	100.0	$N=20$	100.0	$N=15$	100.0

26. Did their employees know they were franchisees?

	ServiceMaster		Dyno-Rod		Wimpy		Total	
		%		%		%		%
Yes	8	53.3	16	100.0	20	100.0	44	86.3
No	—	—	—	—	—	—	—	—
Non-response/ Not applicable	7	46.7	—	—	—	—	7	13.7
	$N=15$	100.0	$N=16$	100.0	$N=20$	100.0	$N=51$	100.0

If "yes" did this affect their attribute to working for them?

		%		%		%		%
Yes	—	—	3	18.8	1	5.0	4	9.1
No	8	100.0	11	68.8	19	95.0	38	86.4
Other	—	—	2	12.5	—	—	2	4.5
	$N=8$	100.0	$N=16$	100.0	$N=20$	100.0	$N=44$	100.0

27. *Did franchisees experience any problems in their relationship with customers?*

	ServiceMaster		Dyno-Rod		Wimpy			Total
		%		%		%		%
Yes	1	6.7	4	25.0	—	—	5	9.8
No	14	93.3	12	75.0	*20	100.0	46	90.2
	N = 15	100.0	N = 16	100.0	N = 20	100.0	N = 51	100.0

* Occasionally.

Section Three: Advantages and Disadvantages of Franchising

28. *Were there any aspects of franchising that franchisees did not like?*

	ServiceMaster		Dyno-Rod		Wimpy			Total
		%		%		%		%
Yes	12	80.0	15	93.8	16	80.0	43	84.3
No	3	20.0	1	6.3	4	20.0	8	15.7
	N = 15	100.0	N = 16	100.0	N = 20	100.0	N = 51	100.0

29. *Were there any benefits franchisees' customers got from them as a franchise that they would not have got from an ordinary managed branch of a large company?*

	ServiceMaster		Dyno-Rod		Wimpy			Total
		%		%		%		%
Yes	14	93.3	16	100.0	15	75.0	45	88.2
No	1	6.7	—	—	5	25.0	6	11.8
	N = 15	100.0	N = 16	100.0	N = 20	100.0	N = 51	100.0

30. *Were there any ways in which franchisees could perhaps have given their customers an even better service, but could not because of restrictions in their agreements with their franchisor*

	ServiceMaster	%	Dyno-Rod	%	Wimpy	%	Total	%
Yes	5	33.3	*1	6.3	10	50.0	16	31.4
No	10	66.7	15	93.8	10	50.0	35	68.6
	$N=15$	100.0	$N=16$	100.0	$N=20$	100.0	$N=51$	100.0

* Reduce cost.

Part Three

TABLE 1. *Main information sought by franchisees at their first meeting with their franchisor*

	Home Tune %	Prontaprint %	Ziebart %	Total %
Financial returns	36.6	48.4	29.2	38.8
Cost of entry	25.4	29.7	16.7	24.6
Technical aspects	22.5	18.8	16.7	19.7
Franchisor back up	15.5	18.8	14.6	19.7
Franchisor's integrity	9.9	28.1	16.7	18.1
Product's marketability	4.2	20.3	12.5	12.0
Previous employee so little or none requested	7.0	4.7	10.4	7.0
$N=$	71	64	48	183

TABLE 2. *Main type of financial information initially provided to franchisees*

	Home Tune	Prontaprint	Ziebart	Total
	%	%	%	%
Cost of entry	43.7	42.2	31.3	40.0
Pro forma	12.7	51.6	22.9	29.0
Expected returns	32.4	25.0	14.6	25.1
Little or none	9.9	3.1	14.5	8.7
Previous employee so little or none requested	2.8	3.1	16.7	6.6
$N=$	71	64	48	183

TABLE 3. *What financial projections were supplied by franchisor once the franchisee's own territory or site had been agreed upon?*

	Home Tune	Prontaprint	Ziebart	Total
	%	%	%	%
Capital required	93.0	75.6	52.2	77.0
First years trading projections	65.1	57.8	40.0	56.7
Other	2.3	0.0	0.0	0.9
None given specific to own territory or site	4.7	24.4	40.0	20.4
$N=$	43	45	25	113

N.B.: Columns total more than 100% due to multiple responses

TABLE 4. *Were visits made to existing franchisees prior to entry?*

	Home Tune	Prontaprint	Ziebart	Total
	%	%	%	%
Visit made	56.3	90.6	79.2	74.3
None visited	42.3	9.3	18.8	24.6
No response	1.4	0.0	2.1	1.0
	100.0	100.0	100.0	100.0
$N =$	71	64	48	183

TABLE 5. *Did their franchisor advise them to consult an independent third party prior to signing their agreement?*

	Home Tune	Prontaprint	Ziebart	Total
	%	%	%	%
Yes	52.1	70.3	25.0	51.9
No	46.5	26.6	75.0	47.0
Can't recall/ No response	1.4	3.1	0.0	1.6
	100.0	100.0	100.0	100.0
$N =$	71	64	48	183

TABLE 6. *Was the independent third party consulted knowledgeable about franchising? (Franchisee respondents obtaining advice)*

	Home Tune	Prontaprint	Ziebart	Total
	%	%	%	%
Yes	19.6	12.5	27.9	19.3
No	68.6	69.6	44.2	63.3
Other/ Don't know	5.9	5.4	2.3	5.3
No response	5.9	12.5	25.6	12.0
	100.0	100.0	100.0	100.0
$N =$	51	57	43	151

TABLE 7. *Proportion of franchisees' initial funding obtained from a bank*

	Home Tune	Prontaprint	Ziebart	Total
	%	%	%	%
None reported	48.8	35.6	48.0	43.4
Up to 25%	2.3	20.0	16.0	12.4
26% to 50%	11.6	26.7	16.0	18.6
51% to 75%	11.6	15.6	4.0	11.5
Over 75%	18.6	2.2	12.0	10.6
Can't recall/ No response	7.0	0.0	4.0	3.6
	100.0	100.0	100.0	100.0
$N =$	43	45	25	113

TABLE 8. *Did your bank manager appear to understand the concept of franchising?*

	Home Tune	Prontaprint	Ziebart	Total
	%	%	%	%
Understood	58.1	44.4	60.0	53.1
Didn't understand	30.2	42.2	16.0	31.9
Other	0.0	2.2	4.0	1.8
No response/ Don't know	11.6	11.1	20.0	13.3
	100.0	100.0	100.0	100.0
$N =$	43	45	25	113

TABLE 9. *What do you think was your bank manager's attitude towards franchising?*

	Home Tune	Prontaprint	Ziebart	Total
	%	%	%	%
Favourable	53.5	51.1	56.0	53.1
Unfavourable	32.6	26.6	16.0	26.5
Other	2.3	8.9	12.0	7.1
No response/ Don't know	11.6	13.3	16.0	13.3
	100.0	100.0	100.0	100.0
$N =$	43	45	25	113

TABLE 10. *Did you undertake training before starting to operate as a franchisee?*

	Home Tune	Prontaprint	Ziebart	Total
	%	%	%	%
Training undertaken	85.9	89.1	75.0	84.2
No training undertaken	2.8	3.2	8.3	4.4
Prior employee so not required	5.6	3.1	12.5	6.6
Other	2.8	4.7	4.2	3.8
No response	2.8	0.0	0.0	1.1
	100.0	100.0	100.0	100.0
$N =$	71	64	48	183

The Guide to Franchising

TABLE 11. *Franchisee assessments of the quality of franchisor advice*

	Home Tune	Prontaprint	Ziebart	Total
	%	%	%	%
Technical advice				
Good to very good	41.9	71.1	52.0	55.7
Adequate	41.9	24.4	44.0	35.4
Poor to very poor	14.0	4.4	4.0	8.0
Sales advice				
Good to very good	53.5	71.1	12.0	51.3
Adequate	30.2	17.8	20.0	23.0
Poor to very poor	11.6	11.1	64.0	23.0
Not provided	2.3	0.0	4.0	1.8
Financial advice				
Good to very good	39.5	28.9	0.0	26.5
Adequate	34.9	31.1	24.0	31.0
Poor to very poor	14.0	31.1	8.0	19.5
Not provided	9.3	8.9	68.0	22.1
Staffing advice				
Good to very good	16.3	37.8	8.0	23.0
Adequate	20.9	37.8	16.0	26.5
Poor to very poor	14.0	17.8	24.0	17.7
Not provided	44.2	4.4	52.0	30.1
Training advice				
Good to very good	34.9	66.7	64.0	54.0
Adequate	25.6	20.0	24.0	23.0
Poor to very poor	30.2	11.1	12.0	18.5
Not provided	7.0	0.0	0.0	2.7
$N=$	43	45	25	113

N.B.: Column groups may be less than 100% due to non-respondents.

TABLE 12. *Does your franchisor see you primarily as an independent small businessman or essentially as a manager?*

	Home Tune	Prontaprint	Ziebart	Total
	%	%	%	%
Independent	73.1	81.3	79.1	77.6
Managers	19.8	6.2	8.3	12.1
Both	7.0	12.5	12.5	10.3
	100.0	100.0	100.0	100.0
$N =$	71	64	48	183

TABLE 13. *How much individual freedom does your franchisor give you in running your franchise?*

	Home Tune	Prontaprint	Ziebart	Total
	%	%	%	%
A great deal	52.1	46.9	50.0	49.7
A reasonable amount within guidelines	46.5	53.1	43.8	48.1
Very little	0.0	0.0	2.1	0.5
Other	1.4	0.0	4.2	1.6
	100.0	100.0	100.0	100.0
$N =$	71	64	48	183

TABLE 14. *Has there been renegotiation or attempted renegotiation of your territory since you started to operate the franchise?*

	Home Tune	Prontaprint	Ziebart	Total
	%	%	%	%
Territory changed	36.6	10.9	10.4	20.8
Territory unaltered	8.5	1.6	10.4	6.6
None	53.5	85.9	79.2	71.6
No response	1.4	1.6	0.0	1.1
	100.0	100.0	100.0	100.0
$N =$	71	64	48	183

TABLE 15. *Why did the renegotiation of the territory take place?*

	Home Tune	Prontaprint	Ziebart	Total
	%	%	%	%
Expansion of the business	56.3	37.5	50.0	46.0
Area cumbersome/ ill defined	15.6	25.0	0.0	10.0
Franchisor pressure to reduce size	9.4	0.0	20.0	10.0
Various reasons	12.5	25.0	30.0	28.0
Can't recall/ No response	6.3	12.5	0.0	6.0
	100.0	100.0	100.0	100.0
$N =$	32	8	10	50

TABLE 16. *How often do you have direct dealings with your franchisor?*

	Home Tune	Prontaprint	Ziebart	Total
	%	%	%	%
Twice or more weekly	1.4	12.5	20.8	10.4
Once a week	8.5	25.0	18.8	16.9
Fortnightly	8.5	10.9	6.3	8.7
Monthly	32.4	26.6	16.7	26.2
Quarterly or less frequently	46.5	25.0	37.5	36.6
No response	2.8	0.0	0.0	1.1
	100.0	100.0	100.0	100.0
$N =$	71	64	48	183

TABLE 17. *Main instigator of franchisor–franchisee dealings*

	Home Tune	Prontaprint	Ziebart	Total
	%	%	%	%
Mainly franchisee	64.3	42.1	52.2	54.3
Mainly franchisor	32.1	47.4	34.8	37.1
Unsure	3.6	10.5	13.0	8.6
	100.0	100.0	100.0	100.0
$N=$	28	19	23	70

TABLE 18. *What are the main reasons for you contacting your franchisor?*

	Home Tune	Prontaprint	Ziebart	Total
	%	%	%	%
Technical queries	35.2	18.8	47.9	32.8
General queries	23.9	45.3	16.7	29.5
Supply of materials or parts	35.2	3.1	45.9	26.7
Advertising and promotion	16.9	21.9	14.6	18.1
Accounts/finance administration	12.7	10.9	6.3	10.4
Equipment failure/queries	8.5	15.6	2.1	9.3
Feedback and statistics	4.2	1.6	8.3	4.3
$N=$	71	64	48	183

N.B.: Columns may total more than 100% due to multiple responses.

TABLE 19. *What are the main reasons for your franchisor contacting you?*

	Home Tune	Prontaprint	Ziebart	Total
	%	%	%	%
Sales promotions	3.6	26.3	47.8	24.4
Accounts/royalty payments	46.4	10.5	8.7	24.3
General circulars	28.6	31.6	4.3	21.4
General queries/ liaison	25.0	10.5	8.7	15.7
Technical/new methods/new equipment	10.7	26.3	8.7	14.2
New products	0.0	21.1	21.7	12.8
Organise meetings	3.6	31.6	8.7	12.8
Customer liaison/ complaints	17.9	0.0	17.4	12.8
Quality control	0.0	5.3	30.4	11.5
Reports/ statistics	3.6	21.1	8.7	10.0
$N=$	28	19	23	70

N.B.: Columns may total more than 100% due to multiple responses.

TABLE 20. *Does the franchisor respond quickly to your requests for assistance?*

	Home Tune	Prontaprint	Ziebart	Total
	%	%	%	%
Yes	81.4	86.7	64.0	79.6
No	2.3	4.4	24.0	8.0
Depend on type of request	9.3	8.9	8.0	8.8
Other/ No response	7.0	0.0	4.0	3.6
	100.0	100.0	100.0	100.0
$N=$	43	45	24	113

TABLE 21. *How often do your franchisor's representatives actually visit you?*

	Home Tune	Prontaprint	Ziebart	Total
	%	%	%	%
Weekly or fortnightly	0.0	12.5	12.6	7.6
Monthly	0.0	42.2	20.8	20.2
Every 2 months	0.0	28.1	20.8	15.3
Quarterly	1.4	3.1	27.1	8.7
Half-yearly	2.8	3.1	6.3	3.8
Annually	23.9	0.0	4.2	10.4
On request as needed	15.5	3.1	0.0	7.1
Never	50.7	0.0	0.0	19.7
Other	0.0	7.8	6.3	4.4
Can't recall/ No response	5.6	0.0	2.1	2.7
	100.0	100.0	100.0	100.0
$N=$	71	64	48	183

TABLE 22. *How often do you like your franchisor's representatives to visit you?*

	Home Tune	Prontaprint	Ziebart	Total
	%	%	%	%
Weekly or fortnightly	0.0	15.6	20.8	11.0
Monthly	1.4	42.2	29.2	23.0
Every 2 months	0.0	12.5	16.7	8.7
Quarterly	7.0	6.3	6.3	6.6
Half-yearly	12.7	0.0	2.1	5.5
Annually	22.5	0.0	0.0	8.7
On request/ other	11.3	15.7	14.6	13.7
Never	33.8	1.6	8.3	15.8
Don't know/ No response	11.3	6.3	2.1	7.1
	100.0	100.0	100.0	100.0
$N=$	71	64	48	183

TABLE 23. *How long is it since you were last visited by a representative of your franchisor?*

	Home Tune	Prontaprint	Ziebart	Total
	%	%	%	%
Within last week	0.0	32.8	35.4	20.8
Week to fortnight	0.0	20.3	16.7	11.5
Fortnight to a month	1.4	26.6	18.8	14.8
Month to 2 months	4.2	15.6	10.4	9.8
2 months to 6 months	8.4	4.7	6.3	6.5
6 months to 12 months	9.9	0.0	8.3	9.8
Over 12 months ago	29.6	0.0	2.1	12.0
Never visited	45.1	0.0	0.0	17.5
Cannot recall/ No response	1.4	0.0	2.1	1.0
	100.0	100.0	100.0	100.0
$N=$	71	64	48	183

TABLE 24. *Franchisees' ratings of the general quality of their franchisors' assistance*

	Home Tune	Prontaprint	Ziebart	Total
	%	%	%	%
Very good	28.2	21.9	8.3	20.8
Good	23.9	34.4	16.7	25.7
Adequate	23.9	34.4	50.0	34.4
Poor	16.9	6.3	12.5	12.0
Very poor	5.6	0.0	10.4	4.9
No response	1.4	3.1	2.1	2.2
	100.0	100.0	100.0	100.0
$N=$	71	64	48	183

TABLE 25. *Division of day-to-day responsibility for key operational areas (franchisee and franchisor respondents)*

	Home Tune		Prontaprint		Ziebart		Total	
	F'ee	F'or	F'ee	F'or	F'ee	F'or	F'ee	F'or
	%		%		%		%	
Hours of operation								
Franchisor	0.0	0	62.5	3	0.0	0	21.9	3
Equal	2.8	1	6.3	0	0.0	1	3.3	2
Franchisee	97.1	2	31.3	1	100.0	4	74.9	7
Bookkeeping								
Franchisor	4.2	2	21.9	1	0.0	0	9.3	3
Equal	4.2	1	12.5	0	2.1	0	6.6	1
Franchisee	91.6	0	65.6	3	97.9	5	84.2	8
Products/Services								
Franchisor	53.5	3	50.1	4	37.5	5	48.1	12
Equal	14.1	0	32.8	0	16.7	0	21.3	0
Franchisee	29.5	0	16.2	0	45.8	0	29.5	0
Retail prices								
Franchisor	71.8	2	90.6	4	14.6	3	63.4	9
Equal	12.7	0	7.8	0	18.8	1	12.6	1
Franchisee	14.1	1	1.6	0	66.7	1	23.5	2
Local advertising								
Franchisor	4.2	0	1.6	1	2.1	1	2.7	2
Equal	0.0	2	4.7	2	6.3	3	3.3	7
Franchisee	95.8	1	93.8	0	91.7	1	94.0	3
Quality of service								
Franchisor	5.6	1	4.7	3	2.1	0	4.4	4
Equal	16.9	0	20.3	0	14.6	2	17.5	2
Franchisee	77.4	2	75.0	1	83.3	3	78.1	6
Employee number								
Franchisor	1.4	1	1.6	1	0.0	1	1.1	3
Equal	7.0	0	4.7	1	0.0	1	4.4	2
Franchisee	85.9	2	93.8	2	100.0	3	92.3	7
Employee wages								
Franchisor	4.2	1	1.6	0	0.0	0	2.1	1
Equal	11.3	0	0.0	0	0.0	0	4.4	0
Franchisee	60.4	2	98.4	4	100.0	5	88.0	11
N =	71	3	64	4	48	5	183	12

Some column groups do not total 100% as the proportions of non-respondents are not included.

TABLE 26. *Closeness with which franchisees' claim to follow their franchisors' stipulated procedures*

	Home Tune	Prontaprint	Ziebart	Total
	%	%	%	%
Very closely	56.3	37.5	54.2	49.2
Fairly closely	39.4	53.1	39.6	44.3
Neither closely nor loosely	4.2	3.1	4.2	3.8
Fairly or very loosely	0.0	4.7	2.1	2.1
No response	0.0	1.6	0.0	0.5
	100.0	100.0	100.0	100.0
$N=$	71	64	48	183

TABLE 27. *Has your franchisor ever given you special assistance because your business was experiencing difficulties?*

	Home Tune	Prontaprint	Ziebart	Total
	%	%	%	%
Yes	23.9	45.3	39.6	35.5
No	73.2	53.1	60.4	62.8
No response	2.8	1.6	0.0	1.6
	100.0	100.0	100.0	100.0
$N=$	71	64	48	183

TABLE 28. *What type of assistance was provided?* (*Those receiving special assistance*)

	Home Tune	Prontaprint	Ziebart	Total
	%	%	%	%
Marketing/ promotion/ advertising	23.5	27.6	26.3	26.2
Extended credit	52.9	0.0	42.1	26.2
Technical assistance	11.8	13.8	10.5	12.3
Financial guidance	0.0	20.7	5.3	10.8
Personnel/ administrative	0.0	20.7	5.3	10.8
General advice	0.0	13.8	0.0	6.2
Other	5.9	3.4	10.5	6.2
No response	5.9	0.0	0.0	1.5
	100.0	100.0	100.0	100.0
$N=$	17	29	19	65

TABLE 29. *Was it a real help in overcoming the problems?* (*Those receiving special assistance*)

	Home Tune	Prontaprint	Ziebart	Total
	%	%	%	%
Yes	88.2	75.9	84.2	81.5
No	0.0	13.8	5.3	7.7
Still in progress	5.9	10.3	5.3	7.7
Don't know	5.9	0.0	5.3	3.1
	100.0	100.0	100.0	100.0
$N=$	17	29	19	65

TABLE 30. *How useful are national conferences?*

	Home Tune	Prontaprint	Ziebart	Total
	%	%	%	%
Very useful	41.9	55.6	16.0	41.6
Fairly useful	37.2	26.7	24.0	30.1
Not very useful	11.6	4.4	24.0	11.5
Not useful at all	0.0	4.4	12.0	4.4
No response	9.3	8.9	24.0	12.4
	100.0	100.0	100.0	100.0
$N=$	43	45	25	113

TABLE 31. *How useful are regional conferences?*

	Home Tune	Prontaprint	Ziebart	Total
	%	%	%	%
Very useful	18.6	37.8	8.0	23.9
Fairly useful	20.9	33.3	20.0	25.7
Not very useful	2.3	20.0	24.0	14.2
No response/ not applicable	58.1	8.9	48.0	36.3
	100.0	100.0	100.0	100.0
$N=$	43	45	25	113

TABLE 32. *Does your franchise have a joint franchisor–franchisee committee?*

	Home Tune	Prontaprint	Ziebart	Total
	%	%	%	%
Yes	57.7	17.2	16.7	32.8
No	7.0	79.7	77.1	50.8
In the past	32.4	0.0	6.3	14.2
Don't know no response	2.8	3.1	0.0	2.2
	100.0	100.0	100.0	100.0
$N=$	71	64	48	183

TABLE 33. *Use of joint committees to make representations to their franchisor (Respondents reporting having joint committees)*

	Home Tune	Prontaprint	Ziebart	Total
	%	%	%	%
Committee used	26.5	14.3	14.3	22.9
No use made of committee	73.5	85.7	71.4	75.0
Can't recall	0.0	0.0	14.3	2.1
	100.0	100.0	100.0	100.0
$N =$	34	7	7	48

TABLE 34. *Should a joint franchisor franchisee committee be instituted?*

	Home Tune	Prontaprint	Ziebart	Total
	%	%	%	%
Already have joint committee	57.7	17.2	16.7	32.8
Should institute a committee	7.0	46.9	50.0	32.2
Committee not wanted	32.5	31.3	33.3	32.2
No response	2.8	4.7	0.0	2.7
	100.0	100.0	100.0	100.0
$N =$	71	64	48	183

TABLE 35. *Strictness with which their franchisor enforces the terms of the franchise agreement*

	Home Tune	Prontaprint	Ziebart	Total
	%	%	%	%
Very strictly	0.0	1.6	12.5	3.8
Fairly strictly	12.7	6.3	27.1	14.2
Neither strictly nor leniently	28.2	53.1	18.8	34.4
Fairly leniently	22.5	21.9	12.5	19.7
Very leniently	14.1	3.1	2.1	7.1
Some parts strictly, some leniently	19.7	14.1	25.0	19.1
Don't know/ no response	2.8	0.0	2.1	1.6
	100.0	100.0	100.0	100.0
$N=$	71	64	48	183

TABLE 36. *What parts of the contract does your franchisor most strictly enforce?*

	Home Tune	Prontaprint	Ziebart	Total
	%	%	%	%
Declaration/ payment of royalty	67.9	52.6	0.0	41.4
Use of foreign materials	0.0	5.3	78.3	27.2
Corporate image/ cleanliness	25.0	52.6	0.0	24.3
Quality of product/service	17.9	5.3	13.0	12.9
Territorial boundaries	10.7	10.5	0.0	7.2
Non-authorised work/competing business	10.7	0.0	4.3	7.2
Use of non-standard equipment	3.6	10.5	4.3	5.7
Exploitation of territory	3.6	0.0	8.7	4.3
$N=$	28	19	23	70

N.B.: Columns may total more than 100% due to multiple responses.

TABLE 37. *Franchisees' satisfaction with way their franchisor carries out his contractual obligations*

	Home Tune	Prontaprint	Ziebart	Total
	%	%	%	%
Very satisfied	30.2	20.0	8.0	21.2
Fairly satisfied	37.2	53.3	28.0	41.6
Neither satisfied nor dissatisfied	25.6	24.4	36.0	27.4
Fairly dissatisfied	2.3	0.0	4.0	1.8
Very dissatisfied	0.0	2.2	24.0	6.2
No response	4.7	0.0	0.0	1.8
	100.0	100.0	100.0	100.0
$N =$	43	45	25	113

TABLE 38. *Are there any sections of the contract which you feel should be altered?*

	Home Tune	Prontaprint	Ziebart	Total
	%	%	%	%
Yes	42.3	23.4	33.3	33.3
No	53.5	70.3	58.3	60.7
No response/ don't know	4.2	6.3	8.4	6.0
	100.0	100.0	100.0	100.0
$N =$	71	64	48	183

TABLE 39. *Areas in which changes sought (Those wanting contract alterations)*

	Home Tune	Prontaprint	Ziebart	Total
	%	%	%	%
Termination clauses	36.7	26.7	18.7	29.5
Payments to franchisor	13.3	46.7	18.7	23.0
Balance of the agreement	10.0	0.0	25.0	11.5
Territory	13.3	0.0	6.3	8.2
Equipment ownership	10.0	0.0	6.3	6.6
Other	13.3	20.0	18.7	16.4
No response	3.3	6.7	6.3	4.9
	100.0	100.0	100.0	100.0
$N =$	30	15	16	61

TABLE 40. *Outcomes of requests made by franchisees for negotiation?*

	Home Tune	Prontaprint	Ziebart	Total
	%	%	%	%
Changes obtained	5.6	1.6	39.6	13.1
Changes refused	7.0	9.4	10.4	8.6
Changes being discussed	1.4	1.6	4.2	2.2
No changes requested	85.9	87.5	45.8	76.0
	100.0	100.0	100.0	100.0
$N =$	71	64	48	183

TABLE 41. *What parts of the contract do you think should be open for negotiation? (Those responding in favour of negotiation)*

	Home Tune	Prontaprint	Ziebart	Total
	%	%	%	%
Whole of the contract	39.1	0.0	47.4	31.6
Territory	8.7	73.3	15.8	28.1
Advertising	13.0	0.0	0.0	5.3
Prices	4.3	0.0	5.3	3.5
Other	21.7	13.3	31.6	22.8
Don't know/ no response	13.0	13.3	0.0	8.8
	100.0	100.0	100.0	100.0
$N=$	23	15	19	57

TABLE 42. *Do you think it is unlikely that you may want to stop operating* your franchise before your contract comes up for renewal?*

	Home Tune	Prontaprint	Ziebart	Total
	%	%	%	%
Yes	11.3	31.3	43.8	26.8
No	85.9	65.6	47.9	68.9
Don't know/ no response	2.8	3.2	8.3	3.3
	100.0	100.0	100.0	100.0
$N=$	71	64	48	183

* This would usually be through the sale of the outlet

TABLE 43. *Main grounds for franchisor termination of the agreement*

	Home Tune	Prontaprint	Ziebart	Total
	%	%	%	%
Poor quality workmanship	46.5	21.9	39.6	36.1
Non-payment of royalty	32.4	39.1	6.3	27.9
Underutilisation of territory	26.8	4.7	27.1	19.1
Use of foreign materials	0.0	3.1	62.5	17.5
Poor corporate image	18.3	12.5	2.1	14.2
Doing unauthorised work	18.3	3.1	2.1	8.8
$N=$	71	64	48	183

N.B.: Columns total more than 100% due to multiple responses.

TABLE 44. *Estimated period of grace to put right any breaches of their contract*

	Home Tune	Prontaprint	Ziebart	Total
	%	%	%	%
Up to 2 weeks	0.0	0.0	14.6	3.8
3 weeks	0.0	0.0	2.1	0.5
4 weeks	8.5	10.9	27.1	14.2
6–12 weeks	4.2	7.9	14.6	8.2
13–52 weeks	2.8	1.6	2.1	2.2
No period specified	38.0	32.8	18.8	31.1
Little or none/ it depends on breach	5.6	4.7	10.4	6.6
Don't know	38.0	39.1	8.3	30.6
No response	2.8	3.1	2.1	2.7
	100.0	100.0	100.0	100.0
$N=$	71	64	48	183

TABLE 45. *Do you think that your franchisor has ever terminated contracts?*

	Home Tune	Prontaprint	Ziebart	Total
	%	%	%	%
Terminations known of	88.7	64.1	87.5	79.8
No terminations known of	4.2	18.8	2.1	8.7
No response/ don't know	7.0	17.2	10.5	11.4
	100.0	100.0	100.0	100.0
$N=$	71	64	48	183

TABLE 46. *Extent to which the time taken for franchisees to establish their business conformed, or was expected to conform, with their franchisor's predictions*

	Home Tune	Prontaprint	Ziebart	Total
	%	%	%	%
Longer than predicted	38.0	29.7	35.4	34.4
As predicted	11.3	45.3	14.6	24.0
Quicker than predicted	7.0	9.4	8.3	8.2
Don't know yet	2.8	3.1	6.3	3.3
No prediction made	35.2	9.4	27.1	24.0
Can't recall/ no response	5.6	3.1	8.3	6.0
	100.0	100.0	100.0	100.0
$N=$	71	64	48	183

TABLE 47. *If you feel at all dissatisfied with your profitability, is the main problem the general level of sales or the profit margin on those sales? (Those dissatisfied with their profitability)*

	Home Tune	Prontaprint	Ziebart	Total
	%	%	%	%
Level of sales	73.7	57.7	52.9	61.3
Profit margin	10.5	15.4	23.5	16.1
Combination	10.5	26.9	23.5	21.0
No response	5.3	0.0	0.0	1.6
	100.0	100.0	100.0	100.0
$N=$	19	26	17	62

TABLE 48. *Practical advantages of franchising to their franchisors*

	Home Tune	Prontaprint	Ziebart	Total
	%	%	%	%
National coverage for low capital outlay	38.0	53.1	41.7	44.3
Royalty/fees	36.7	29.7	14.6	28.5
Franchisee more dedicated than a manager	23.9	23.4	22.9	23.5
Fewer head office and field staff/ lower overheads	5.6	6.3	4.2	5.4
No/less day-to-day management of outlets	4.2	6.3	8.3	6.0
Franchisees captive customs	0.0	0.0	20.8	5.4
Other	9.9	7.8	10.4	9.9
No response/ don't know	7.0	7.8	4.2	6.5
$N=$	71	64	48	183

N.B.: Columns total more than 100% due to multiple responses.

TABLE 49. *Practical disadvantage of franchising to their franchisors*

	Home Tune	Prontaprint	Ziebart	Total
	%	%	%	%
Lack of absolute control/inability to dictate policy	19.7	43.8	25.0	29.5
None or few	32.4	20.3	20.8	25.1
Poor franchisees	0.0	3.1	18.8	6.0
Individuality of franchisees	8.5	3.1	6.3	6.0
Maintenance of corporate image	8.5	0.0	0.0	3.3
Other	11.3	12.5	22.9	14.8
Don't know	8.5	1.6	0.0	3.8
No response	11.3	15.6	6.3	11.5
	100.0	100.0	100.0	100.0
$N=$	71	64	48	183

TABLE 50. *Do you think that relevant prior experience contributes to the success of franchisees within your franchise?*

	Home Tune	Prontaprint	Ziebart	Total
	%	%	%	%
Not of particular help	32.6	82.2	52.0	56.6
Helpful	55.8	13.3	24.0	31.9
Helpful at the start	7.0	0.0	4.0	3.5
Don't know/ no response	4.7	4.4	20.0	8.0
	100.0	100.0	100.0	100.0
$N=$	43	45	25	113

TABLE 51. *Franchisee opinions of the British Franchise Association*

	Home Tune	Prontaprint	Ziebart	Total
	%	%	%	%
Know too little about it to hold an opinion	40.8	28.1	41.7	36.6
Didn't know it existed	0.0	3.1	37.5	10.9
A good idea	21.1	17.2	2.1	14.8
Helps keep up standards	9.9	18.8	6.3	12.0
Operates solely for the benefit of franchisors	8.5	7.8	6.3	7.7
Other	8.5	6.3	4.2	6.6
Don't know/ no response	11.3	18.7	2.1	
	100.0	100.0	100.0	100.0
N =	71	64	48	183

TABLE 52. *Awareness by franchisees of their franchisor's membership of the British Franchise Association*

	Home Tune	Prontaprint	Ziebart	Total
	%	%	%	%
Franchisor is a member	88.7	78.1	60.4	77.6
Franchisor not a member	0.0	3.1	37.5	10.9
Don't know	9.9	10.9	0.0	7.9
No response	1.4	7.8	2.1	3.8
	100.0	100.0	100.0	100.0
N =	71	64	48	183

TABLE 53. *Should franchisees also have a place in the British Franchise Association?*

	Home Tune	Prontaprint	Ziebart	Total
	%	%	%	%
Yes	67.4	60.0	60.0	62.8
No	2.3	11.1	4.0	6.2
Don't know	23.3	26.7	32.0	26.5
No response	7.0	2.2	4.0	4.4
	100.0	100.0	100.0	100.0
$N=$	43	45	25	113

TABLE 54. *Should franchisees form a national, cross franchise, association similar to the B.F.A?*

	Home Tune	Prontaprint	Ziebart	Total
	%	%	%	%
Yes	43.7	34.4	35.4	38.3
No	39.4	42.2	52.1	43.7
Don't know	15.5	20.3	10.4	15.8
No response	1.4	3.1	2.1	2.2
	100.0	100.0	100.0	100.0
$N=$	71	64	48	183

Arbitration

PART I

"Any dispute or difference of any kind whatsoever which arises or occurs between the parties in relation to any thing or matter arising under out of or in connection with (Clauses   of) this Agreement shall be referred to arbitration under the Arbitration Rules of the Chartered Institute of Arbitrators."

PART II

The Chartered Institute of Arbitrators
Arbitration Rules
(adopted to take effect from 1 March 1981)

Where any agreement, submission or reference provides for arbitration under the Rules of the Chartered Institute of Arbitrators ("the Institute") the arbitration shall be conducted in accordance with the following Rules, or such amended Rules as the Institute may have adopted to take effect before the commencement of the arbitration.

Request for, or Notification of, Arbitration

1. (1) Any party wishing to commence an arbitration under these Rules shall send to the Registrar of the Institute ("the Registrar") a written Request for arbitration, which shall include, or be accompanied by:

   (a) the names and addresses of all the parties to the arbitration;
   (b) copies of the contractual documents under which the arbitration arises;
   (c) any separate submission or reference to the arbitration;
   (d) a brief statement of the nature and circumstances of the dispute;
   (e) a statement of any matters on which the parties have previously agreed as to the conduct of the arbitration;
   (f) the fee prescribed in the Schedule of Costs;

   and shall confirm to the Registrar that copies have been sent to all the other parties.

   (2) Where the agreement, submission or reference to arbitration provides for the appointment of the arbitrator (or all the arbitrators, if there is more than one)

by any person or body (including the parties themselves) other than the Institute, Rule 1(1) above and Rule 2 below shall not apply, but the arbitrator when so appointed (or, if there is more than one, their Chairman) shall promptly send to the Registrar a Notification of arbitration, which shall include, or be accompanied by:

(a) a copy of his or their appointment, and of any documents referred to therein;
(b) a brief statement of the nature and circumstances of the dispute;
(c) a statement of any matters on which the parties have previously agreed as to the conduct of the arbitration, and of any steps taken in the arbitration since the appointment;
(d) the fee prescribed in the Schedule of Costs.

Appointment of Arbitrator

2. (1) On accepting the Request, the Institute (unless all the parties have previously agreed to appoint a specified single arbitrator) will elect and appoint an arbitrator or arbitrators to determine the dispute, and will notify the parties accordingly.
    (2) If the parties have each nominated an arbitrator, the Institute will appoint those arbitrators together with a sufficient number of additional arbitrators selected by the Institute to ensure that the total number of arbitrators is uneven.
    (3) The Institute will appoint the arbitrator (or one of the arbitrators) it selects as the Chairman.
    (4) If any arbitrator, after appointment, dies, refuses, fails or in the opinion of the Institute becomes unable or unfit to act, the Institute will, upon request, appoint another arbitrator in his place.
    (5) In selecting arbitrators, the Institute will, so far as possible, have regard to the nature of the contract and the nature and circumstances of the dispute.

Independence and Impartiality of Arbitrators

3. All arbitrators (whether or not nominated by the parties) conducting an arbitration under these Rules shall be and remain at all times wholly independent and impartial, and shall not act as advocates for any party.

Communication between Parties and Arbitrator

4. (1) In the following Rules, the expression "the arbitrator" includes all the arbitrators where more than one has been appointed.
    (2) Unless the Institute directs otherwise, all communications between a party and the arbitrator shall be made through the Registrar. Where the Institute does so direct, all further references in these Rules to the Registrar shall thereafter be read as references to the arbitrator.
    (3) Where the Registrar, on behalf of the arbitrator, sends any communication to one party, he will send a copy to each of the other parties.
    (4) Where any party sends any communication (including any Statement under Rule 6) to the Registrar, he shall include a copy for each arbitrator, and he shall also send copies to all the other parties and confirm to the Registrar that he has done so.
    (5) The addresses of the parties for the purpose of all communications during the proceedings shall be those set out in the Request for or Notification of arbitration, or such other addresses as the parties shall later agree, or as any party concerned shall at any time notify to the Registrar and to all the other parties.

Jurisdiction and Procedure in the Arbitration

5. (1) The arbitrator shall have the jurisdiction, and the powers to direct the procedure in the arbitration, necessary to ensure the just, expeditious, economical and final determination of the dispute, as set out in the Schedule of Jurisdiction and Powers of the Arbitrator.

   (2) In the absence of any other directions, the procedure will be that set out in Rules 6 and 7.

Submission of Written Statements

6. (1) Within thirty days of the notification of appointment of the arbitrator the party or parties who requested the arbitration ("the Claimant") shall send the Registrar a Statement of Case setting out in sufficient detail the facts and contentions of law on which he relies, and the relief that he claims.

   (2) Within thirty days of the receipt of the Statement of Case, the other party, or parties if there is more than one ("the Respondent"), shall send the Registrar a Statement of Defence stating in sufficient detail which of the facts and contentions of law in the Statement of Case he admits or denies, on what grounds, and on what other facts and contentions of law he relies. If he has a Counterclaim, he shall set it out in his Statement of Defence as if it were a Statement of Case.

   (3) Within thirty days of receipt of the Statement of Defence, the Claimant may send the Registrar a Statement of Reply.

   (4) Where there is a counterclaim, the Claimant shall send the Registrar a Statement of Defence to it within thirty days of its receipt, to which the Respondent may reply within a further thirty days of receipt.

   (5) All Statements of Case, Defence and Reply shall be accompanied by copies (or, if they are especially voluminous, lists) of all essential documents on which the party concerned relies and which have not previously been submitted by any party, and (where practicable) by any relevant samples.

   (6) After the submission of all the Statements, the arbitrator will give directions for the further conduct of the arbitration.

Meetings and Hearings

7. (1) The arbitrator may at any time fix the date, time and place of meetings and hearings in the arbitration, and the Registrar will give all the parties adequate notice of these. Subject to any adjournments which the arbitrator allows, the final hearing will be continued on successive working days until it is concluded.

   (2) All meetings and hearings will be in private unless all the parties require otherwise.

   (3) Provided he gives the Registrar and the other parties not less than ten days' prior notice, any party may be represented at any meeting or hearing by a legal or other professional practitioner.

The Award

8. (1) The arbitrator will make his award in writing and, unless all the parties otherwise agree, his reasons will be set out or referred to in the award.

   (2) The arbitrator will send his award to the Institute as soon as practicable after the conclusion of the final hearing. Thereupon the Institute will notify the parties that the award is ready to be taken up.

9.   Where there is more than one arbitrator and they disagree on any matter or question, they will decide by a majority. Failing a majority, the Chairman alone decides.

Costs of the Arbitration

10.   (1) The costs of the arbitration will be in accordance with the Schedule of Costs.

    (2) From the commencement of the arbitration, all the parties shall be jointly and severally liable to the Institute for these costs until they are paid.

    (3) The arbitrator will specify the total amount of the costs of the arbitration in his award. Unless all the parties shall agree otherwise, he will determine (in the exercise of his absolute and unfettered discretion) which party shall pay them, and whether any party shall pay all or part of any other costs incurred by any other party.

11.   (1) After notification by the Institute, any party may take up the award upon payments to the Institute of any costs of the arbitration then still outstanding.

    (2) If the award has not been taken up within ten days of the notification, the Institute may by action recover all outstanding costs of the arbitration from any or all of the parties.

    (3) If the arbitrator has determined that all or any part of the costs of the arbitration shall be paid by any party other than a party which has already paid them, that party shall have the right to recover the appropriate amount from that other party.

12.   If the arbitration is abandoned, suspended or concluded, by agreement or otherwise, before the final award is made, the parties shall pay to the Institute the costs of the arbitration incurred up to that time, in such proportions as between them they shall agree or, failing agreement, as the arbitrator shall determine.

Simplified Procedure

13.   Where the value of all matters in dispute between the parties does not exceed £5000, or in any other arbitration where the parties so agree,

    (1) the Registrar will appoint a single arbitrator;

    (2) the arbitrator may determine the dispute at an informal hearing attended by all the parties;

    (3) alternatively, the arbitrator may determine the dispute by the parties, voluntarily or on his direction, without any hearing.

Exclusion of Liability

14.   (1) Neither the Institute nor the arbitrator shall be liable to any party for any act, omission in connection with any arbitration conducted under these Rules, save that the arbitrator (but not the Institute) shall be liable for the consequences of any conscious and deliberate wrongdoing on his own part.

    (2) After the award has been made (and any accidental mistake or omission corrected), the arbitrator shall be under no obligation to make any statement to any person about any matter concerning the arbitration, nor shall any party seek to make him a witness in any legal proceedings arising out of the arbitration.

Schedule of Jurisdiction and Powers of the Arbitrator

A.   By submitting to arbitration under the foregoing Rules, the parties shall be taken to have conferred on the arbitrator the following jurisdiction and powers, to be exercised by him so far as English law allows, and in his absolute and unfettered discretion, if he shall judge it to be expedient for the purpose of ensuring the just, expeditious, economical and final determination of the dispute referred to him.

B. The arbitrator shall have jurisdiction to
   (1) determine any question as to the validity, extend or continuation in force of any contract between the parties;
   (2) order the correction or amendment of any such contract, and of the arbitration agreement, submission or reference, but only to the extent required to rectify any manifest error, mistake or omission which he determines to be common to all the parties;
   (3) determine any question of the law arising in the arbitration;
   (4) determine any question as to his own jurisdiction;
   (5) determine any question of good faith, dishonesty or fraud arising in the dispute;
   (6) order any party to furnish him with such further details of its case, in fact or in law as he may require;
   (7) proceed in the arbitration notwithstanding the failure or refusal of any party to comply with these Rules or with his orders or directions, or to attend any meeting or hearing, but only after giving that party written notice that he intends to do so;
   (8) receive and take into account such written or oral evidence as he shall determine to be relevant, whether or not strictly admissible in law;
   (9) make one or more interim awards;
   (10) order the parties to make interim payments towards the costs of the arbitration;
   (11) hold meetings and hearings in England and elsewhere;
   (12) express his awards in any currency;
   (13) award interest on any sum from and to any date at such rates as he determines to be appropriate;
   (14) correct any accidental mistake or omission in his awards.

C. Unless all the parties shall at any time agree otherwise, the arbitrator shall have power, on the application of any of the parties or of his own motion, but in either case only after hearing or receiving any representations from the parties concerned, to
   (1) allow other parties to be joined in the arbitration with their express consent, and make a single final award determining all disputes between them;
   (2) allow any party, upon such terms (as to costs and otherwise) as he shall determine, to amend his Statement of Case, Defence or Reply;
   (3) extend or abbreviate any time limits provided by these Rules or by his directions;
   (4) rely on his own expert knowledge and experience in any field, or appoint one or more advisors or experts on any matter (including law) to assist him in the conduct of the arbitration;
   (5) direct the parties to submit to the Registrar, for subsequent exchange, written statements, whether or not verified by oath or affirmation, of the evidence of witnesses, and direct which of the makers of such statements are to attend before him for oral examination;
   (6) conduct such enquiries as may appear to him to be necessary or expedient;
   (7) order the parties to make any property or thing available for his inspection, and inspect in it in their presence;
   (8) order the parties to produce to him, and to each other for inspection, and to supply copies of, any documents or classes of documents in their possession or power which he determines to be relevant;
   (9) order the preservation, storage, sale or other disposal of any property or thing under the control of any of the parties;
   (10) make interim orders for security for any party's own costs, and to secure all or part of any amount in dispute in the arbitration.

D. In addition, the arbitrator shall have such further jurisdiction and powers as may be allowed to him by the laws of England, the contract between the parties, and any place outside England in which he holds hearings or in which witnesses attend before him.

Arbitration Rules of the Chartered Institute of Arbitrators

SCHEDULE OF COSTS

Court's Charges

(a) The fee payable with the Request or Arbitration (Rule 1(1)) is £75, which covers all costs up to and including the appointment of the arbitrator.

(b) If the arbitrator(s) has been appointed by any person or body (including the parties themselves) other than by the Institute Rule 1(2), the fee payable with a Notification of Arbitration is £10.

(c) Thereafter, the administrative costs of the arbitration will be calculated by reference to the work done by the Institute in connection with the arbitration.

(d) Work done by the Institute's administrative staff will be charged at the rate of £30 per hour.

Arbitrator's Fees

(e) The arbitrator's fees will be calculated by reference to the work done by him in connection with the arbitration, and will be charged at rates appropriate to the particular circumstances of the case, including its complexity, and any special qualifications of the arbitrator. These rates will be established by the Institute after consultation with the parties before the appointment of the arbitrator (unless they have been agreed previously in circumstances where the arbitrator(s) has been appointed by the parties or another appointing authority).

(f) Where the arbitrator takes over the administration of the proceedings under Rule 4(1) above; time spent by him on administration thereafter will be charged at the hourly rate of his fees.

Expenses

(g) Specific outgoing expenses incurred by the Institute or the arbitrator in connection with the arbitration—for travel, subsistence, hire of arbitration rooms, postage, telex, cable, telephone, copying, recording and transcribing services, reports of experts and advisors, and any other items—will be charged at cost.

Special Arrangements

(h) By special arrangement, where the parties prefer this, an inclusive fee for all the work done in the arbitration may be agreed with the Institute, based on a percentage of the amount in dispute.

Value Added Tax

(i) Value Added Tax will be added where appropriate.

Notes

By way of guidance, the rates of the arbitrator's fees on 1 March 1981 fall, in most cases, within the following range:

Time for meetings or hearings (including travelling time, and time wasted by late postponement or cancellation)—£250 to £750 per day or part of a day.

Other time spent on the arbitration—£30 to £100 per hour.

However, in exceptional cases the appropriate rates may be higher or lower. In small claims cases (under £5000) they will normally be lower.

Index